CULTS,
TERRITORY,
AND THE ORIGINS OF
THE GREEK
CITY-STATE

၎ ❋ ၇

❧ ✻ ❧

CULTS, TERRITORY,
AND THE ORIGINS OF
THE GREEK CITY-STATE

~ ❋ ~

François de Polignac

TRANSLATED BY JANET LLOYD
WITH A NEW FOREWORD BY CLAUDE MOSSÉ

THE UNIVERSITY OF CHICAGO PRESS
CHICAGO AND LONDON

François de Polignac is chargé de recherches in the Centre national de la recherche scientifique, associated with the Centre Louis Gernet de Recherches Comparées sur les Sociétés Anciennes in Paris. Janet Lloyd is an accomplished translator of French whose works include *Cunning Intelligence in Greek Culture and Society* by Marcel Detienne and Jean-Pierre Vernant (Chicago, 1991).

The University of Chicago Press, Chicago 60637
The University of Chicago Press, Ltd., London
© 1995 by The University of Chicago
All rights reserved. Published 1995
Printed in the United States of America
04 03 02 01 00 99 98 97 96 95   5 4 3 2 1

ISBN (cloth): 0-226-67333-2
ISBN (paper): 0-226-67334-0

First published in French under the title *La Naissance de la cité grecque,*
© Editions La Découverte, Paris, 1984.

This translation was published with the assistance of the French Ministry of Culture.

Library of Congress Cataloging-in-Publication Data

Polignac, François de.
 [Naissance de la cité grecque. English]
 Cults, territory, and the origins of the Greek city-state /
François de Polignac ; translated by Janet Lloyd with a new foreword
by Claude Mossé.
     p.   cm.
 Includes bibliographical references.
 ISBN 0-226-67333-2
 1. Cults—Greece—History. 2. Cities and towns, Ancient—Greece—
History. 3. Greece—Antiquities. I. Title.
DF122.P6513 1995
307.76'0938—dc20   94-46009
                                                                              CIP

CONTENTS

❧ ✳ ❧

FOREWORD

꧁ ✳ ꧂

The publication, in 1984, of François de Polignac's book marked an important turning point in the analysis of the origins of the specific form of social and political organization constituted by the Greek city-state. Up until then, particularly in French historiography, the emergence of the city was linked to the development of political institutions set up in the place of "clan" structures based on birth and kinship. That analysis was based on Aristotle's reflections in the *Politics* where, partially taking over Plato's explanations in the *Republic*, he took man's "need," his inability to live on his own, to be the catalytic element in the constitution of first the family, then the village, and eventually the city. But that analysis was based essentially upon the Athenian "model" and the developments described by Aristotle in the *Constitution of Athens*.

François de Polignac deliberately broke away from that model by showing, in the first place, that the Athenian example was purely relative and that historians of Greece needed to free themselves from Athenian discourse and seek information elsewhere; and secondly that this "elsewhere" might better be revealed by archaeology than by repeated readings of the literary documentation.

And what could a historian learn from the excavations carried out not only in mainland Greece but also in the islands and the colonial world? These showed that, from the end of the ninth century on, a reoccupation of the land took place along with rapid demographic progress. The appearance of numerous deposits of offerings was the most visible sign of this. And, con-

trary to what the traditional schema of analysis suggested, it was
not in the center of the urban space of future cities that these
offerings accumulated, but on the edges of the territory. Athens
in fact constituted an exception. The second and longest chapter
of the book was accordingly devoted to a study of these "extraurban" sanctuaries. Polignac showed what an important role
these sanctuaries played, both in defining the city's space and in
integrating members of the civic community, and on this basis
suggested that the city was in the first place a religious community. His demonstration, centered on mainland Greece and the
islands, was then extended to the western colonial world, even
though the presence of indigenous communities gave settlements
there particular characteristics of their own. As for the political
dimension, this was reintroduced in the last chapter, in connection with the development of heroic cults. The conclusion drawn
by Polignac was that "what we call the *polis* resulted from the
progressive establishment of social cohesions and hierarchies,
which took the form of a quest for agreement on the choice of
mediating cults and the modalities of participation in their rites."
The mediating cults consisted of, first, those devoted to the deities who protected the territory, but also, at the heart of the urban
space, others that the community addressed to its heroes—the
real or mythical founders of the city. At the two poles of the civic
space, the extraurban sanctuaries and the heroes' tombs thus
combined to confirm the domination exerted over the territory
by those who were committed to defending it.

Polignac's thesis was attractive and was recognized to be so.
But it also provoked reservations, even criticisms of a more or
less acerbic nature from various quarters. To some, the emphasis
placed on the religious factor seemed excessive, and they criticized the new French "model," as it has sometimes been called,
for losing sight of the political factor at the origin of the city and,
by stressing participation in the religious cults in the definition
of citizenship, erasing the distinctions that existed between citizens and other inhabitants of the civic territory.

Furthermore, some archaeologists' works, in particular the
most recent publications on the "dark ages," seemed to be call-
ing into question any overall interpretation of the "birth" or rise
of the Greek city. Finally, it now seemed that the heroic cults

were, after all, not so closely linked to the rediscovery of Mycenaean tombs as had been thought.

In the English-language edition of his book, Polignac takes
these criticisms and new approaches into consideration. He freely
recognizes that the dark ages do not constitute an absolute void,
as had been thought, and that the rhythm of evolution certainly
varied from one region to another, with some retaining ancient
structures for longer than others. He nevertheless remains con-
vinced that the eighth century was a period of great upheavals
and that the settlements established then did prefigure the structure of the Greek world of the late Archaic and Classical periods.
It is, however, necessary to recognize that the transformations
came about more gradually and, in particular, that extraurban
sanctuaries in some cases continued to be used in common by
several communities, since the appropriation of frontier zones
was completed only at a relatively late date, toward the end of
the Archaic period. Similarly, offerings of weapons in sanctuaries do not antedate the seventh century. The origin of the Greek
temple also turns out to be more complex than it seemed ten
years ago, when the miniature terra cotta model found in the
Heraion of Perachora was regarded as evidence of the existence
of temples as early as the eighth century. In reality, the distinction between domestic architecture and religious architecture
was not as evident in the eighth century as it was to become in
the sixth and fifth centuries. That is a revealing example of Polignac's new view of the rise of the Greek city. The city should be
regarded not as a structured State formation, but rather as "an
agent that developed various modes of participation in ritualized social practices." Hence the difficulty, with regard to the
origin of the temple, of distinguishing between, on the one hand,
altogether new architectural creations and, on the other, edifices
that derived from the "banqueting halls" where the ritual meals
of the aristocracy were held. The phenomenon of warfare also,
to a certain extent, stemmed from these ritualized practices, and
on this point too Polignac takes into account the necessary distinction between the "symbolic" functions and the "strategic"
functions associated with the extraurban sanctuaries.

This less strictly institutional approach to the city is reflected
in the revised handling of the last chapter. In the English version,

much deeper emphasis is laid upon the funerary practices of the end of the Middle Geometric period, for these introduce new distinctions within the aristocracies of many regions of the Greek world. The problem that Polignac raises is that of the transition from heroizing funeral rites to the establishment of cults. The comparison between the "royal tomb" of Lefkandi and, three centuries later, the tomb of the "prince of Eretria" is revealing in this respect. In both cases a dynastic necropolis was formed close to the tomb of the "founder," but only at Eretria did a heroic cult appear, a fact that suggests that the settlement here was of a different nature. It is, however, important to point out that the Eretrian cult was not necessarily a "public" cult right from the start. Again stress is laid on the need to resist reducing the political element, in its archaic form, to the establishment of institutions: the ritual banquets that were a manifestation of the cult, even if this involved only an aristocratic group more or less linked with the descendants of the "prince," were nevertheless an essential element in the definition of Eretrian citizenship.

Similarly, the question of the appearance of heroic cults at Mycenaean tombs turns out to be less simple than it seemed. Even if dispersed traces of veneration can be found at these tombs, in some cases they disappear quite rapidly from the beginning of the seventh century on. And even where proof of the heroization of the mythical founder does exist, its link with an ancient tomb is not systematic. In many instances it was engineered later, as in the case of the Heroon of the Seven at Argos.

Clearly then, François de Polignac has modified his original text on a number of important points. He certainly remains faithful to a demonstration that opened up new perspectives for the analysis of the origins of the Greek city. But he now introduces new passages that take account of not only the most recent archaeological discoveries but also another way of approaching the emergence of politics. His new approach is reflected in the question that he asks in his conclusion: Is it right to speak of the emergence of the city in the eighth century? The answer lies not in a Manichean choice between a break and continuity but in the very definition of what is understood by a city at the beginning of the Archaic period. For, while new forms of solidarity accompanied by the development of various ritual practices undeniably did appear, these at first involved no more than a tiny fraction of society. On the other hand, participation in the religious rites was to make it possible to organize this society in new ways and to define an early form of citizenship within a space that was both civic and religious.

As can be seen, the French model of this new version not only stands up to criticism but is defined more clearly by virtue of its anthropological dimension and, thanks to this, prepares the way for new research perspectives capable of leading to a more accurate perception of the nature of the Greek city at its beginning.

CLAUDE MOSSÉ

PREFACE TO THE ENGLISH EDITION

❧ ✳ ☙

Any general analysis that attempts to account for phenomena previously considered only in isolation runs the risk of elaborating a model of interpretation that is too rigid, oversimplifying a reality that is always more varied and complex than the explanations put forward for it. But an analysis that furthermore makes a wide use of archaeology also, more or less consciously, exposes itself to the danger of being contradicted by new discoveries that call into question data previously accepted. So far, purely by chance perhaps, the ideas put forward ten or so years ago in this work on the origin of cults set up in outlying territory and the role that they played in the formation of the cities of the archaic period have not been formally contradicted by the discoveries made by excavations in the meantime. But in an investigation of this kind, readjustments are inevitably made necessary by evolving knowledge and interpretations, the more so in view of the fact that the past decade has seen the appearance of many essential works that correct, modify, or complement the present study. Its publication by the University of Chicago Press thus presents an excellent opportunity to integrate the latest data and also to refine some of the theories put forward in my analyses. Those theories were based upon notions that seemed to go without saying: "city" (*polis*) and "territory" are terms so familiar to a historian of ancient Greece that no precautions seemed necessary in using them. Nevertheless, despite the concern I several times expressed not to allow myself to become confined by categories forged in the context of classical Greece, it must be admitted that those categories did impose limits that needed to be breached in order to obtain a wider view of the problems.

Thus, the concept of a "territory," in the classical sense of a bounded space within which an exclusive sovereignty was exercised, should be used with caution in connection with the Greece of the end of the Geometric period. At that time, the establishment of strict boundaries to "the citizens' space" and the political elaboration that this presupposes were not always as definite as in the late archaic and classical periods. The formulation of relations between the various communities in strictly political terms such as "confrontation" or "submission," "citizens" and "foreigners," "inside" and "outside" the territory is often too vague or too rigid because they are based on concepts that are anachronistic for situations that were still fluid and relatively unformalized. Thus, the very notion of a *polis*, together with all the institutional background that it incorporates in the vocabulary of a historian, needs to be used with caution if it is not to impose upon the communities of the late Geometric and early archaic periods modes of thought taken over from the classical world. Not that we should follow the current of historiography that denies the existence of any decisive turning points in the transformations of this period, content to see the transition from the late Bronze Age to the Greece of the cities as a regular form of evolution so gradual and progressive that it presents none of those significant ridges that catch the eye and stimulate the thought of a historian. In short, while it may be true that an abuse of notions linked with the image of a "Greek renaissance" could well lead to a reductive view of Geometric Greece, in which only the eighth century would be important, to err in the opposite direction would be to dilute that same world in so long a duration that it would become ahistorical, a *morne plaine* into which only archaeologists in search of typologies would dare to venture. As it endeavors to show that it is possible to conceive of the city not exclusively from the point of the view of the formation of a state, but also as the agent organizing various modes of participating in ritualized social practices, this book hopes to avoid both these pitfalls. The reader must be the judge of whether it succeeds and should be assured that the improvements made to the present edition were largely inspired by the suggestions and criticisms kindly made by colleagues and friends too numerous to name, while the guesses and errors that it still contains are solely the result of my own negligence.

PREFACE

⟋⟍ ✳ ⟋⟍

This text emerged from the reworking of a *doctorat de 3e cycle*, presented at the Ecole des hautes études en sciences sociales.[1] Certain terms that have a more restricted sense in current usage are here given an extra, specific meaning. As in all studies on the ancient Greek world, the word "city" renders the term *polis* in its usual sense (which, however, only approximates ancient usage): the social unit established on a territory with a central inhabited area, where its political institutions are located. These, however—along with politics in the modern and restricted sense of the term—constituted but one particular aspect of the political or civic organization, which affected a number of the domains of collective life.

My debt to all those who helped me to complete my thesis has increased in the course of its revision. I should like first of all to express my gratitude to Claude Mossé who, after kindly acting as my supervisor, continued to guide and oversee my revision of the thesis. This could never have been completed without the unfailing encouragement and advice of Pierre Vidal-Naquet, whom I should like to thank once again. I enjoyed most fruitful discussions with the late Moses I. Finley and with Anthony Snodgrass when I studied at the University of Cambridge, and with Ettore Lepore and Georges Vallet, both deeply missed in the world of ancient history and archaeology, when I was at the

1. In June 1979, before a jury presided over by Pierre Vidal-Naquet and composed of Claude Mossé (the supervisor), Nicole Loraux, and Juliette de La Genière.

French School of Rome. Finally, I have greatly profited from many suggestions and comments from Anton Bammer, Claude Bérard, Bruno D'Agostino, Marcel Detienne, Pierre Ellinger, Michel Gras, Emmanuelle Greco, Guenter Kopcke, Juliette de La Genière, Christian Le Roy, Nicole Loraux, Irad Malkin, Ian Morris, Pauline Schmitt Pantel, Claudio Sabbione, Alain Schnapp, Jean-Pierre Vernant, Giuseppe Voza, and Beritt Wells, to all of whom I offer my warmest thanks.

INTRODUCTION

⟋⟍ ✳ ⟍⟋

The city represented a major form of social organization in the Greek civilization of the classical period and has, on that account, been a subject to which modern historians have paid particular attention. Numerous studies, many of them highly authoritative, starting with Fustel de Coulanges' famous *Cité antique* and following on with the renewal of interest aroused by Gustave Glotz's *Cité grecque* (to mention only the French historiography), have tried to define the Greek city's identity, describe its institutions and trace its evolution.[1]

However, despite the fact that any concept of the *polis* must surely be derived closely from the reasons and modalities of its formation, these have remained shrouded in uncertainty, for they have been reconstructed on the basis of extremely fragmentary knowledge of an essentially literary nature and, what is more, largely dependent upon schemata suggested by the philosophers of antiquity, Aristotle in particular. The birth of the city has thus been presented as resulting from the disintegration of a society based upon private solidarity, dominated by noble clans organized into phratries and tribes, and placed under the authority of a monarchical institution that was progressively dismantled as, within the confines of the territory, a community based on public law developed. This community was supposed to have absorbed all the precivic groups and institutions and, as it did so, reduced their political, juridical, and even economic

1. The historiography of the city and the pertinence of the questions posed are analyzed by M. I. Finley in "The Ancient City from Fustel to Weber and Beyond" (1977).

privileges, meanwhile maintaining their traditional cults but subordinating them to the community's own cults, in particular that of the deity who was the protector of the city.

The construction of this deity's temple, in the heart of the city, on the acropolis, which was believed previously to have been the seat of royal power, was considered to testify to a transition from human to divine sovereignty.[2] The attributes of the shattered monarchy were dispersed within the civic body yet rested symbolically in the hands of the god or goddess who had become the sole authority in the new community. The city was thus believed to have developed in a concentric fashion, with the city territory spreading out around the town, which was the seat of the city, and the prestigious acropolis and temple where the city cult ensured and expressed the unity of the group.

This interpretation, which saw the nascent city as a state set up as a result of the weakening of the distinctions that used to characterize a clanic and tribal society, was first challenged when certain of the concepts upon which it rested came to be reconsidered. Studies devoted to the *genos,* phratry, and tribe showed that, far from constituting the essential framework of precivic society, these institutions, as we know them, only came to be fully developed once the *polis* was already formed.[3] So they were not vestiges of a past age but, on the contrary, constituted the indispensable means of expressing the cohesion and *philia* that united the citizens.

Furthermore, both the painstaking reconstitution of the dislocation of monarchy and the image of the city centered upon its

2. Victor Ehrenberg is the author of the much quoted statement: "The god himself took the place of the king." It appears in Bérard and Altherr-Charon, "Erétrie" (1981), p. 237, and in Nenci, "Spazio civico" (1979), p. 464, in connection with the *città monocentrica.*

3. Bourriot, *Recherches sur le génos* (1974); Roussel, *Tribu et cité* (1976). Some *genē* were even flourishing in the latest phases of the history of the city. The most that seems likely in the "dark ages" is tribal grouping of a relatively loose nature from which the *ethnos* of the classical period may have derived (Snodgrass, *Archaic Greece* [1981], pp. 25–28 and 42). It was in the eighth century that groups of what were probably the graves of a single family began to appear, suggesting that kinship ties among the aristocracy were being tightened (Hägg, "Burial Customs" [1983] pp. 28–29 [Argos]); But even in the Athens of the classical period, funerary solidarity was a much more restricted circle than what is imagined to have been a *genos:* see Humphreys, "Family Tombs" (1980).

acropolis are all too neatly evocative of Athens, the paragon and model of a Greek city in the eyes of both the Athenians of the classical period and many modern scholars, and also of what Aristotle had to say about Athens.[4] Should we really accept that Athenian model without reservations, when it comes to considering the genesis of the Greek *polis* generally? And should we really read the texts of philosophers relating to the early days of the city as though they were transparent historical accounts or immediate interpretations of the situation? What makes it all the more necessary to question them is the fact that, to describe and explain the origins of the city, all the literary texts employ a terminology and concepts elaborated from the "final" result of the phenomenon that they set out to analyze. That terminology and those concepts are confined by the meaning attributed to them by those who were examining the city of the classical period, for it is to that city that they are more or less adapted. Instead of constituting familiar references all ready for use, the notions of city and citizen can, on the contrary, be properly understood only once the nature of the social formation that gave rise to them has been elucidated. We must make an effort to forget the institutional image of the Greek city if we are to understand the true nature of a historical phenomenon yet to be defined. To answer these questions and make progress in an investigation into the formation of the city, we must set aside the theories elaborated in the past and adopt a different way of proceeding, one that has a chance of shedding true light upon the phenomenon by considering it from a new angle.

That is the aim of the present study. The period to which it is devoted—the end of the ninth century to the early seventh, that is to say, the end of the period known as "Geometric" and the first decades of the archaic period—is the one in which the Greek world acquired what were to be the essential features of its "classical" civilization. It did so in the course of a series of concomitant upheavals: the reappearance of writing, an increasingly general regular use of maritime routes and long-distance trading, hitherto limited to the pioneers of the Levant, in particular the Phoenicians and the Euboeans, a renaissance in monu-

---

4. On the elaboration of the Athenian model, see Loraux, *Invention of Athens* (1986).

mental architecture, the emergence of the historical cities of the
Greco-Aegean world, and the colonial foundations of southern
Italy and Sicily. Our knowledge of this period is progressively
improving thanks to the refinement of archaeological techniques
and a consequent wealth of new documentation. The eighth century is now recognized to have been a critical time of social
growth, the demographic aspect of which has been the first to be
well documented.[5]

Greece seems to have undergone a pronounced population
decline at the time Mycenaean civilization disappeared. The violent fighting, traces of which have been found, the migrations
that followed, and the collapse or gradual decline of the palace
system of government upon which large sectors of economic activity depended, not only in the domains of large-scale trade and
craftsmanship but also in that of agriculture, ushered in a down-
wardly spiraling recession accompanied by a population decline. It is known for certain that in the thirteenth century B.C.,
320 sites were inhabited, whereas only 120, 40, and 100 are
known to have been occupied in the twelfth, eleventh, and tenth
centuries respectively.[6] Even allowing for the hazards and lacunas of archaeological excavation, the tendencies suggested by
these figures are clear enough. The Greeks of the "dark ages"
apparently lived in smaller and poorer groups, which occupied
only a limited proportion of the available space.

In contrast, two facts seem to testify to rapid population
growth in the eighth century: the number of known sites increased (110 in the ninth century, 220 in the eighth); and each
was more densely occupied, as can be deduced from their larger
burial grounds. An examination of those discovered in Attica
has made it possible to calculate the average number of burials
per theoretical generation in each period of the "dark ages":
fewer than 30 or so for each thirty-year cycle in the ninth century
(Ancient and Middle Geometric I); about 45 for the first third of

5. In particular by Anthony Snodgrass, *Dark Age* (1971), *Archaeology* (1977),
Archaic Greece (1981), and Nicholas Coldstream, *Geometric Greece* (1977), conclusion. The figures given by these two authors, which I have repeated here, need
to be revised and increased in view of recent discoveries.

6. Snodgrass, *Dark Age*, p. 364, *Archaic Greece*, pp. 20–24; Coldstream, *Geometric Greece*, p. 357.

the eighth century (Middle Geometric II), 150 for the last third (Late Geometric II).[7] Even allowing for correctional factors (such as the destruction of old burial grounds by more recent ones), these figures seem to indicate a population increase that gathered pace as the century proceeded. One hypothesis advanced to explain this is that agricultural practices changed: essentially pastoral activities over an extensive area, which made for a precarious balance between the meager resources and the small, possibly nomadic population gradually gave way to more intensive agricultural methods.[8] The change, imperceptible at first, is supposed to have upset that balance toward the end of the ninth century, allowing demographic growth to take off. That growth, in its turn, is believed to have speeded up the transformation of erstwhile pastures into arable land, thereby creating a cycle of growth that was self-perpetuating. The growing diversity and number of the objects deposited in tombs and cult sites are likewise thought to testify to the increase in resources that is also detectable in the progress of artisan activities and the importation of precious objects from the Middle East.

However, this picture needs to be modified. In the first place, the idea of a spectacular demographic explosion has been called into question by a number of studies, in particular that by Ian Morris, which have drawn attention to the shortcomings of an exclusively quantitative analysis of the archaeolgical data and have suggested different interpretations: the variations observed in the number and the density of the Attic necropolises were probably also occasioned, to an extent that is hard to determine, by an evolution in funerary practices and the archaeological visibility in which these resulted.[9] Furthermore, the increasing number of discoveries made recently show that the so-called dark ages were not uniformly dark everywhere, especially in regions that, either on their own initiative or through the mediation of Cypriot or Levantine seafarers, maintained or soon reestablished contact with Cyprus and the Near East. The excavations at Lefkandi in Euboea have also revealed a world that does not exactly correspond to the image of a Greece so radically impoverished,

7. I have simplified the data provided by Snodgrass, *Archaeology,* pp. 10–11.
8. Ibid., p. 15. See also J. Sarkady, "Development of Greek Society" (1975).
9. Morris, *Burial and Ancient Society* (1987).

isolated, and reduced to a state as primitive as was imagined twenty years ago.[10] Noticeable regional differences thus characterize the state of the Greek world at the beginning of the Iron Age, differences that for the most part favor the Aegean coast and the islands.

The crisis of growth in the Greek world in the last years of the Geometric period cannot therefore be considered as an accidental overpopulation in which a stable and limited level of resources was automatically exceeded by a demographic excess, which the movement of colonization then progressively reabsorbed. Certainly, the limited space available for land clearance distinguished some areas—such as mountainous regions (the Peloponnese, Locris) and the islands, from which so many of the colonial expeditions were launched—from the larger or more fertile territories where internal colonization may have sufficed to absorb the extra numbers of inhabitants (Attica, Boeotia, Thessaly).[11] But the movement of colonization began in the regions that were the first to engage in maritime trading and in a quest for new resources, particularly through mining, to provide bronze for metallurgical production. It is certainly not by chance that the Euboeans, even if they did not establish a proper trading post at al-Mina in Syria, were the first to travel to the western Mediterranean, no doubt following in the wake of the Phoenicians, in the early eighth century at the latest, then settling along the coasts of Italy and Sicily; the Corinthians, who had been visiting the Adriatic (Epirus, Otranto) since the same period, joined them there one generation later. It is thus clearly because it was a period of exploration and expansion that the eighth century witnessed the opening up of new opportunities and the introduction of new tensions, the origin of which should be traced to the very structure of Greek society in the Geometric period.

This was a society dominated by a warrior aristocracy estab-

10. Popham, Sackett, and Themelis, *Lefkandi I* (1979–80); Popham, Calligas, and Sackett, *Lefkandi II* (1990); and Popham, Touloupa, and Sackett, "Further Excavations" (1982). The impact upon Geometric Greece of relations with the Cypro-Levantine world and the western Mediterranean is the theme of the studies collected together in Kopcke and Tokumaru, *Greece between East and West* (1992).

11. In Attica, the resettlement of the *chōra* seems to have involved more people than the expansion of urban Athens: Snodgrass, *Archaeology*, p. 13. In Boeotia, the property of Hesiod's father at Ascra is a well-known example.

lished around *basileis*, the heads of, not *gene*, but *oikoi*, houses or domains similar to the one in Ithaca described in the *Odyssey*.[12] The noble *oikos* was composed of the immediate family of the *basileus*, his companions, clients, and servants (distinguished from one another by the degree of their dependence), his flocks, and his treasure. The latter consisted of an accumulation of richly worked bronzes and enabled him, through the exchange of gifts, to maintain the links of hospitality and the network of kinship and marriage alliances that constituted the bases of his power and prestige quite as much as did his personal valor and his wealth in the form of domesticated animals. Whatever the area devoted to cereal cultivation on these domains,[13] from the eleventh century on, rivalry for the control of land, whether possessed from ancient times or newly acquired, must have been sharpened by the need to raise two kinds of animals: cattle, which remained a symbol of prosperity right down to the time of the poets of the archaic period; and horses, the distinctive status symbol of the warrior nobility and quite indispensable to whoever needed to manifest his rank in agonistic and military activities and through ceremonial displays.

Similarly, far from constituting the specific activity of a group of merchants that, through them, discovered its own autonomy and a new source of wealth and influence, naval expeditions and long-distance trading were very often initiated by the warrior aristocracy itself, and in difficult situations, some of its members even played an active part in them.[14] The many opportunities

12. Although it gives an overcoherent view of the "Homeric world" (cf. Snodgrass, "An Historical Homeric Society?" [1974]), Finley's analysis, *World of Odysseus* (1977), is most illuminating on this point. To translate *basileus* as "king" is to risk introducing total confusion: these "masters of *oikoi*," the leaders of the warrior group, were kings only to the same extent as any man who was *primus inter pares* and who dominated the group by virtue of his valor, wealth, and connections.

See the remarks of Mossé in "Ithaque" (1980), pp. 12–15, 18, and Quiller, "Homeric Society" (1981), on the factors of disintegration and instability undermining "Homeric" power.

13. Illustrated, according to Snodgrass (*Archaeology*, p. 15, and *Archaic Greece*, p. 36) by the placing of terra-cotta models of a new type of barn in the finest Attic tombs, from about 850 on.

14. The forms of aristocratic participation in maritime trading has been the subject of a debate between Mele, *Commercio greco arcaico* (1979), and Bravo,

offered to the Greeks by the broadening of their horizon and the remarkable new sources of wealth and influence they could promote in the most enterprising of the cities thus helped to accentuate phenomena of rivalry over prestige and power, particularly within the aristocracy from which, in the eighth century, we find groups emerging that are distinguished by their increasing opulence and their adoption of new status symbols.[15]

Access to new resources, conflicts over their appropriation, and tensions within the nobility: such are the features peculiar to the surge of growth experienced by the Greco-Aegean world at the end of the Geometric period and the context within which there appeared, as a historical agent, the form of community that we customarily call the "city," the *polis*, without any clear idea of what the term really denotes at that date. Now the changes that can be seen to have taken place in another domain, that of religious life, would appear to throw some light upon the emergence of the *polis*. In the eighth century, profound and lasting changes affected Greek religious concepts and practices. New types of offerings appeared at the same time as cult sites multiplied, and some of those sites acquired a special importance with the construction of monumental edifices that came to represent a particular model of sacred space, namely, the Greek sanctuary. We can thus form some idea of the evolution of religious attitudes, which two essential factors make explicit and place at the very heart of the process by which the *polis* was formed: namely, the popularity of the sanctuaries situated outside the main population centers and the emergence of cults of heroes.

The role played in the city by the cults generally known as extraurban and the heroic cults is a problem that has often been addressed in works devoted to the colonial cities of Italy and Sicily, but only within the colonial framework. They have consequently been treated as a purely local peculiarity and without reference to the Greco-Aegean world, where, in contrast, they have been the subject of no systematic study.[16] An investigation

"Commerce et noblesse," (1984), pp. 99–161, an article that also tackles the crucial problem of concepts of "nobility" and "aristocracy."

15. See for example Hägg, "Burial customs," pp. 27–31, on Argolis.

16. Except, recently, on the subject of heroes. Earlier studies in many cases consist of typologies that undertake no more than a superficial examination of the relations between the hero and the city.

that would take in both the old world and the new thus seemed to me bound to prove fruitful, not only on account of the consequent enrichment of our documentation but also by virtue of the potential rewards to be gained from the adoption of a new method.

My procedure, then, will take the form, first, of an archaeological inquiry aimed at discovering the nature and scope of the changes that affected the religious behavior of the Greeks in regions where they had long been established and also at showing how major sanctuaries appeared there, located out in the countryside or on the borders of the main habitations that were to become the future urban centers. In the light of this data and the features of the eighth century sketched in above, the myths and rituals attached to these sanctuaries and the legends and events connected with the earliest days in the history of the Greek cities will then reveal how the *polis* was established through, on the one hand, the religious definition of a new representation of space—the city territory—and on the other, the elaboration of a new civic community, thanks to rites of social integration: both being changes connected with the development of nonurban cults. The conclusions drawn from that inquiry will make it possible to tackle the case of colonial foundations from a new angle and, looking beyond the variants produced by the interplay of purely local factors and circumstances, to extrapolate certain features fundamental to the emergence of the Greek city generally. Finally, an analysis of the simultaneous flowering of heroic cults and their significance within the given context will complete and sharpen our understanding of how, through the orientation of public religious life, it became possible to elaborate a form of society whose strengths and weaknesses the Greek civilization demonstrated with such far-reaching consequences.

CHAPTER ONE

Cults, Offerings, and Sanctuaries

༷ ✳ ༺

I n the eighth century, on the Greek mainland, the Aegean islands, and the coast of Asia Minor, not to mention Rhodes
and Crete, sites that had either never been inhabited or, as in
most cases, no longer reveal any traces of habitation after the end
of the Mycenaean period (Late Helladic IIIC) appear unques-
tionably as consecrated to religious purposes. This large-scale
development, which is indicated by the earliest deposits of what
became continuous series of offerings, mostly earthenware or
bronze, is in sharp contrast with the situation in the dark ages of
the twelfth to the ninth centuries. To be sure, the frequent absence of material vestiges from that period does not necessarily
prove that no religious rituals were carried out. However, a profound change now took place.

New Sites and New Religious Practices

The first and most remarkable indication of that change is the
proliferation of votive deposits. Even if recent discoveries and
studies do fill out the list of objects found, the fact remains that,
to date, nonperishable offerings from the Geometric period have
been discovered in only a few sites.[1] The only cults attested in
this fashion with relative certainty for the end of the tenth cen-

1. The frequently isolated nature of the most ancient objects, the often impre-
cise chronology, before the eighth century, of certain regional items of pottery
and also of bronzes found without stratigraphy make the identification and dating of many of the earliest votive deposits a very chancey business. That is the
case in Sparta, for the cults of Athena Chalkioikos, Artemis Orthia, and the Heroon: ninth century? See most recently Coulson, "Dark Age Pottery of Sparta"

tury are those of Olympia and Kombothekra in Elis, Amyclae in
Laconia, Isthmia near Corinth, Mount Hymettos and Mounychia
in Attica, the Cabirion near Thebes, Kalapodi in Phocis, Aetos
and Polis in Ithaca, Aya Irini in Ceos, probably Aegina (Aphaia);
Kommos, Kato Symi, and a number of caves (Ida, Dicte, Prasos,
etc.) in Crete; and dating either from that time or from shortly
after, those of Tegea (Alea), the Heraion of Samos, and probably
Brauron in Attica. A new generation of cult sites appear, ar-
chaeologically speaking, toward the end of the ninth century:
Delphi, Delos, the acropolis of Athens, the Heraion of Argos, and
possibly Perachora.

We should not assume that the scanty nature of these discoveries is simply due to archaeological lacunas, for the contrast
with what we know of the following period is too striking. The
number of cult sites identified for the eighth century, particularly
for the late Geometric period (second half of the century) is increasing all the time. In 1977, Nicholas Coldstream counted
more than eighty, and many other sanctuaries have been discovered since then.[2] Their geographic distribution covers the entire
area of "classical" Greek civilization—the eastern half of Greece
(Thessaly, Boeotia, Euboea, Attica, Corinthia, Argolis, and Laconia, where almost half the religious deposits are to be found),
the Cyclades, the eastern Aegean, eastern Crete—and scattered
around the western edges of this Greco-Aegean area are six sites,
some of which were destined to acquire a Panhellenic reputation
(Olympia, Delphi, Dodona).[3]

(1985), and on Pheres in Thessaly, Kilian, *Fibeln in Thessalien,* (1975), p. 170f. Another unknown factor is the length of time that may have elapsed between the
making of certain objects and their consecration (pins, fibulae, etc.); cf. Philipp,
Bronzeschmuck aus Olympische (1981), pp. 9–23.

2. See the list in Coldstream, *Geometric Greece* (1977), pp. 318–20, to which
should be added Mounychia, Kommos, Kombothekra, Tyros (Laconia), Bassai
(Arcadia), Koukounaries (Paros), and many other local cults such as the mountaintop cults of Attica and Corinthia.

3. These, all situated on the borders of the Greece of city-states, obviously
found their Panhellenic role growing from the eighth century on, precisely because they were located a long way from the scenes of warfare and appropriation
that marked the emergence of those states. They are, for that reason, only of in-
direct relevance to the present study. However, Morgan's *Athletes and Oracles*
(1990) makes a more detailed study of them.

The material evidence alone thus testifies to an astounding increase in the number of places where the Greeks took to making regular deposits of objects intended as offerings. In the overwhelming majority of cases, there are no traces of any earlier cult, even in the form of animal sacrifices, which, wherever practiced frequently and over a fairly long period, leave considerable layers of ashes and semicarbonized bones. In most cases, signs of such sacrifices only appear along with other material traces of religious activity, such as vestiges of ritual meals (dishes, *obeloi*) and deposits of offerings (various earthenware and bronze figurines): pins, fibulae, brooches, figurines, and tripod cauldrons in the larger sites, where jewelry, ivory pieces, and (mainly from the seventh century on) arms and armor were also consecrated.[4] The same sequence is detectable in most of the sites, although the chronology may vary from one to another.

The archaeological evidence is certainly insufficient to tell us much about the religious life of the Greek society of the dark ages, and the absence of remains proves, not that no religious rites were practiced, but simply that they were maintained in forms and at levels too close to daily life to have left any identifiable traces. So the important thing is not always to decide when a cult site began to be used, given that if it was only frequented in an informal fashion no traces may remain.[5] Rather, we should try to see when and why the cult took on a form that rendered it more visible both materially and socially. Now, the double phenomenon of, on the one hand, the proliferation of religious sites and, on the other, the increasing richness of the deposits of offerings that testify to their existence would be inadequately accounted for by a mechanistic explanation that saw them simply as a reflection of the general sudden flowering of this society. For one thing, such a hypothesis would not explain why it was that offerings of this kind were previously strictly limited to a hand-

4. The need to distinguish between offerings and utensils has been clearly shown by Tomlinson, "Perachora" (1992), pp. 343–46, who suggests banning the use of the word "votive" to qualify all the objects found in sanctuaries.

5. These discreet traces may sometimes have escaped the attention of archaeologists in the past, although more recent excavations have revealed them: for example, the temporary structures found in the sanctuary of Poseidon at Isthmia (Gebhard and Hemans, "Excavations at Isthmia" (1992), pp. 13–14.

ful of very specific sites and were not to be found, even in the more modest forms to be expected of the dark ages, throughout the Greek world, which cannot, on that account, be assumed to have lacked all forms of religious life.[6]

One fact in particular proves that the proliferation of traces of religious life in the eighth century also resulted from a new attitude toward the sacred, which had the effect of converting religious practices into a more autonomous and specific component of social life: most of the kinds of offerings that make their appearance on religious sites in the Geometric period were also deposited in graves. Now, in the course of the eighth century, many of these progressively disappear from the tombs, in particular the bronze objects that thereafter increasingly came to occupy a larger place in the sanctuaries.[7] Given the prestige value of this metal, the principal element in aristocratic treasure stores, its presence in increasing quantities probably does indicate that the Greek world now had at its disposal greater wealth and many more material goods. But what it shows above all is that such riches were now increasingly destined for the gods. Personal ornaments such as pins and fibulae, a few of which would be placed in tombs and sanctuaries until the end of the ninth century, after this time appeared in large numbers in sanctuaries.[8] Cauldrons and basins, always rare in tombs, now constituted the major type of offering in the larger religious sites.[9] And the last burials of warriors accompanied by their arms and armor date

6. No consecration of offerings accompanied what appears to have been the dominant custom: the animal or plant sacrifice (cf. *Iliad* 1.460f. and *Odyssey* 3.1f., among others).

7. Coldstream, *Geometric Greece*, p. 332f. The same phenomenon has been noted in the Latium of the late seventh/early sixth century, in the context of an overall evolution identical to that described here (Pourcet, "Latium protohistorique" [1978], pp. 556–601).

8. Snodgrass, *Dark Age* (1971), p. 75f., and *Archaic Greece* (1981), pp. 52–54 (with a table). The contrast is particularly striking at Olympia, Argos (Heraion), Lindos (Athenaion), and Pheres in Thessaly (Artemision).

9. Cauldrons were used as receptacles for the ashes of the deceased, as in the tombs of the small western burial ground of Eretria (Bérard, *L'hérôon à la porte de l'Ouest* [1970]). As for bowls with a stand or a tripod, their presence in Greek tombs is exceptional: one case in Crete from the proto-Geometric period (Brock, *Fortetsa* [1957], Tomb 11, no. 17 [Cnossos]) and one in Athens at the beginning of the seventh century (Kübler, *Kerameikos VI* [1959], Tomb 74).

from the end of the eighth century, just as pieces of armor also were beginning to be used as votive offerings.[10] This phenomenon is accentuated by the fact that objects destined to be offerings now gradually evolved toward forms that detached them from their original function and rendered them unsuitable for any but a votive use. Ornaments formerly used for securing clothing reached outsize proportions (pins of up to 0.80 meters have been found in the sanctuary of Hera in Argolis). Tripod basins, which until this time had remained on the borderline between useful objects and items of symbolic prestige, now definitively shed their former useful function: they, too, now took on outsize proportions (some may have stood more than one meter high), and as they proliferated, they also displayed increasingly intricate ornamentation. A greater proportion of the surface area would be decorated, motifs became more varied, figurines were added to ornamental handles, and the repoussé work became more sophisticated: all this testified to the care that was lavished on the creation of these impressive offerings.[11]

A specific category of objects with an exclusively votive function was thus created, and these artifacts now diversified, enriched, and ennobled the rites of consecration in places where cults were established. Correlatively, certain tombs of the late Geometric period were also characterized by lavish furnishings and ornaments, particularly in Attica, Argolis, and Cyprus, although a sharp decline in the number of offerings finding their way into funerary deposits occurred at the turn of the eighth and seventh centuries. This transfer to the gods of an ever increasing proportion of the society's products, on an ever increasing number of sites, testifies to a change in religious behavior. Greek society now seemed to be manifesting a new devotion toward the gods, with offerings that took forms designed to be durable.

That devotion is also attested by the third element in these religious changes: sanctuaries were now constructed, a new way of using space set aside for purely religious purposes. The ritual

10. See the parallels drawn by Courbin for the "tomb with armor" in Argos, "Tombe géométrique d'Argos" (1957), and Hägg, "Burial Customs" (1983), pp. 27–31.

11. Coldstream, *Geometric Greece*, pp. 335f.; Olympia: Maas, *Geometrischen Dreifüsse* (1978); Delphi: Rolley, *Les trépieds* (1979).

world of the dark ages, as conveyed to us by certain passages in
the *Iliad* and the *Odyssey*, seems to have been characterized by a
relative lack of spatial determination, with no clear differentiation between sacred space and profane space. Thus, when the
bard describes a great sacrifice to Poseidon, it takes the form of a
ceremony with all the solemnity befitting a high point in religious life, yet no sanctuary consecrated to the god is involved.[12]
The entire ritual takes place on the beach, and there is no mention even of any space that is reserved, marked out by any
boundary post or other sign.[13] Proximity to the sea, the god's
own domain, seems to be the most important consideration.
Once the sacrifice is completed, the spot where it was carried out
can revert to being a place like any other, not differentiated in
any way from its surroundings—except perhaps in the memories of those who were present, which may account for the
lingering respect felt for certain sites. However important
the ritual, though, no sacred space was either defined or
institutionalized.

In point of fact, the kind of sacred space most often mentioned
in the Homeric poems is the sacred wood, *alsos,* a site to be
classed with those places (pools, caves, mountains) that, simply
by virtue of their natural qualities, seemed fitted to shelter some
daimōn, rather than a space strictly defined, arranged, and organized.[14] Many such places reserved for piety of a generally hum-
bler or more local type remained throughout antiquity unim-
proved and hardly identified, in contrast to the sanctuaries set
up for the community as a whole.[15]

It was during the Geometric period that the three constituent
elements of the "classic" Greek sanctuary were elaborated: the
altar, the temple (which housed statues and offerings), and the

12. The sacrifice of the Pylians, *Odyssey* 3, lines 1–68.

13. Ibid., 5.5: *Toi d'epi thini thalassēs hiera rhezon . . .*

14. See ibid., 9.196, 20.276–79. *Naoi* are rare and are usually mentioned in
texts that already reflect the religious changes of the late Geometric period in
general, as in the passage where, before taking the cows of the Sun, Eurylochos
promises: "If ever we reach our homeland in Ithaca, our first act shall be to build
Hyperion the Sun-god a rich temple (*naon*) and fill it with precious offerings
(*agalmata*)" (*Odyssey* 12, lines 345–47, translated by E. V. Rieu, Penguin Classics
[Harmondsworth, 1948]).

15. Like the Eumenides' wood, in which Sophocles sets his *Oedipus at Colonus.*

precinct wall, which marked out the sacred area. Of the three, the altar seems, from the evidence, to have been the first to appear. It was necessary for making burnt offerings in the open air and was in many cases the first stable component of the religious site. In the sanctuary of Artemis at Kalapodi, layers of ashes dating from the proto-Geometric period covered a small Mycenaean structure described as an "altar," but it is not certain that the rites of the Mycenaean period ascribed the same role to the altar as the rites of the historical period did; at any rate, in the middle Geometric period the installation took the form of a cone of ashes. The most ancient altar known to date from the Geometric period may be the one in the Heraion of Samos. It took the form of a stone rim surrounding a hole in the earth.[16]

The monumental temple, where the deity resided, may well have been a creation of the eighth century, but its origins remain confused. It seems to have been as unknown to the Greeks of the Mycenaean period as to those of the dark ages.[17] The small-scale earthenware models deposited in the sanctuaries of Hera, the earliest in about 800 at Perachora, later ones in Argolis (Prosymna) and Samos, represent a building of wood and rough bricks in the form of an apsidal hall surmounted by a steeply sloping roof and fronted by a porch supported by two pillars. These have been interpreted as reproductions of the earliest temples, but they may simply be models of houses.[18] In several sanctuaries, traces of absidal buildings dating from the eighth century have been found. Some were quite short (Perachora, the

16. The dating is controversial (ninth century?); Walter, *Das Heraion von Samos* (1976), pp. 32–47. Kalapodi: Felsch, "Kalapodi" (1987), pp. 4–5. On the role of the altar and Mycenaean sacrificial rites: Bergquist, "Archaeology of Sacrifice" (1988); Marinatos, "Imagery of Sacrifice" (1988); Etienne, "Autels et sacrifices" (1992), pp. 311–12. "Hard" altars in some cases only replaced those formed by the accumulation of ashes at a fairly late date, or even not at all, as at Olympia (Rupp, "Development of Altars" (1983).

17. The wide variety of Helladic cult-sites is now better known, but neither the refurbishment of rural sanctuaries, nor the urban sanctuaries, nor the palace *megara* of the Mycenaean period can be assimilated to the classical community temple; see the studies collected in Hägg and Marinatos, *Sanctuaries and Cults* (1981); Renfrew, *Archaeology of Cult* (1985); Rutkowski, *Cult Places of the Aegean* (1986).

18. Schattner, *Griechische Hausmodelle* (1990). For the dating of the earliest temples, see Kalpaxis, *Früarchaische Baukunst* (1976).

"Daphnephoreion" of Eretria, Eleusis, Olympia, and probably
Asine/Barbouna), others more elongated (Mycenae, Paros/
Oikonomos, Solygaea-Galataki in Corinth, and the first temple
of Eretria, which was the longest of all). In truth, the dividing
line between domestic and religious architecture was still very
tenuous in this period and the first absidal "temples" were derived from the great "public halls" or "banqueting chambers" of
the Geometric period, where the ritual meals of the aristocracy
took place, the prototype of which seems to be represented by
the Megaron A (late Bronze Age?) of Thermon and the building
at Toumba in Lefkandi (about 1000 B.C.).[19] In these cases, as in
those of the elongated rectangular temples that made their appearance in the early to mid eighth century on, for example,
Samos and Thermon—which, once the length had been fixed at
one hundred feet, the central colonnade had been replaced by
two lateral ones, and the peristyle had been generally adopted,
were at the origin of the archaic canon—it is not so much a problem of determining what architecture was the source of their in-
spiration. Rather, the question is where, when, and how did a
more specialized use of these places introduce a clear distinction between the temple and other buildings, even if the temples
did remain a similar shape. Now it is often hard to determine
exactly where the activities associated with religious practice
took place in the eight-century sanctuaries. We find buildings
possibly designed for ritual meals—although this is a controversial matter—alongside small *oikoi* (possibly chapels or treasure
stores) that may have housed the deity's statue, rich offerings,
and precious relics; and some of these buildings may have combined both kinds of function.[20] It was only at the end of the
Geometric period or at the beginning of the archaic that a clear

19. These buildings are sometimes called "ruler's dwellings," for example by
Mazarakis-Ainian ("Architecture religieuse," [1985], "Early Greek Temples"
[1988], who, however, includes in that description edifices of very different types
and functions; besides, it is an idea that can only be applied to urban sites. The
semantic imprecision certainly reflects the difficulties of interpretation, where
remains from the Geometric period are concerned, as soon as it is no longer a
matter of necropolises or obvious sanctuaries. See also Drerup, *Griechische Baukunst* (1969); Toumba: Popham, Calligas, and Sackett, *Lefkandi II* (1990).
20. That is the case of a type of rectangular temple with an inner hearth and
a stone bench running along the end wall, where statuettes and offerings were

functional separation is seen to operate, with the chief edifice exclusively designed to house the god and his treasure, while ritual meals were shifted to other buildings (*hesitiatorion*) and spaces specially arranged for this purpose.[21]

Meanwhile, measures were taken to define the religious space more precisely: terraces and the *temenos* wall were constructed. All the principal centers of worship were thus now enclosed in some way, whether it was a matter of separating the ritual precinct from the inhabited area, as at Delphi, Eleusis, and Delos, or from the natural environment, as in the case of the Heraion of Argos, which is, furthermore, set on a terrace supported by a particularly massive wall, or from surrounding marsh, as in the case of the Artemision of Sparta.[22]

In this way, certain religious sites, which started out simply as places where sacrifices were performed and were subsequently equipped with an altar, were gradually turned into sanctuaries in the course of the eighth century, when temples, extra buildings, or even a *temenos* wall were added. But it was only at certain sites that this happened.

Once again, while it is true that such transformations could only be carried out within the framework of a society that by now possessed the necessary resources, the problem should not be considered solely from a quantitative point of view. Such construction work also presupposes the existence of centers of de-

---

placed. It was probably modeled on the ancient Minoan sanctuaries and it was particularly common in Crete (Dreros, Amnisios, Prinias, Gortyn, Kavousi, Kommos) and in the Cyclades (Delos, the first Heraion; Paros, Koukounaries). The first religious building of Kalapodi, dating from the second half of the ninth century, and the two protoarchaic temples also featured an inner altar hearth, but no bench. See Marinatos, "Temple géométrique de Dreros" (1936); Coldstream, *Geometric Greece*, p. 280; Schilardi, "Athena on Paros" (1988), p. 47, for an interpretation favoring temples; and *contra*, Bergquist, "Sympotic Space" (1990), who suggests that some of these edifices should be seen as banqueting halls rather than temples. On the distinction between temples and treasures, Fågerström, *Iron Age Architecture* (1988), p. 160f.

21. Bergquist, "Sympotic Space"; Perachora: Tomlinson, "Upper Terraces" (1977), pp. 197–202; Samos: Kron, "Kultmahle" (1988); Aegina: Sinn, "Kult der Aphaia" (1988), pp. 149–59; Halieis: Bergquist, "Temple Function" (1990), pp. 23–37.

22. Cf. Bergquist, *Archaic Greek Temenos* (1967), pp. 19, 26, 30, and 47; Mylonas, *Eleusis* (1961), p. 56; Boardman, "Artemis Orthia" (1963).

cision capable of mobilizing those resources and implies deliberate choice, since the building took place only at a limited
number of the many sites mentioned above.[23]

The appearance of sanctuaries implies a definite change in
people's perception of space, for in the first place, it put an end
to the relative indeterminacy of religious sites. Now the space
was organized and divided up and a frontier was clearly drawn
between what was sacred and what was profane. It is interesting
that, as the Heraion of Argos and the Artemision of Sparta show,
the sacred aura of woods or marshland was now deemed inadequate for the protection of the religious quality of these holy
places. At the same time, the creation of a sanctuary stabilized
the cult, rooting the ritual in the earth, in this parcel of land consecrated to the deity and situated at once within the surrounding
territory and apart from it: the site was, par excellence, a place
of mediation between the men and the gods who, together, were
attached to this particular territory. In this manner, a vision of
space was forged that was clearly oriented in relation to the car-
dinal points represented by these permanent and fixed manifestations of the god's presence. All this was made even clearer by
the erection of a temple, for not only was the temple one of this
period's major architectural achievements, but it also symbolized
the insertion of the sacred universe into the earthly countryside.
The topographical importance that the sanctuary came to assume draws attention to the ordering of the day-to-day environment by means of the establishment of certain cult sites
constantly and deliberately represented as the objects of the
community's particular concern and pride.

Which cult sites were these, then, and why them in particular?
Why and how did religious life become oriented toward certain
deities who were typically honored by having their *temenos* de-
limited and dwellings for them built, to store the offerings
brought to them? The emergence of the sanctuary was another
phenomenon that cannot be reduced to a mechanical consequence of the growth that took place generally in the eighth century. In this society, which had already become richer in cults
and more generous with offerings than in the past, a hierarchy

23. In fact, the building of a monumental temple has sometimes been considered as a *polis'* "birth certificate" (Snodgrass, *Archaeology*, p. 26).

becomes distinguishable in the divine world. The interesting thing is that, in the movement that entailed building archaic sanctuaries, it was the cult sites situated at some distance from the towns that were particularly affected.

The Importance of Nonurban Sanctuaries

In the Greco-Aegean world of the eighth century, "towns" often consisted of loose groups of villages or clusters of houses that the first elements of urbanization were, at the end of the century, just beginning to pull together in an organic fashion (above all by creating spaces reserved for public use), just as they were expanding as a result of demographic growth.[24] A number of these towns, including some very famous ones, for a long time retained a somewhat disorganized air, even when their truly urban character could not be doubted: Sparta was, of course, one of these, but others were Athens, Corinth, and probably Argos and Tegea.[25] It is thus quite legitimate, where the documentation makes it possible, to start by locating the central inhabited area and from there to proceed, city by city, to pinpoint the position of the principal sanctuaries that appeared at the end of the Geometric period, provided that, for the moment, we limit our consideration to those sanctuaries whose importance has been established purely by archaeology.

Let us first distinguish the sanctuaries that have traditionally been regarded as the most important in the city: the sanctuaries set on an acropolis, whether or not this was truly centrally situated, and those placed at the center of an agglomeration, where they functioned as the focus of growth and urban organization. In Athens, Sparta, Argos, Mycenae, and probably Tiryns, Miletus, Phocaea, and the cities of Rhodes (Lindos, Camiros, Ialysos), the urban sanctuaries of Athena (often accompanied by Zeus) were perched on an acropolis. But the sanctuaries of

24. The most ancient traces of early urbanization have been found in Asia Minor (the layout and walls of "Old Smyrna"), in Crete (the agora of Dreros), and in Eretria. Cf. Martin, *Urbanisme* (1974), p. 289; *Recherches sur l'agora* (1951), p. 59; Altherr-Charon and Bérard, "Erétrie" (1981), pp. 230–36.

25. Snodgrass, *Archaeology*, pp. 28–29; Roebuck, "Aspects of Urbanization in Corinth" (1972).

Apollo in Corinth, Eretria, Dreros (together with Artemis), and Gortyn, all in the vicinity of the agora, belong to the second variety.[26]

Next, we may distinguish the group of suburban or periurban sanctuaries located on the margins of the inhabited area. These were constructed either right on the edge of the town or just a little way off, and they were originally separate from the urban area, although some were subsequently swallowed up by it as it expanded. A marginal position of this kind was occupied by the sanctuaries of Apollo in Thebes (Ismenion), Argos (Deiras), Halieis (Porto Cheli), Paros, and Naxos; the sanctuaries of Artemis in Sparta, Thessaly, Pheres, Delos, and Ephesus; and the sanctuary of Athena in Delphi.[27] Although less monumental, the sanctuaries of Demeter (discovered in Eleusis, Corinth, and Cnossos) were also suburban.

The last group comprises sanctuaries that were, quite literally, extraurban. The most notable of these were seldom situated less than five or six or more than twelve to fifteen kilometers from the town, and although too far away for the more ordinary, daily demonstrations of piety, they were still relatively accessible. Deities honored in this fashion, away from the urban centers, in the outlying territory (*chōra*) were Hera in Argos, Samos, Megara, and Corinth (Perachora), Pisa and Elea (Olympia, together with Zeus); Apollo in Epidauros, Sparta (Amyclae), Acraiphia (Ptōon), Megara (Tripodiscos), Chios (Phanai), Colophon (Claros), and Miletus (Didyma); Poseidon in Athens (Sunium, with Athena), Corinth (Isthmia), and Calauria; Zeus in Cleonae (Nemea); and Aphaia in Aegina. Also in this category are the outlying sanctuaries of Artemis situated on seashores (or river-

26. In Delphi, too, the earliest sanctuary of Apollo seems to have been situated in the heart of the settlement: in the seventh century still, houses appear to have stood on the site of the "Rhodians' Chariot," to the east of the temple, where the *peribolos* wall was built in about 600–590 (*BCH* 115 [1991]: 691–97); the extension of the sanctuary then pushed the settlement out toward the southwest (*BCH* 105 [1981]: 721–40).

27. The little sanctuary of Athena at Koukounaries (Paros), at first suburban in relation to the Geometric settlement, became rural when the site was abandoned in the seventh century; Schilardi, "Athena on Paros." The same occurred at the sanctuary of Apollo on the top of Mount Barbouna at Asine: Wells, "Apollo at Asine," (1985).

banks) (Mounychia, Brauron) or in the mountains (Kombothekra in Elis, Volimnos in Laconia, Lousoi in Arcadia, Kalapodi). In regions where habitations remained dispersed, with no large urban center being developed, these rural sanctuaries served as rallying points for the populations in the neighborhood: for instance, Olympia for the western Peloponnese, Thermon for Aetolia, Dodona in Epirus, and in Arcadia, the sanctuary of Athena Alea, around which the synoecism of Tegea took place.[28]

Set out in this way, the list reveals a fact to which attention is seldom drawn: many of the Greek world's most famous sanctuaries fall into the nonurban category. What the literary sources will confirm is already perceptible from an examination of the purely archaeological documentation, even taking into account the particularly extensive damage suffered by many urban sites that are also not easily accessible. For instance, it is interesting to note that, so far as chronology goes, urban sanctuaries do not in general seem to go back to a date that would immediately mark them out as being the city's primordial place of worship. The list of sanctuaries of the proto-Geometric and early Geometric periods shows clearly that it is on nonurban sites that the most ancient traces of religious practices have been found. The same goes for the earliest features typical of sanctuaries and for the appearance of the first buildings designed for exclusively religious purposes. Finally, the construction of the first of the large temples took place on rural sites (the Heraion of Samos, possibly in about 800 or 750; Thermon, Megaron B, possibly in about 750), as well as on urban ones (Tiryns, possibly in about 750; Eretria, in about 750).[29] As I have already pointed out, what this indicates above all is that the religious activities within the inhabited areas

28. It is also the role of the mountain cults of Zeus, in particular that of Mount Ida in Crete, distinguished by the sumptuous nature of its offerings from those of mountaintops in Greece (Mounts Hymettos and Parnes in Attica, Apesas in Corinthia, Arachnaion in Argolis, Lykaion in Arcadia); cf. Langdon, *Zeus on Mount Hymettos* (1976). Olympia: Morgan, *Athletes and Oracles*, pp. 49–56, 92–99; Thermon: Fågerström, *Iron Age Architecture*, pp. 151–53; Tegea: Jost, *Sanctuaires d'Arcadie* (1985), pp. 145–46, 151–54; Voyatsis, *Athena Alea* (1990).

29. The dating of "Megaron B" of Thermon and the "temple" of the acropolis of Tiryns is controversial, however, for both are sometimes considered to be edifices dating from the end of the Mycenaean period (discussion in Mazakaris-Ainian, "Architecture religieuse" pp. 12–14, 37).

for a long time revolved around practices and places that are hard to distinguish from those used in everyday life, whereas the rural sanctuaries—particularly in a few outstanding instances—became distinctive and conspicuous much earlier, by reason of their deposits of material offerings and the first attempts made there to organize the space specifically for religious purposes. It is precisely these differences and the selection of sites that accompanied them that we should investigate.

Furthermore, even in the absence of any monumental temple, a comparison of the deposits of offerings similarly reveals how very rich the nonurban sanctuaries were: many of them have yielded extremely large collections of bronze and ivory objects and figurines. In the whole of Argolis, there is no sanctuary richer or more impressive than the Heraion. That this was the foremost sanctuary of Argos and that Hera was the primordial goddess of the Argives, as she was for the Samians, is amply attested by the huge effort that must have gone into building the temple terrace and its supporting wall, and the quantity as well as the quality of the offerings dating from the eighth and seventh centuries (in particular the tripod cauldrons, the bronze figurines, the hundreds of fibulae, pins, outsize or not, *obeloi*, and steatite seals). Hera's sanctuary on Samos is equally unrivaled on that island. The antiquity of this, the first Greek *hekatompedon* to be constructed (and the speed with which reconstruction work was completed following the flooding of the Imbrasos in about 660) and the abundance, first, of terra-cotta and bronze figurines, then, in the seventh century, of eastern ivories, together with the variety of their origins, all testify to the fact that Hera was as much revered by the Samians as by the Argives and enjoyed pride of place both on the island itself and in the surrounding Aegean, where she seems to have been the patron of the world of seafaring and trade.

A similar demonstration could be undertaken to emphasize the preeminence of nonurban sanctuaries such as that of Artemis Elaphebolos at Hyampolis (Kalapodi) in Phocis and, in Boeotia, that of Apollo Ptoieus at Acraiphia, which seems to have contained some remarkable tripod cauldrons of eastern origin as well as its famous sets of tripods and *kouroi* of later date, or the sanctuary dedicated to Aphaia on Aegina. As is shown by the objects discovered in the Heraion of Perachora (in particular some very fine ivories found among the more ordinary offerings), this sanctuary was a major center of Corinthian religion at the end of the Geometric period, as was the Poseidonion of the Isthmus in the archaic period.[30]

So, without relying entirely upon the general dearth of comparable archaeological data for urban sanctuaries, it can be shown that the formation of the *polis* was accompanied by the development of large extramural sanctuaries that, in most cities, were at least as numerous and as imposing as their urban counterparts. This modest conclusion in itself calls into question the monocentric image of the city created under the exclusive aegis of the deity worshiped on its acropolis, particularly since the nonurban cults were addressed to a perfectly coherent group of deities of major standing.

Deities and Offerings: A Mismatch or a Coherent Pattern?

Athena, Hera, Apollo, and Artemis were the four deities most involved in the wave of sanctuary-building, and some of them are associated with specific religious locations. Thus, Hera is the extraurban deity par excellence, while Athena is the goddess of the acropolis. A great Olympian like Poseidon is less common, and Zeus is at once very much present by virtue of his great interregional sanctuaries (Olympia, Dodona, and Mount Ida) and his many small mountaintop sanctuaries and yet much less involved in the religious systems peculiar to every city, which did not directly reflect the hierarchy and attributes of the family of the gods as elaborated and presented in the Homeric and Hesiodic poems.[31] In several instances, the areas of action ordinarily associated with these deities seem to bear no relation to the places where their cults are located. Why is it that Hera, the god-

30. For an overall view of the groups of offerings and their origins in these sanctuaries, see Kilian-Dirlmeier, "Fremde Weihungen" (1985); Strøm, "Evidence from the Sanctuaries" (1992). The importance of the rural sanctuaries has been well established in other studies, for example, Jost, *Sanctuaires d'Arcadie* and *Sanctuaires ruraux* (1992).

31. See, similarly, Robert, "Dieux d'Homère" (1977), p. 417f.; Schachter, "Policy, cult" (1992), pp. 37–51.

dess of matrimonial and domestic life and, very often, Apollo,
the *archēgetēs* (founder) god, the protector of well-organized
societies, are honored right out in the countryside? And conversely, why is it that we find urban and suburban sanctuaries
consecrated to Artemis, a goddess more usually relegated to the
frontiers of the wild?

A similar lack of differentiation also seems to characterize the
choice of offerings that confers unity upon these deities as a
group rather than distinguishing between the attributes of each
one separately. All of them are recipients of bronze tripods, the
most precious of all treasures and booty, symbols of victory that
evoke the *agōn* and competition in all its forms, including warfare, as is underlined by the presence also of arms and figurines
representing warriors.[32] All these deities also received figurines
of animals, which evoke power over the natural world, particularly figurines representing horses and bulls. And all the goddesses, not just Artemis, were offered representations of wild
animals (deer, birds, and various other wild creatures). The two
principal categories of offerings typical of sanctuaries consecrated to goddesses are, first, objects closely linked with feminine and domestic life—in particular anything to do with clothing, such as fibulae and pins[33]—and second, terra-cotta figurines
representing, in a conventional, quasi-uniform fashion, either
the goddess herself (wearing a *polos* on her head) or, more rarely,
the female dedicator. In the extent of their powers, goddesses
thus appear to outshine even the gods. Indeed, many hymns do
celebrate the universality of the feminine deities who, in many
places, are regarded as the figures who hold supreme power,

32. The religious symbolism of the tripod (and more specifically Mantic symbolism in the oracular sanctuaries of Apollo) does not exclude its agonistic aspect. The two are inseparable. The scenes of "the fight for the tripod"—in particular the depiction on a tripod leg (Maas, *Geometrischen Dreifüsse* pp. 55–58),
which it is tempting but perhaps inexact to interpret as the fight between Apollo
and Herakles for possession of the Delphic tripod—clearly convey rivalry over
the establishment of power of a religious as well as a political nature, based upon
possession of the sacred *agalma* of which Gernet writes in *Anthropology of Ancient
Greece* (1981). It is, in my opinion, precisely that rivalry that presides over the
formation of the city.

33. As Herodotus reminds us (5.85) in an etiological myth of the cult of Damia
and Auxesia in Aegina.

whether they happen to be called Hera or Artemis, who "loves . . . the slaying of wild beasts in the mountains, . . . and dancing and thrilling cries and shady woods and the cities of upright men"; or Gē, who ensures the fecundity of the earth and the flocks and prosperity and justice in the opulent city that nurtures its vigorous youth; or, come to that, Hecate, who, for Hesiod, is the true queen of the universe, the mistress of the earth, the sky, and the sea.[34] It is she who, having escaped the disastrous fate of the Titans, dispenses riches and success— whether in the agora, on the battlefield, or in athletic competitions—keeps watch over justice, and protects the growth of the young (*kourotrophē*) and the flocks.

These apparent—but as we shall see, no more than apparent—peculiarities or anomalies have led some historians, struck by the undeniable continuity between many religious notions and practices of the Mycenaean (or even Minoan) period and those of the historical period, to extend that continuity indiscriminately to the religious sites. It is quite true that virtually all the sanctuaries, particularly the nonurban ones, were—in most cases quite deliberately—built on the top of ruins from the Bronze Age.[35] It has, on that account, sometimes been unreservedly accepted that most of the historical cults of Hera, Athena, Artemis, and Zeus (let alone Poseidon, Aphaia, etc.) were simply a perpetuation, on the very same sites, of Helladic cults that had survived the dark ages complete with their own myths, attributes, and rites.[36]

On the other hand, archaeologists sensitive to the hiatus that they detected in the occupation of most of the sites between the end of the Bronze Age and the Geometric period have stressed the discontinuity between those two phases, particularly since the Helladic vestiges on top of which the Geometric sanctuaries

---

34. *Homeric Hymn to Aphrodite*, line 15f. (trans. Hugh G. Evelyn-White, Loeb Classical Library [London and Cambridge, Mass., 1967]; *Homeric Hymn to Gē*, Hesiod, *Theogony*, lines 411–52.

35. The best-known exceptions are the urban and suburban sanctuaries of Eretria, Corinth, Argos, and Sparta.

36. The works of M. P. Nilsson, in particular *Minoan-Mycenean Religion and Its Survivals* (1950), have systematized this thesis, which is also defended, albeit from a different point of view, by Lévêque, "Continuité et innovations" (1973), and Dietrich, *Tradition in Greek Religion* (1986).

are constructed may in some cases be ordinary habitations, where no particular religious activity is detectable (their possible domestic cults having left no trace). And in places where a cult of the Mycenaean period truly did seem to have preceded one in the Geometric period, the attitude of the Greeks of the ninth eighth century sometimes seems to suggest more a return to places still remembered than an uninterrupted continuity. Thus, the use of relics from the Mycenaean period (figurines, ivory objects, pottery, etc.) as possible foundation deposits beneath the Artemision of Delos or the sanctuary of Athena Pronaia in Delphi, the reuse of the head of a Minoan goddess for a cult statue of Dionysus in the sanctuary of Aya Irini in Ceos, and even the careful way in which eighth-century altars and temples reused or preserved Helladic structures—whether a sanctuary, as in Epidauros (Mount Kynortion), a palatial *megaron*, as in Tiryns (assuming a late date for the "temple"), or a complex with an indeterminate function, as in Eleusis—could all have been prompted by a kind of religious archaeology, a desire to connect with a prestigious past by effacing all the breaks that had really intervened. In other words, the continuity in such cases may have been not so much real as professed.[37]

There was thus, for a while, a tendency to underline the breaks in continuity, at the price of overestimating the force of arguments based on the absence of material traces (see above) and underestimating the role clearly played by the memories that survived of particular cults and religious sites.[38]

The shortening of the chronological hiatus in the occupation

37. A very clear account is given by Le Roy, "Mémoire et tradition" (1984). Gallet de Santerre has put forward new arguments in favor of the existence of a Mycenaean Artemision in Delos: "Statuettes de bronze" (1987); Eleusis: Darcque, "Vestiges mycéniens," (1981); Epidauros: Lambrinoudakis, "Remains of the Mycenaean Period" (1981).

38. The most trenchant positions are those of Rolley, *Les trépieds*, pp. 131–46 (Delphi), and "Sanctuaires panhelléniques" (1983). A similar problem is posed by certain types of offerings that, given that they reappear in the Geometric period, suggest the perpetuation of the "memory of the artisan" (Le Roy, "Mémoire et tradition," p. 165), the material nature of which is unknown; but certain regions where the Mycenaean cultural tradition remained the strongest (Arcadia, Cyprus) may have played a determining role in these types of transmissions (Voyatsis, "Votive Riders," [1992], pp. 259–79).

of sites that has been suggested by recent research (in Isthmia and Tegea, for instance) and even the hypothesis of a strict continuity in the case of the sanctuary of Artemis at Hyampolis (Kalapodi) could well be seen as so many arguments reinforcing the opposite thesis. But in my view, what they indicate above all is the need to escape from a sterile and ill-conceived debate that persists in limiting itself to the clash of two opposed and mutually exclusive theses. What needs to be done is not to decide once and for all whether there was a general "break" or a general "continuity" in religious sites, practices, and architecture, but rather to try to see what part was played by both breaks and continuity in the history of each sanctuary and each cult, and to understand their implications in the history of the society concerned. The case of Olympia, the subject of fierce disagreement between those who ascribe a Mycenaean background to the cult and those who deny any such thing, emphasizing that the Altis was not frequented at all between Ancient Helladic III, or the mid Helladic period (the early second millenium B.C.), and the tenth century, is typical: if one cannot totally exclude the possibility that a (modest) Mycenaean cult of Zeus existed, it would have to have been located on the top of Mount Kronos, whereas the sanctuary of the historic period materialized in the plain, probably centered on the remains of a tumulus that was already a thousand years old and that "fixed" the legend of Pelops—and that "refoundation" seriously alters the nature of the cult.[39] Similarly, in the context of an overall continuity—which, however, started only in the period of Late Helladic IIIC, that is to say, after the collapse of the Mycenaean palaces, a fact that in itself implies that a displacement of either populations or religious practices had already taken place—the history of the cult of Artemis Elaphebolos at Hyampolis is punctuated by significant changes. The cult may have taken place in the open air, directly on top of the late Mycenaean structures until the middle Geometric period, but new arrangements in the second half of the ninth century created a new religious center in the northern building, which housed a hearth / altar. When temples were built in about 700, the southern temple, constructed above a pit that

39. Kyrieleis, "Neue Ausgrabungen in Olympia" (1992).

may have been the center of the Mycenaean cult, incorporated earlier features that preserved the sacredness of the place. However, it was the northern temple that, after a phase of relative equality between the two buildings, eventually acquired the greater importance in the sanctuary, to such a degree that it alone was reconstructed in the fifth century after the destruction of the Persian Wars.[40] Each of these phases was also characterized by different types of offerings: here, as elsewhere during the earliest phase, even the perpetuation of the cult did not prevent typically Myceneaen offerings (figurines, rhyton, bronzes, etc.) from disappearing; it was after the "refounding" of the ninth century that material offerings once again began to appear in large quantities, particularly metal objects.[41] So continuity, though certainly an important factor, was no more than relative and is not enough to explain the status and role of a cult at any particular period.

All kinds of different cases were thus possible: a Helladic cult might be perpetuated in situ or a sanctuary created ex novo; a cult site might have lain more or less unused for part of the dark ages, either abandoned but not forgotten or visited occasionally in an informal fashion, or where the cult took a purely domestic form; and the renaissance of such a site involved either the ancient deity associated with it (as in the case of the Athenas of acropolises where they were heiresses to a palace goddess) or else the introduction of a new deity (a frequent situation, as at Amyclae, Epidauros, Tegea, Delphi-Athena, possibly Delos, and Ceos). Alternatively, an ancient cult might be moved to a new site, no doubt with many changes introduced into the rites and the cult's significance. Or finally, many different kinds of vestiges might be consecrated purely on account of their antiquity, which sufficed to lend them a sacred aura (as modern archaeologists are well placed to appreciate) and made it possible to give the foundation of a cult there the appearance of a refoundation (as may have happened at Isthmia, the Heraion of Argos, and Eleusis, although the nature of the underlying Mycenaean sites has not yet been determined). However that may be, the history of a cult does not tell us absolutely everything about its significance,

40. Felsch, "Kalapodi" and "Tempel und Altäre" (1992).
41. Felsch, "Geometrischer Bronzen aus Kalapodi" (1983).

and the existence of a Mycenaean background is not enough to explain the importance that certain sites acquired.

It is accordingly more important to stress whatever is specific to Greek religious behavior in the eighth and seventh centuries than to dilute it in some vast religious continuum. The determining phenomenon in that pattern of behavior was the proliferation of cults addressed to deities such as Athena, Hera, Artemis, and Apollo, of whom only Athena was a principally urban deity, while the others often (if not in general) presided over the establishment of great sanctuaries situated on the borders of the inhabited area or at some distance from it. In most cities (with the notable exception of Athens), the importance of these sanctuaries and the correlative local primacy of the deities they housed—regardless of the Olympian hierarchy and with no attempt to define the special attributes of the deity concerned by relating them to the choice of the sanctuary's site or the type of offerings deposited there—are by no means anomalies that can only be explained by the Helladic legacy. Rather, they become perfectly coherent within the framework of the change that was then taking place in the Greco-Aegean world: namely, the formation of the *polis*.

CHAPTER TWO

The Nonurban Sanctuary and
the Formation of the City

꙾ ✳ ꙾

*Men came together by cities and by tribes, because they naturally tend to hold
things in common, and at the same time because of their need of one another;
and they met at the sacred places that were common to them for the same
reasons, holding festivals and general assemblies; for everything of this kind
tends to friendship (*philia*), beginning with eating at the same table, drinking
libations together, and lodging under the same roof.*

Strabo 9.3.5 (419)

The obscurity that surrounds many urban sanctuaries is
not caused solely by archaeological lacunas. The literary
sources, too, have so very much more to say about the nonurban
sanctuaries of the archaic period, as they relate the myths that
were passed down there, the festivals and rituals that took place
there, and the events in which they played a part. This wealth of
documentation makes it possible for us to take into account sanctuaries of which scarcely any other traces remain. Research can
thus be extended to take in a wider spread of religious sites, the
importance of which must be evaluated in relation to that of the
respective cities that controlled them. In every *polis* of the early
archaic period, the sanctuary was the one place where monumental architecture was erected, on whatever scale the community could manage. The sanctuary thus became the principal

Epigraph translation by Horace Leonard Jones, Loeb Classical Library (London and Cambridge, Mass., 1978).

place of communication between the human and the divine worlds, being a part of both at the same time, clearly defined, securely established, and highly valued as a result of the collective effort that had gone into its construction. As such, the sanctuary would both reflect and, conversely, influence the way the Greeks represented their own space, organizing it around this point where superior powers were anchored in human reality. A more detailed study of the locations of sanctuaries may thus illuminate the spatial concepts of the Greek world of the early archaic period and, over and above this, also its modes of social organization.[1]

The Sanctuary, the Land, and the Territory

Extraurban sanctuaries are particularly revealing. I earlier characterized them by the distance that separated them from the preurban habitations. However, that is no more than a relative consideration, which varies according to another factor: namely, the area of the land controlled by the community upon which the sanctuary depended. The point is that the sanctuary was often situated *right on a threshold to the territory.*

That positioning is clearly perceptible in the Greek landscape, which so often consists of little plains surrounded by hills or mountains, the "ideal" natural setting for many of the ancient cities. The most illuminating case is that of the Heraion of Argos, a model sanctuary on several counts. It is situated right on the edge of the plain of Argos, looking down over it from the top of a foothill backing onto the mountain range that borders the eastern side of Argolis, which is roughly triangular in shape. The site could be seen from many points, but was particularly visible from Argos, whose inhabitants could not fail to notice the sanctuary and its temple whenever they looked out to the east: when they did so, it was the only large construction immediately visible, for Mycenae lay further to the north and Tiryns and Nauplia further to the south.

Many sanctuaries are situated in just such ex-centric positions, toward the edge of a plain on which an inhabited area is located

---

1. Similarly, see Nenci, "Spazio civico" (1979), pp. 460–61 and 474.

opposite: the sanctuary of Amyclae is to the south of the "Lacedaemonian hollow"; that of Amarynthos is on the east of the
Eretrian plain; the Poseidonion of the Isthmus is out in the direction of the mountains that, in the northeast, separate the Corinthian plain from that of Megara, and is not far from the sea. The
sanctuary of Didyma marks out the southern boundary of the
territory of Miletus; at Samos, the presence of the Imbrasos, flow-
ing through the plain to the southwest of the town, just beyond
the Heraion, marked a kind of limit. In the cities, some large (Argos, Samos, Eretria, Corinth, Sparta), others small (like Phlius),
where the sanctuary was visible, if not from the town itself, at
least from its acropolis, the gaze of whoever looked out over the
plain would be attracted to this material marker, which indicated two kinds of limit: the limit of human implantation and
the limit of the city's control over the terrain.[2]

Now, the conditions of Greek development in the ninth and
eighth centuries confer a precise significance upon this positioning. This was the time when, in the plain, a sparse occupation of
the area—with large portions left indeterminate as fallow or pas-
ture land—gave way to dense occupation with agricultural exploitation predominating and other activities (hunting, the rais-
ing of large herds) being pushed out to the more hilly land. On
the edge of this area, now humanized, ploughed, and organized,
the extraurban sanctuary thus marked the outer limit of the ad-
vance of agrarian civilization and drew attention to its takeover
by setting it in opposition to the neighboring domain of the
mountains and forests (or the sea). The frontier that the sanctuary thus indicated was of considerable symbolic significance.

In the eyes of the Greeks, that spatial distinction reflected the

2. It is obviously more difficult to appreciate this nowadays, since the buildings have disappeared, but on certain sites there can be no doubt on the subject.
It is worth remembering that when thinking about the perfect city, Aristotle
takes into account the criterion of a clear view, as a means of protection: "The
territory . . . must be well able to be taken in at one view, and that means being a
country easy for military defence" (*Politics* 7.5.2.1327a, trans. H. Rackham, Loeb
Classical Library, [London and Cambridge, Mass., 1972]). However, that ideal
picture should not make us forget the sanctuaries separated from the settlement
by hills, in territories that are less "perfectly" laid out, but with an identical role:
Nemaean Zeus at Cleonae; Apollo Maleatas at Epidauros, Ptoieus at Acraiphia,
Claros at Colophon, Aphaia at Aegina, all visible from far away.

contrast and complementarity between two systems of values that, when kept in balance and related by clearly defined means of temporary interchange, presided over the successful functioning and reproduction of human societies. On the side of civilization, a complex of order-imposing actions and institutions (which Greek thought associated and interwove at various levels in such a way that it was impossible to conceive of the existence of one without that of all the others) underpinned and protected the stability and cyclic regularity of human life, which evolved at just the right distance from both nature in the wild and the gods. In contrast to a state of disorder, in which the relations between beings of different kinds are characterized either by too great proximity or by too great distancing, the state of society is stabilized by the simultaneous existence of precise demarcations and codified practices, which make it possible for controlled relations to be established between the various worlds that are thus distinguished.

In opposition to the two extremes represented by, on the one hand, beings springing asexually from the earth and, on the other, indiscriminate promiscuity with its multiple unions, marriage and procreation (both signs of the mortal nature of human beings and conditions of their survival) establish those necessary, correct distances, just as do the abandonment of cannibalism and its inevitable corollaries: the domestication of animals, in particular the ox (for ploughing and the consequent consumption of cereals and also for the consumption of meat following the institutionalized violence of sacrifice). Sacrifice, which the theft of fire rendered at once possible and necessary, reveals the irremediable separation of the gods from men and at the same time perpetuates the links between their respective worlds and proves to be the generator of social life, given that it introduces sharing and the acquisition of speech that this entails.

However, the civilized space thus created and marked out is confronted by the wild world in which the exact reversal of civilized values strengthens their validity, guaranteeing their preservation in society. The extraurban sanctuary thus appears as a symbolic bulwark erected against the domain of all that is undifferentiated, disordered, and ephemeral, all that is dominated by abnormal relations and placed under the sign of cunning and noninstitutionalized violence: relations without mediation between men and gods (forbidden visions, phenomena involving possession) and between human beings themselves (misanthropy, misandry, and misogyny, forms of uncontrolled aggression, anthropophagy, and sexual violence) and between men and animals (hunting).[3]

The sanctuary, the place where two worlds meet, is accordingly seen as the stable point where a controlled passage from the one to the other is possible. So the category of cult sites in "relatively" borderline positions must be expanded to include those that occupy "absolutely" extreme positions: situated at the heart of the wild world, these sanctuaries manifest the integration of deities who, from being potentially hostile, become beneficent for the community that makes room for them within its religious life. These sanctuaries are, as a rule, both more modest and more distant than the "relatively" distant ones; they are isolated at the "world's end," out in the *eschatiai*. The deities most frequently honored by this type of sanctuary are Artemis (Elaphebolos at Hyampolis, Brauronia in the hills of Attica, close to the sea, Limnatis in the Taygete region and in Elis, and Caryatis and Hemerasia in the mountains of Arcadia), and sometimes Apollo (also at Hyampolis and at Kosmas in Kynouria).[4]

Now, many of these sanctuaries also mark a frontier, but a political one. The fact is, of course, that the "otherness" upon which the protective sanctuary looks out, either warding it off or rehabilitating it, was constituted not only by a disturbing and hostile nature, with its own untamed deities, but also by other human beings: in other words, a neighboring society. So the concept of territory, as well as that of land, is relevant: the organization of space is defined not only by the relationship of man to his natural environment, but also by the relations between different groups of human beings.

3. I am here briefly summarizing what has already been illuminated and to a large extent explained in numerous studies (in particular those by Jean-Pierre Vernant and Pierre Vidal-Naquet).

4. However, the Heraion of Perachora, a cult site that is famous but set in an isolated position on its promontory, is closer to this type than to the sanctuaries of Hera at Samos and Argos. See Pausanias 4.4.13 (Limnatis), 3.10.7 (Caryatis), 8.19.7 (Hemerasia); Kosmas (Pythaean or Maleatas Apollo): Faklaris, *Archaia Kynouria* (1985), pp. 218–25.

From this perspective, the position of the extraurban sanctuary is every bit as significant. Let us return to the example of the Heraion of Argolis, which lies between Argos, Mycenae, and Tiryns, situated about eight, five, and nine kilometers from those three towns respectively. It has the air of a central spot, a meeting place for the entire region. Its position made it the ideal place for the demonstrations of ritualized competition (including sacrifices and offerings that vied in lavishness) that appear to have developed in the eighth century among some Greek aristocracies, and it thus became the locus for the symbolic expression of the regional supremacy of Argos.[5] In similar fashion, the sanctuary of Amyclae constitutes a statement of Sparta's domination over the Lacedaemonian plain, while the sanctuaries of Isthmia, Amarynthos, Nemea, Epidauros, Aegina, Samos, Didyma, and Claros proclaim the power of the respective social bodies that set them up in the territories they occupy.

Peremptory symbols of this kind were complemented by the establishment of sanctuaries right on the boundaries of the city territory. For Corinth, the sanctuaries of Perachora, Solygaea, and Tenea are so many points of reference that mark out how far the *chōra* extends to the north and the south. In Kynouria, the sanctuaries of Apollo Tyritas and Pythaean/Maleatas mark out the path leading from Prasiai to Tyros and from Prasiai to Laconia proper; the sanctuary of Artemis Elaphebolos in the Hyampolis pass indicated the northern frontier of the city and also of the whole area of Phocis; an Aphrodision was built between Lato and Olonte in Crete; on the island of Ceos, the sanctuaries of Apollo Sminthaea and Athena Nedussa stood, one on each side of a valley, respectively marking the boundaries of the territories of Coressia and Poïeessa.[6] But in some cases, a cult would be shared by two adjacent cities: that of Artemis Hymnia by Orchomenos and Mantinaea in Boeotia, that of Artemis Hemerasia by Pheneos and Cleitor, in Arcadia. The cults of Artemis that proliferated along the mountainous borders of Arcadia and Argolis in

5. Antonaccio, "Argive Heraion" (1992), pp. 85–105; Polignac, "Cité et territoire" (forthcoming).

6. Kynouria: Faklaris, *Archaia Kynouria*, pp. 209–25; Crete: Van Effenterre, "Querelles crétoises" (1942); Ceos: Strabo 9.5.6. Other examples are given by Daverio-Rocchi, *Frontiera e confini* (1988), pp. 54–56.

the seventh century were probably frequented by the neighboring populations of both regions, just as initially the cult of Artemis Limnatis must have been shared by the Spartans and the Messenians and that of Poseidon of Onchestos by Orchomenos and Thebes, in Boeotia.[7] In areas where no major city was strong enough to eclipse the other communities or cities, sanctuaries situated at equal distance from them all continued to be shared: on Lesbos, the island's four cities shared the sanctuary situated at its center, where the poet Alcaeus was obliged to take refuge when he was exiled beyond the frontiers of his territory.[8]

This ordering of space again brings to mind the agricultural conquest of the land. The notion of territory in a society dominated by pastoral activities was not the same as it was where agriculture predominated. In the former case, grazing land, watering points, and paths had to be kept open and accessible. Agreements and compromises were necessary to guarantee freedom of movement. The protection extended over a flock as it moved about, not over the land that it moved over. In the latter case, the notion of frontiers was crucial: the important thing was to mark out precisely the space where one particular group of people reserved the right to plant and harvest their crops, and to do so it was necessary to exercise control over access routes and to defend the land itself.[9]

Now, it is very noticeable that most of the cult sites that appeared from the tenth century on were situated either in regions where habitations were dispersed, where they served as meeting places for the populations whose offerings sometimes testified to their pastoral way of life (as at Olympia and at the Cabirion of Thebes), or else close to a shore or a port. The most ancient generation of sanctuaries thus corresponds to a phase during which

7. Cf. note 4 and Pausanias 8.13.1; 9.37.1.

8. Cf. Robert, "Recherches épigraphiques" (1960), pp. 300–315. Some of these sanctuaries in a position of equidistance from a number of settlements became the seat of the federal institutions for their region, as did the sanctuary at Onchestos for Boeotia in the Hellenistic period (cf. Roesch, "Onchestos" [1977], pp. 82–83).

9. On the frontier in antiquity, see the articles in *Ktèma* 4 (1979), in particular Sartre, "Aspects économiques et aspects religieux," and Daverio-Rocchi, *Frontiera e confini*. On pastoralism in Greece, Osborne, *Classical Landscape* (1987), pp. 47–52.

contacts and trading possibilities were being sought out and stabilized, following the contraction of the preceding centuries. These contacts might be established either between neighboring cantons and populations (Olympia, Kombothekra, Tegea, Cabirion, Hyampolis, Hymettos, maybe Amyclae, and in the Cretan mountains) or with passing seafarers (the Heraion of Samos, Mounychia, possibly Brauron, Polis in Ithaca, Kommos in Crete). Where space and society were organized in this fashion, cult sites were, as a rule, shared. But such sharing could only be perpetuated in the case of the borderland cults that specialized in rites of inversion, in which adolescents who had reached the stage of being formally admitted into society left civilized and civic space for a while, the better to be reborn in their new status. The cultural indetermination of a space adjacent to two cities made it possible for certain sanctuaries to straddle a political boundary.[10] On the other hand, the situations where cult sites, initially shared, passed under the control of a single community, which set up its own border sanctuaries, testify to the impact of the territorial problem upon the agrarian societies of the late Geometric period. The heavy demand for land at this time made it necessary for societies to strengthen their control over space— a process facilitated by the very demographic expansion that was at its origin—in order to ensure that the land involved would permanently be exploited for the exclusive benefit of those who continued to live there. The sanctuaries that appeared in the eighth century, or the beginning of the archaic period, were far more likely to be the product of preoccupations of this kind. Agrarian tension thus played its part in the shaping of a new concept of space that affirmed the common interest of all those who lived in it, first and foremost among them the holders of authority, whether they resided in the center of that space or on its periphery.

Now, once this solidarity took shape, first through the frequenting, then through the appropriation of a cult site that marked the boundary of the relevant space, an essential step had

10. Polignac, "Mediation, Competition, and Sovereignty" (1994). It is worth noting that most of the known cases of a perpetuation of such a division are situated in regions, such as Arcadia, where pastoralism always played an essential role.

been taken toward the unification of all the society's components into a single entity: namely, a city. That unification culminated in the erection of a sanctuary for the principal deity, positioned within the territory but on the edge of the cultivable area. The social space was thus structured around two poles: the inhabited area and the sanctuary, the separation/combination of which formulated a new definition of the community on a territorial basis.

That duality, the effect of which was to impose order upon the social unit, was sometimes given material representation in the form of a solemn pathway. The great paths that linked the urban centers with their principal peripheral sanctuary were constructed with particular care. These axes of the civic territory, tangible traces of the fundamental connection between the two poles of the city, constituted the stage upon which great processions took place. In these, at regular intervals, the social body as a whole performed for itself, parading from the town to the sanctuary and thereby periodically reaffirming its control over the territory, a control that was exercised according to the norms of agrarian civilization. The processions of the Argives, the Plataeans, and the Samians for the Heraia, and the Lacedaemonians' procession for the Hyacinthia are among the most famous of these great "political" demonstrations.[11] But others are also worth mentioning: the procession of the Hermionians for the festival of Demeter Cthonia and all the other celebrations that gathered whole cities together in their extraurban sanctuaries (for example, the sanctuary of Apollo Maloeis in Mytilene on Lesbos, and that of Dionysus at Smyrna).[12]

All these celebrations consecrated the solidarity of the group, by gathering together the *dēmos* and its leaders and, around them, the nonwarrior population usually excluded from public life: dependents of every kind, women and adolescents. They

---

11. Led by their magistrates, all the cities made their internal hierarchy manifest in this way. In Lacedaemonia, the road to the sanctuary was known as the "Hyacinthos Way" (Athenaeus 4.173f.). The sacred way that linked Miletus and its sanctuary of Apollo at Didyma has been partially uncovered: Tuchelt, "Heiligtümer von Didyma" (1991), pp. 91–98.

12. Pausanias 2.35.4; Thucydides 3.3; Herodotus 1.150. On the Eleusinia and the Eleusinian Sacred Way, see below.

may have been a legacy from ancient practices,[13] but even if they were, they now acquired a new, civic dimension with the construction of a great sanctuary within the territory, on a religious site whose essential functions are revealed by the characteristics of the celebrations themselves.

The Agrarian Space: Fecundity and Kourotropheia

One of the best known of these processions, that of the Heraia of Argos, is also one of those most charged with meaning. Its first characteristic feature is the part played in it by a particularly highly valued domestic animal, the ox. The chariot that carried the priestess of Hera was drawn by a team of oxen. Upon the basis of this custom was grafted the famous story of Cleobis and Biton, who once filled in when oxen were unavailable and thus drew their mother, who was then the priestess, to the Heraion.[14] A second factor is that Hera was believed to have been brought up by the three daughters of the river Asterion (which flowed alongside her sanctuary), and one of them, Euboia, was supposed to have given her name to the mountain that rose behind the Heraion: a name "propitious to the bovine."[15] Finally, the complex of myths surrounding Io and the Danaids, which constitutes a great discourse on the subject of marriage seen as the basis of the civilized order and was probably drawn from the *hieros logos* of the sanctuary, begins with the metamorphosis of Io, the Argive priestess of the goddess Hera, who changed her into a white cow in a vain attempt to keep her out of the clutches of Zeus.[16]

The ox was par excellence the animal that drew the plough, as well as being the perfect victim for sacrifice.[17] When Cleobis and

13. Cf. *Odyssey* 20.270–79; sacrificial victims were led to the wood of Apollo the Archer, where the people were assembled.

14. Herodotus 1.31.

15. Pausanias 2.17.

16. Aeschylus *Suppliant Women* 1.291–301.

17. The place of the ox in the combination of ploughing-sacrifice with the orientation and foundation of civilized society (assimilated by the Greeks to the world of the *polis*) is examined by Durand, *Labour et sacrifice* (1986). The significance of ploughing in the symbolic and the real appropriation of a space in which wandering is banished and the part played both by the agricultural cart (*arotron*)

Biton were obliged to submit themselves to the yoke (*zeuglē*), it
was because the oxen had not yet returned from the fields to the
town, which was the starting point for the procession now due
to set off toward those very fields, passing through them by way
of the great, solemn path that led to the sanctuary. In other
words, the ox would leave one particular field to lead the Heraia
procession through the communal fields that constituted the cultivated territory whose boundary was marked by the sanctuary:
the Argive *pompē*, a slow, dignified progress of the social body
escorting the priestess and her oxen, can be seen as a collective
sacred ploughing, in which the processional route represents a
symbolic furrow leading from the dwelling place of human beings, in the center, to the dwelling place of the deity on the edge
of the plain now taken over by agricultural civilization.

   This agrarian mediation between the people of Argos and
their goddess evoked the first form of protection that they de-
sired from her: namely, fertility, as has already been suggested
by our study of the offerings deposited in the sanctuary. As we
have just seen, this means the fertility of the fields whose expanse could be surveyed from the Heraion, from which one
could also "preside" over their exploitation; and it also means
the fertility of the flocks and herds, whose maintenance guaranteed the goddess her annual sacrifices, as is widely attested by
the important part played by bovines in all the mythology pertaining to her.[18] Hera's role as protectress of the herds may well
have constituted one of the most ancient attributes of the goddess. But through the image and importance of the domesticated
ox, she became first and foremost the protectress of the agrarian
space—and hence also of those who drew their subsistence from
it, perpetuating the imprint of civilized life there—for the sovereignty of Zeus' wife was also exercised over another funda-

---

and the chariot (*hamaxa*) pulled by oxen are underlined in chapter 6 ("Lieurs de
boeufs et labours sacrés"). Meanwhile, in the *chōra*, seen as a "single furrow" but
one that turned back on itself (*boustrophēdon*), the processional path, a single
straight line, was an effective way of marking the fundamental axis of the
territory.

   18. Cf. the legend of Io, "Hera's cow," watched over by the irreplaceable
guardian constituted by Argos, "which sees everything"; only Hermes, the thiev-
ing god of herds (cf. *Homeric Hymn to Hermes*) can get the better of it.

mental institution of humanized space, marriage, so her protection also extended to human fecundity.

But there is another aspect to that fecundity. The hope of see-
ing its fruits come forth would be vain if they were not preserved
thereafter. As an extension of the protection that she affords
to the earth and its products, the great matrimonial goddess
watches over not so much the birth of beings as their growth; she
is even more concerned to preserve the household than to ensure
the fertility of marriage. Above all, she nurtures the young, and
this function of the *kourotrophē* is worth examining further.[19]

It is a function shared by all the deities honored by the erection of great sanctuaries in the early archaic period, but in particular by the feminine deities whose names vary from one place
to another and whose extensive powers have been mentioned
above. Foremost among them is Hera, in Argos, Perachora, and
Samos and also in Plataea, where the great Daidala procession,
which celebrated a "reconciliation" between Hera and Zeus,
passed right through the territory, from the city to the river Aso-
pos and thence on to Mount Citheron, sharing many points in
common with the procession in Argos.[20] But they also include
the goddesses whom the hymns praise for their omnipotence in
the particular region or city where they are honored. As we have
noted, Hecate and Gē dispense "fine children and fine har-
vests."[21] Nor does even Artemis' rebarbative virginity disqualify

19. See Hadzisteliou-Price, *Kourotrophos* (1978).

20. The sanctuary of Plataea: Herodotus 9.52. Daidala: Pausanias 9.3. Hera
was both Teleia (The Spouse) and Nympheuomene (Promised in Marriage) (Pausanias 9.2.7). The carts that carried the *daidala* (pieces of wood roughly sculpted
and bedecked with feminine ornaments) were no doubt drawn by oxen, as is
indicated by the etiological myth. But although the Dedalia were played out as a
ritual of hierogamy, there were many other aspects to them, and the *daidalon* was
probably not a statue of the goddess: cf. Frontisi-Ducroux, *Dédale* (1975), pp. 193–
216. In the Roman period, the whole of Boeotia was represented at the Great
Dedalia, every fifty-nine years; but the remarks of Pausanias on the repercussions
of the political events of the classical and Hellenistic period suggest that the archaic festival was probably chiefly Plataean and was also held more frequently,
possibly as often as the minor Dedalia that were celebrated when the *daidalon*
was made. Hera the Kourotrophos: Hadzisteliou-Price, *Kourotrophos*, pp. 143–45,
179–81.

21. *Eupaidēs te kai aukarpoi* (*Homeric Hymn to Gē*, line 5). Hecate the Kourotrophos: Hesiod *Theogony*, lines 450 and 452.

her from this domain,[22] where she operates not as its sovereign
but as the guardian of its boundaries and points of contact with
the antinomic and complementary world of the disordered fertility of nature in the wild and the rejection of marriage. Her role
in this capacity, which is particularly evident at the critical moment of transition between adolescence and adulthood, operates
in both directions, for by safeguarding the balance between civilized space and wild space, Artemis presides over the harmoni-
ous preservation of both these worlds.[23] The protection that she
affords to beings committed to a wandering kind of life (shep-
herds, hunters, nondomesticated animals) is thus indissociable
from that which she extends to the growth of human beings up
to the point of their initiation when, for a short time, she acts as
their guide in the chaotic expanses of the frontier regions. And
even when he is integrated into the stable, organized, agrarian,
civic world, an adult can only preserve its cultural bases with the
help of the goddess who watches over its frontiers.[24]

Her brother Apollo, meanwhile, was the major masculine deity
and the principal god to take on this kourotrophic role, which
was sometimes accompanied by agrarian preoccupations.[25] In
Sparta, he was associated with a "hero of vegetation," Hyacinthos, and the Hyacinthia, the greatest of the Spartan celebrations, lasted for three whole days, following a death-mourning/
renewal-joy pattern: the day devoted to the hero's death was
followed by first a solemn procession from Sparta to Amyclae,
then a festival that featured various exercises (gymnastics, dancing) performed by adolescent boys and girls, and last, the sacrifice with its ritual meal, in the course of which the summer
produce of the earth (grain, beans, fruit) was sampled, to mark

22. No more than Athena, in her few extraurban sanctuaries, as at Troezen
(Schmitt Pantel, "Athena Apatouria" [1977]). It was she who received the
greatest number of consecrated statues of young girls: over half the archaic
korai have been discovered in her sanctuaries (cf. Ducat, "Kouros et Kolossos,"
[1976]).

23. Cf. below, p. 60.

24. Frontisi-Ducroux, "Artémis bucolique" (1981); Vernant, in *Annuaire du
Collège de France*, 1981–82, pp. 400–420; 1982–83, pp. 443–457; Vernant "Artémis
Orthia" (1984).

25. Hesiod *Theogony*, lines 346–47. Locally, only the Cretan Zeus and Poseidon (Phytalmios at Troezen, cf. Pausanias 2.32.7) can be compared to him.

the end of the harvest season.[26] In Laconia, Apollo played the same role as Hera in Argos: he guaranteed the fertility of the earth and nurtured and protected the young. It is certainly this last aspect of his activities that was acknowledged, with remarkable majesty, by the offerings of the famous archaic *kouroi* to be found in most of the sanctuaries of this god, the foremost beneficiary of this custom.[27] These statues represented a ritual form of consecration of the city's young people, the purpose of which was to obtain the god's protection over the society of which they were the future or new full members: the Apollo Kourotrophos, who ensured that the norms of civilization were passed on from one generation to the next, thereby became a "political" god as those norms came to define the city space.[28]

In that Apollo and the feminine deities were responsible for two frequently combined tasks, the protection of fertility and the nurturing of the young, they seem to have been committed in particular to the renewal of the vital forces of society; but perhaps we should venture a little further. The notion of *trophē* was rich in nuances, incorporating a number of different images of growth: *trephein* meant not only to nourish and to bring up but also to gel, crystallize, and cohere similar elements.[29] The great deities of the *trophē*, who watched over the survival and vitality of the groups that honored them, acted as protectors of the cohesion and agglomeration of the individuals who made up the society, by gathering them all around their cult. The fact that they did so provided the grounds for their intervention in two other domains: warfare and initiation.

The Territory: Warfare, Appropriation, and Sovereignty

Vigilence was also exercised from the extraurban sanctuaries over the other threat that hung over the land: human aggression.

---

26. Athenaeus 4.138f. See the study by Calame, *Choeurs de jeunes filles* (1977) p. 305f.; and Pettersson, *Cults of Apollo* (1992), pp. 9–41.

27. As in the case of the *korai* for Athena, half the *kouroi* discovered have been dedicated to him. Cf. Ducat, "Kouros et Kolossos," p. 239.

28. Ibid., p. 243f. But I do not think that this should be seen as an attenuated form of *ver sacrum*.

29. Démont, "Remarques" (1978), p. 358–84.

Within the framework of the changes taking place in the eighth century, this took on a new intensity and assumed new forms. The military nature of some of the sanctuary offerings has already been noted.[30] From the end of the Geometric period and throughout the archaic period, panoply items (in particular, helmets, greaves, and shields) and arms (swords, spear- and arrow-tips) were deposited in sanctuaries such as Olympia, Delphi, Isthmia, Tegea, and Philia and, to a lesser degree, Amyclae, Hyampolis (Kalapodi), and Aegina (Aphaia). In certain sanctuaries, etiological rites and stories appear to have developed out of this practice. In Argolis, the *pompē* that led from Argos to the Heraion seems to have included armed participants, and a whole corpus of rites and myths concerning the shield was elaborated around the sanctuary. In the classical period, a bronze shield was the prize to be won in the games consecrated to Hera, perhaps for an armed race of the type known to have taken place in a number of festivals consecrated to this goddess.[31] From the first century B.C. on, these games were accordingly known quite simply as *ex Argous aspis*. According to one tradition, the institution of this prize went back to the time of the Danaid dynasty: the arms of Danaos were supposed to have been passed on first to his son-in-law, Lynceus, then to his grandson, Abas. At Abas' death, the mere sight of these arms had been enough to quell a rebellion by the peoples subjected to the Argives. The shield of Danaos was at this point consecrated to Hera, and this was the episode from which the *aspis* originated.[32] According to another legend, the sons of that same Abas, Acrisios and Proitos, were the ones who invented the shield in the course of their fratricidal struggle for the throne of Argos—or at any rate invented the Argive shield represented on the pyramidal structure situated between Argos and Epidauros, which commemorated their duel.[33] In Argive stories, after the "golden age" of rivers and the dynasty of Phoronides, which introduced the first human beings

30. Cf. chap. 1 above.

31. Hera Prodromia in Sicyon (Pausanias 2.11.2), Dromia in Thera (*IG* 13.3.513). Cf. Ringwood-Arnold, "Shield of Argos" (1937), pp. 436–40; Amandry, "Concours argiens" (1980).

32. Hyginus *Fab.* 273.

33. Apollodorus 2.2.1; Pausanias 2.25.6.

into this region, Danaos, his ancestor Io, and his descendants thus came to represent the mythical establishment of two fundamental institutions of civilization: marriage and warfare, both of which are associated with Hera.

Apollo, who was the recipient of offerings of arms in Delphi and Delos, also received them at Amyclae, where, in the course of the Hyacinthia, those taking part in the festival were shown the breastplate of Timomachos, the Aegeid who was supposed to have conquered Amyclae for the Spartans and founded the Lacedaemonian military organization; and the most ancient bronze tripods deposited in the sanctuary were believed to be the tithe from the Messenian Wars.[34] The anecdote about Pythagoras claiming to recognize the shield of his "ancestor" Euphorbos, consecrated by Menelaos in the temple of Apollo of the Branchidai at Didyma also testifies to the practice of making offerings of this kind to this god.[35]

In Sparta again, in the suburban sanctuary of Orthia, many figurines of warriors have been discovered, testifying to the protection the goddess afforded fighting men. And the sanctuary of Artemis at Amarynthos, to the east of Eretria, contained the text of an agreement concluded between the Eretrians and the Chalcidians to ban the use of projectile weapons in their battles (which many identify as the famous Lelantine War), found alongside a *stēlē* commemorating an Eretrian military *pompē* of 3,000 hoplites, 600 horsemen, and 60 chariots.[36]

However, many of these traditions and documents are of late date and may reflect changes that mostly took place after the archaic period. Thus, the predominant position assumed by the shield in the Argive games and the corresponding myths (Abas, Acrisios, and Proitos) does not appear to go back beyond the end of the Hellenistic period, although the presence of the shield

---

34. Aegeids: Pindar *Isthmian* 7.13–15; Aristotle *Rep. Lacedaem.* (frag. 532 Rose, Schol. Pind. Isthm. 7.18a). Tripods: Pausanias 3.18.7; when the Athenians and the Spartans signed the Peace of Nicias, the latter placed the *stele* upon which the agreement was engraved in the sanctuary of Apollo, and on the occasion of the Hyacinthia, Athenian deputies came there to renew the alliance (Thucydides 5.18, 23).

35. Diogenes Laertius 8.1.4f.

36. Strabo 10.1.10, 12.

among other competition prizes, such as tripods and other
bronzes, may go back further.[37] The intervention of Timomachos
and the Aegeids (which, in any event, other traditions associate
not with Amyclae but with the conquest of Laconia by the
Heraklids) might also be a late intervention, and there is no evidence to determine to which conflict the agreement between the
Eretrians and the Chalcidians related.[38] However, legends such
as these can only have developed on the basis of precise data.
Frequently, they reflect the particular association of a city to a
piece of weaponry upon which, ever since the archaic period, its
reputation had rested (the shields of Argos; the swords of the
Euboeans, made famous in the war associated with them).[39] But
above all, the appearance of pieces of weaponry in the archaic
sanctuaries coincides with the changes that were taking place
from the second half of the eighth century on: notably, the switch
from "heroic" warfare, a matter of raids and individual exploits,
to a stable and collective form of combat from which the hoplite
phalanx was to emerge.

At the turn of the eighth and seventh centuries, weaponry was
affected by modifications that testify to the progressive elaboration of new tactics, in which a fighting man no longer sought out
encounters and single combat of the "Homeric" type, but was
expected to integrate himself in a fighting body whose very
weight and unshakable solidity were the factors that made it
possible to win the day. Whether attacking or resisting without
retreating, the phalanx derived its success from its compact
mass. As a result, the items of a fighting man's panoply underwent a change: breastplates and helmets were redesigned for the
purposes of combat in close formation, using spears and swords.
But it was the shield known as the "Argive shield" that became
the most important piece of defensive equipment: this round
shield, now held by means of a double handle on the inner side,
through which the left forearm and the hand passed, was the
essential item in the cohesion of the hoplite phalanx. The wall of

37. The games of Hera are only definitely attested from the Argive reconquest
of the 460s, but that does not necessarily mean that there was no form of the
games in the archaic period; cf. Amandry, "Concours argiens" p. 242.

38. Timomachos: Cartledge, *Sparta and Laconia* (1979), p. 108.

39. Archilochus frag. 9 CUF.

shields, each one overlapping the next, ensured the protection of the whole line of men, instead of each separate shield protecting a single individual.[40]

But this development itself stemmed from other more general changes. It resulted largely from changes in the ways in which the land was occupied. Homeric raids and the high deeds of champions, professional warriors, belonged to the world of the *oikoi* chieftains of the Geometric period, *basileis* who were more or less independent within a mainly pastoral society. As the land became increasingly used for agricultural purposes, prompting a new concept of the territory and its frontiers, the fundamental objectives of warfare gradually changed. It was no longer a matter of launching a swift expedition to seize domesticated animals. Instead, what became increasingly important was the constant defense of the arable land against invasion, for the effect of such an invasion would be to paralyze agricultural activities and destroy the crops. This was a task that could not be carried out by making swift, isolated raids. The need for constant protection obliged those who wished to reserve the land for their own use to take collective action. This took the form of group tactics, by means of which the enemy could be repulsed in a pitched battle on the plain. Conversely, territory could only be seized by dint of a common and sustained effort to ensure permanent possession of the land, rather than a temporary chance for pillage. In this way, the basic elements of archaic and classical warfare were elaborated: two armies drawn up in serried ranks would confront each other within a defined area, a plain, from which each would attempt to eject the other so as to remain in occupation of the terrain.

In this context, the consecration of pieces of weaponry in a sanctuary does not necessarily confer a warrior nature upon the deity concerned, but rather underlines the particular kind of protection expected or obtained from her in armed conflict. The

40. There is a wide bibliography from which it is particularly worth noting the following: Snodgrass, *Early Greek Armours and Weapons* (1964), and "Hoplite reform" (1965); Courbin, "La guerre à haute époque" (1968); Detienne, "La phalange" (1968); Garlan, "Défense du territoire" (1973), and *Recherches de poliorcétique grecque* (1974), pp. 20–44; Greenhalgh, *Early Greek Warfare* (1973); Cartledge, "Hoplites and Heroes" (1977).

end of the Geometric period certainly did see the eruption of a long series of territorial conflicts in Greece, some of which may have developed proportions and a ferocity unprecedented since the wars of the Mycenaean period: the wars between Chalcis and Eretria (the Lelantine War), supported by their respective allies (the Thessalians and Samians and the Milesians); possibly between Megara and Corinth; between Argos and its neighbors, Asine, destroyed in about 710, and Sparta (the Kynourian and Thyreatid Wars); between Sparta and Amyclae and between Sparta and the Messenians; and later, probably in the archaic period, between Thebes and Orchomenos. Their geographic distribution coincides exactly with the area of diffusion of the archaic *polis*, and all, one way or another, imply the existence of an extra-urban sanctuary.

As we have seen, a sanctuary of this kind was itself sometimes the cause of the conflict: in Boeotian traditions, which are marked by lengthy struggles between the two great rivals Thebes and Orchomenos for control of the rich plains of the region, the Orchomenian king, Clymenos, is said to have been killed by the Thebans during the festival of Poseidon Onchestos, whose sanctuary, halfway between the two cities, seems to have constituted a no-man's-land. The Theban action was a sacrilegious attempt to gain possession of the site.[41] It was also over a sanctuary initially shared that the First Messenian War broke out. The sanctuary was that of Artemis Limnatis, and it was there that the crime presented as the cause of the war was committed. According to the Lacedaemonian version, the Messenians attacked some young Spartan girls and killed the king, Teleclos; according to the Messenians, a plot was hatched against the Messenian *aristoi*, who were attacked by young Spartans disguised as girls. The two versions of the incident can be seen as a historization of two myths concerning the foundation of the cult of Artemis and its rituals designed for adolescents (dressing up, initiatory deaths).[42]

41. Pausanias 10.37.1. These episodes of legendary wars between Thebes and Orchomenos, echoes of possible confrontations in the Helladic period, were actualized in the conflicts of the archaic period, probably in the sixth century, when Thebes was establishing its authority over central Boeotia: Schachter, "Boiotia in the Sixth Century" (1989), p. 80.

42. Pausanias 4.4.1; Calame, *Choeurs de jeunes filles*, p. 253ff.

But whatever the circumstances may have been, the sanctuary clearly was involved in the outbreak of hostilities.

The case of these sanctuaries initially shared by different peoples is instructive, for the conflict that breaks out over possession of a sanctuary and its takeover by a single community reflects the crystallization of the notions of territory and frontiers and show how these were being applied. The history of the sanctuaries of the Isthmus provides another illustration. A number of different traditions would appear to allude to ancient frontier conflicts between Megara and Corinth and the existence of a double cult: the cult of Hera Acraia / Hera Limenaia, in the sanctuary of Perachora, has been interpreted as the sign of a switch in sovereignty, the abandonment of the former being seen to reflect Corinth's assumption of power toward the end of the eighth century.[43] However, there was in truth only one cult at Perachora; the second temple seems, rather, to have been a *hestiatorion* built at the beginning of the seventh century, when the lower cult site became too cramped.[44] Nevertheless, the territorial consolidation of the two cities was a determining factor in the evolution of cults in the region: a geographical limit and at the same time a reference point for Corinth, the sanctuary of Perachora in the eighth century was the major rallying spot of the Peraians. The offerings there, like those in the Heraion of Samos, also testify to the considerable trading activity of the Corinthians, and its establishment enabled the city to assert its sovereignty on the promontory, whether or not this had been claimed by the Megarians. On the other side, the sanctuary of Poseidon at Isthmia had, ever since the proto-Geometric period, been a modest cult site frequented by the local populations and by travelers passing on a road alongside. But in the eighth century, the status of this sanctuary, too, changed, with the appearance of prestige offer-

43. For example, Dunbabin, "Hera Akraia at Perachora" (1951). The mention of Heraia and Peraia, two sites on the promontory of Perachora, among the five villages whose synoecism is supposed to have resulted in the formation of the city of Megara (Plutarch *Quaest. Graec.* 17) may be an indication of the subsequent conquest of this region and the sanctuary by the Corinthians; see also, below, the legend of Coroibos and Orsippos. But those traditions were certainly enriched, if not actually elaborated, at the time of the fifth-century conflicts; cf. Piccirilli, *Megarika* (1975), pp. 6–7.

44. See above, page 19, and note 21.

ings (a number of tripod cauldrons) and the first weapons there (helmets). The various building operations that accompanied this change (the creation of the first terraces with a long altar and the eventual construction of the first temple, in the first half of the seventh century) clearly demonstrates the importance that Corinth attached to this sanctuary, which from this time on would testify to its domination in the region.[45] This affirmation of the Corinthian presence in the Isthmus—whether rapid or gradual—may, in reaction, have encouraged the founding or expansion of the cult of the Megarian Apollo at Tripodiscos (Little Tripod), a village situated at the foot of the Geranian mountains and hence on the edge of a "wild" place that also constituted the frontier with Corinth. The tomb of its mythical founder, the hero Coroibos, used to be pointed out in the agora of Megara, where it was flanked by that of the legendary athlete Orsippos, believed to have been the Olympic champion in 720, that is to say, at the time of the legendary war between Megara and Corinth.[46] According to tradition, Orsippos had also reconquered a frontier territory. The history of the cult at Tripodiscos might thus represent the Megarian reaction to the expansion of the cults of the Isthmus upon which the Corinthians had embarked.

The Heraion of Argos illustrates another kind of connection between a territory's sanctuary and war and sovereignty. This was the cult site of a sovereign Hera, mistress of the plain of Argolis, which was spread out at her feet. Its central and dominating position made it, initially, one of those regional sanctuaries situated at the heart of the common activities by which neighboring communities were linked: one tradition had it that it was at first shared by the peoples of Mycenae and Argos.[47] On that

45. Perachora: Morgan, "Corinth" (1988), pp. 335–36; Sinn, "Das Heraion von Perachora" (1990); Isthmia: Gebhard and Hemans, "Excavations at Isthmia," pp. 11–23; Morgan, "Sacral Landscape" (1994).

46. Pausanias 1.43.7–44.1; Piccirilli, *Megarika*, p. 127–30; Rigsby, "Megara and Tripodiscus" (1987). Coroibos had been ejected from Argos for having resisted vengeance taken by Apollo. The Delphic oracle, to appease the wrath of the god, ordered him to take a tripod and found a sanctuary for Apollo wherever the object slipped from his hands; this happened at a place that was thenceforward known as Tripodiscos.

47. Strabo 8.6.10 (C 372). This tradition and the one according to which the first *xoanon* of the Heraion had been brought from Tiryns after the destruction of

very account, it was also the stake in the struggles for influence between these two communities, and the sanctuary, its foundation myths, and the organization of its rites (in particular the procession) as early as the archaic period testified to Argos' determination to manifest its sovereignty there. However, the process of appropriation did not in this case take the form of a territorial war and the exclusion of neighboring cities (Mycenae, Tiryns, Nauplia) from the cult (which Argos was to take over later, at the time of the Argive reconquest, after 460). Instead, it was more or less voluntarily recognized by these cities that the Argives had won supremacy, first in the ritualized aristocratic competition (to make the richest offerings and the most lavish sacrifices) for which the sanctuary seems to have provided a venue in the eighth century, and later in the political organization of the plain and its immediate tangible expression, namely, the monumental refurbishing of the Heraion and the administration of the cult.[48] And if one accepts the date of the late eighth century for the construction of the great upper terrace, one cannot fail to notice the coincidence between the beginning of those building operations and a more violent manifestation of Argive power: the destruction of Asine. In fact, one wonders whether this war eliminating a close rival, and a "dryopian" city to boot, alien to the world of the plain of Argos, its political organization, and its cults, did not provide the Argives with both the opportunity and the means to turn the shared sanctuary into a symbol of their victory and their now unchallenged supremacy.[49]

---

the town by the Argives (Pausanias 2.17.5) nevertheless bears the mark of the fifth-century conflicts in Argolis.

48. Morgan and Whitelaw, "Pots and Politics" (1991); Polignac, "Cité et territoire"; all the studies show that Mycenae remained the city least dominated by the supremacy of Argos, although it did not have the means to avoid that domination completely.

49. However, this dating of the megalithic terrace is sometimes challenged: the Mycenaean hypothesis remained defended by Plommer, "Argive Heraeum" (1984); on the other hand, others tend to date it to the seventh century (the middle or third quarter), as does, most recently, Antonaccio, "Argive Heraion" (1992), pp. 90–98, who, while failing to resolve the problem, at least challenges the idea of a deliberate "pseudo-Cyclopaean" imitation put forward by Wright, "Old Temple Terrace" (1982). One of the difficulties involved in this problem is the lack of correlation between the construction of the terrace and that of the "first

What is more, this conflict directly affects the history of another cult associated with the determination of territorial boundaries: the cult of Pythaean Apollo.[50] The temple that the people of Asine had built on the Barbouna hill around the mid eighth century was destroyed at the same time as the city of Asine, in about 720–710. It was immediately replaced by a new building in which the cult of Pythaean Apollo was either installed or perpetuated; a cult that appeared simultaneously in Argos itself, on the outskirts of the town, in the Deiras sanctuary. It is hard to tell whether what occurred on this occasion was the appropriation of an Asinean cult by the Argives or the implantation of an originally Argive cult in Asine. Whatever the case may be, the Barbouna cult now testified to Argive expansion.[51] Now, two frontier sanctuaries of Apollo in Kynouria—one on the coast between Tyros and Prasiai (Apollo Tyritas, attested from the late seventh century on), the other at Kosmas in the Parnon area, on the edge of Kynouria and Laconia (Apollo Maleatas, which appeared toward the end of the seventh century)—both revealed sixth-century dedications to a "Pythaeius," who can be identified as either Pythaean Apollo or his son, who according to Argive traditions founded this cult. In this case, the cult seems to testify to the increasing influence of Argos over the small coastal cities that were later conquered by Sparta following its victory over Argos in the famous Battle of the Champions in 546.[52]

This contest between 300 Argives and 300 Spartans, which

temple," the date of which is equally uncertain (see Bergquist, *Archaic Greek Temenos,* pp. 19–20; *contra,* Kalpaxis, *Früarchaische Baukunst,* pp. 43–44; Strøm, "Argive Heraion" [1988]; Billot, "Terres cuites d'Argos" [1990], pp. 96–100).

50. The history of the cult of Pythaean Apollo has recently attracted renewed interest: Piérart, "Oracle d'Apollon à Argos" (1990); Christien, "De Sparte à la côte est" (1992), 165, both tend to favor an Argive origin for the cult; Billot, "Apollon Pythéen et l'Argolide" (1989–90), the Argive appropriation of the Asinean cult, supported by patchily convincing arguments.

51. Asine and Argos: see the references for each site in the Bibliography, in particular, for Asine, Wells, "Asine Sima" (1990).

52. Faklaris, *Archaia Kynouria* pp. 209 and 223. The association of Pythaean Apollo with thresholds and frontiers is also emphasized by the fact that in the town of Hermione, the temple of Pythaean Apollo stood next to that of Apollo Horios (Protector of Frontiers): Pausanias 2.35.2.

was but one episode in the continuous battles between Argos and Sparta over the Thyreatis, seems to belong to a stream of confrontations of both a hoplite and a "chivalrous" nature, the regular features of which have been revealed by Angelo Brelich.[53] These battles, which involved groups of elite warriors in constantly disputed frontier regions, were regulated by preagreed conventions, which tended to limit their ferocity, and one of their characteristics was that they were frequently associated with deities, sanctuaries, and festivals of an initiatory nature. It may have been after the 546 victory that the Spartans set up the cult of Pythaean Apollo on the agora, on the spot known as the *chō-ros*, the scene of the *Gymnopaedia*, one of the functions of which was, according to one tradition, to commemorate the Thyreatis victory.[54] Furthermore, it was in the seventh century that the two sanctuaries of Apollo at Kosmas and Tyros began to receive offerings of weapons and later, from the mid seventh century on, bronze figurines, the most ancient of which is that of a Laconian hoplite, found at Kosmas.[55] It is therefore quite possible that the cult of Pythaean Apollo may have established between the city and these frontier regions, which were still hardly integrated, a link similar to that it had previously established between Argos and the outer limits of its influence. Similarities are noticeable in the conflicts between the Chalcidians and the Eretrians, which were ruled by an agreement banning the use of projectiles: whether there had truly been such a document or it was a tradition invented a posteriori about an ancient and in part legendary

53. Brelich, *Guerre, agoni, e culti* (1961), in particular pp. 22–34 for the Thyreatid wars and Pythaean Apollo: the battles of the Three Hundred (Herodotus 1.82), the episode of the One Thousand in 418 (Thucydides V.41; Pausanias 2.20). Brelich's analysis should be modified or corrected on a number of points (for instance, the cult of Pythaean Apollo in Argos was not "federal" and the cults of Apollo at Thornax, close to Sparta, and at Kosmas, in Kynouria, are confused: pp. 33–34), but it correctly draws attention to the representations that the Greeks created of these frontier conflicts.

54. Pausanias 3.11.9. The history of the Gymnopaedia, particularly concerning their possible link with the Parparonia celebrated by the Spartans on the very spot of their Thyreatid victory, is obscure, however; see Bölte, "Lakonischen Festen" (1929), pp. 124–32; Brelich, *Guerre, agoni, e culti*, p. 31 n. 42; Faklaris, *Archaia Kynouria;* 226–27; Billot, "Apollon Pythéen et l'Argolid," pp. 87–88.

55. Faklaris, *Archaia Kynouria*, pp. 211–14 and 219–22.

conflict, this agreement was certainly intended to confer a "chivalric" character upon it, and the choice of hand-to-hand battle calls to mind Archilochus' allusions to the *douriklutoi* lords of Euboea, who excelled in the use of the short sword.[56] The presence of a *stēlē* in the sanctuary of Amarynthos, situated to the east of Eretria, rather than between the two warring cities, certainly testifies to the attraction that the myths and rites of a deity of the frontier regions and initiations—in this case, Artemis—even when she was distanced from the central theater of operations, exerted on the history and memories of these boundary disputes.[57] They are all part of the same framework of experiences and representations.

The association between boundary disputes and the deities who presided over initiation, always on disputed frontiers and sometimes imperfectly integrated into the city's political territory, is even clearer in cases where the hoplite clash gave place to its opposite: cunning, of an ephebic or Artemisian type. Thus, the historical clashes between Athenians and Boeotians over the frontier district of Panacton (or Oinoe), a perfect example of a canton stranded "between the two frontiers" (*methorios*), constitutes the framework for the legend of the personal duel between Xanthos, king of Thebes, and Melanthos, the Neleid, who symbolized the Athenian *ephēbeia* and triumphed over his opponent by cunning means.[58] And this story, in its turn, provided the etiology for the Athenian festival of the Apatouria, which marked the integration of young people into their phratries. On the Boeotian side, the corresponding legend was that of the clash

56. Cf. n. 37. Archilochus frags. 7 and 9 CUF.

57. Elsewhere, the rise of Eretria at the expense of Lefkandi in the eighth century (possibly following a progressive population transfer: see Bérard and Altherr-Charron, "Erétrie" [1981], pp. 237–38) and the consequential abandonment of the Lelantine plain (Lefkandi was destroyed in about 700) made the sanctuary of Artemis at Amarynthos the principal cult site in the Eretrian territory.

58. Thucydides applies the description *methorios* to contested frontier regions, whether they retained a special status as did Thyreatis—the Spartans installed the exiled Aeginetes there in 431 2.27.2—and Panacton, an area farmed in common with the Boeotians during the archaic period, or whether they were integrated into the political organization of the territory, as were Kynouria (4.56.2) and the Attic deme of Oinoe, bordering Panacton (2.18.1–2); cf. Daverio-Rocchi, *Frontiera e confini*, pp. 33–34 and 180–81, and Munn, "Panacton and the Attic-Boiotian Frontier" (1989).

with the Pelasgoi of Athens, and this was the presumed origin of the annual rite of the Tripodophoria, also strongly marked by "ephebeian" or "cryptic" associations, since it featured the nocturnal theft of a sacred tripod and its secret transfer to Dodona.[59] Also in the tradition of age-old enmity between neighboring peoples was the episode of the "Despair of the Phocidians," in which the latter, under threat of extermination by the Thessalians, won the upper hand through a cunning ploy. Now, this entire episode is dominated by the figure of Artemis, on account of both its extreme features (the threat of extermination, cunning) and the fact that it takes place in the Hyampolis pass, on the northern boundary of Phocis, where the sanctuary of Artemis was situated. Given that the root of this story seems to have been the liberation of Phocis from the Thessalian yoke in about 570, that victory may have occasioned the reconstruction of the temples of Kalapodi (in about 570–560) and the foundation of the great festival of the Elaphebolia, both of which celebrated the frontier sanctuary as the place where the unity and history of Phocis began.[60] And it was no doubt as a result of a similar process that the tales of the origins of the First Messenian War, which also revolved around the theme of cunning and disguise, and the myths and rites of the sanctuary of Artemis Limnatis eventually became totally confused.

The presence of the same deities, essentially Apollo and Artemis, in the same places shows that all these tales of warfare, complementary as much as opposed, in which history, rites, and myths are involved, had to do with the cyclical refoundation of the norms of civilization. Basically, the young people who retreated to the *eschatiai* were complying with the ritual inversion of religious rules that preceded their definitive integration;

59. On Melanthos and the Athenian *ephēbeia*, the fundamental studies are Vidal-Naquet's *Black Hunter* (1986), pp. 106–28, and "Black Hunter Revisited" (1986). Tripodophoria: Strabo 9.2 (C 402); the conflict with the Pelasgians is explicitly situated at Panacton, in Proclos (ap. Photius *Bibl.* 321b32); cf. Munn, "Panacton and the Attic-Boiotian Frontier," p. 240.

60. Ellinger, "Le gypse et la boue" (1978), "Ruses de Guerre" (1984), "Hyampolis" (1987); and *Légende nationale phocidienne* (1993)—all essential works for an understanding of the way in which mythical and religious thought provided ancient Greeks with the categories for "interpretation" and the transmission of history as lived.

whereas the role of the elite phalanxes dispatched to the frontiers was to effect a temporary implantation of civic behavior there and to impose spatial order upon a no-man's-land on the edge of the civic territory. Of course, between these two poles of contrasting patterns of behavior, many combinations were possible, and elements of both were associated in the stories, cults, and myths connected with these local wars, the proliferation and regular repetition of which show that this double-faceted warfare truly constituted a favored way for cities to affirm their existence and perpetuate their cultural norms.

These conflicts fought out around the nonurban sanctuaries afford us a glimpse of how the *polis* came into being. The traditions that surround them show how there came a time when heroic warfare gradually gave way to political warfare, with the appearance of the first, aristocratic, hoplite phalanx, whose distinctive character, within an army now expanded to include a larger fraction of the social body, was preserved by the elite groups of fighting men of the archaic period from which it was composed: the Three Hundred of Sparta and of Argos and the Six Hundred of Phocis, for example.[61] This regrouping of noble warriors into a new fighting force put an end to their ancient behavior as champions, for now, instead of launching themselves upon episodic plundering raids, they had to band together to defend the territory. This signaled the emergence of a new type of social organization and the birth of the territorially based community known as the *polis*, which gathered into a single decision-taking body all the local *basileis* who had previously been more or less independent of one another.

In the *Odyssey* (4.54–55), an image of such a grouping is provided by the city council of the Phaecians. Although an imaginary place, Scheria already has the air of a city, far more than Homeric Sparta or Pylos, and the vagueness surrounding the composition and relations of the various actors in its public life—the *aristoi*, the *hēgētores*, and the *basileis*—reflects a first, fumbling attempt to set up new structures.[62] The switch certainly did not take place all at once or without hesitations. The phalanx

61. Cf. Detienne, "La phalange" (1968), p. 134f. In Sparta, the brotherhood of the Aegeids was supposed to have introduced hoplite tactics, at the time of the war against the Amyclaeans (Aristotle frag. 532 Rose; Pindar *Isthmian* 7.13–15).
62. Cf. Mossé, "Ithaque" (1980), pp. 9–11.

did not spring ready-armed from the earth but was the end result of a long process in which ancient patterns of bellicose behavior lingered for quite a while and temporary fighting forma-
tions of warriors devised for particular campaigns may have
taken some time to be adopted as a permanent form of military
deployment. Some *basileis* or warrior heroes may have refused to
submit to the new disciplines necessitated by the development
of the phalanx (in the second half of the seventh century, still, the
elegies of Tyrtaeus testify to the difficulties involved in imposing
strict cohesion upon the Spartan hoplites fighting against the
Messenians).[63] But that development certainly did constitute a
fundamental change from the Geometric world of the *Odyssey*.
In Ithaca the island nobles, the masters of the neighboring *oikoi*,
were the ones who coveted Odysseus' possessions; and Telema-
chos and Odysseus' only social alliances were with the distant
lords of Pylos and Sparta, with whom links had been forged
through personal relations of hospitality and the exchange of
gifts. But the fact that warfare evolved into permanent occupation of the land gave rise to more closely binding types of territorial solidarity, which sometimes took the form of synoecisms,
that is to say, political unions, to the advantage of the dominant
centers of the region, although this did not put a stop to trading
or marital links between the great families of different cities—a
tradition that was to continue throughout the archaic period.

A number of closely interlinked factors were thus all connected with the appearance of the nonurban sanctuary: the
agrarian crisis, the evolving notion of territory leading to a new
concept of frontiers, the establishment of the aristocratic phalanx, synoecism, and the birth of the city as a social organization
founded upon the unity of a central preurban inhabited area with
a surrounding terrain and constituted around a decision-taking
body based on a group of hoplite nobles all considered equals in
that they all bore arms and so possessed political power.

63. On one possible consequence of this attitude, their participation in the
movement of colonization, cf. Ducat, "Thèmes de la fondation de Rhégion"
(1974), p. 114. In general, the antagonism between "heroic behavior" and "hop-
litic behavior" was only revealed gradually, and certain aspects of the former
persisted in the latter in the archaic period (see also Lonis, *Guerre et religion*
(1979), chaps. 1 and 2, and the review by Asheri in *Revue historique de droit français
et étranger* 59 (1981): 67–68.

As we have seen, the nonurban sanctuary was a key factor in these wars. Religious sites, like the land itself, were the objects of a process of appropriation crowned by the building of a sanctuary that designated the frontier the group claimed for its territory in the face of its neighbor-adversaries. The religious site was an *agalma*, a sacred emblem of the extension of one people's power, and when two peoples fought over it, it resembled the tripod to which both Apollo and Herakles laid claim. The dispute prompted each of the two adversaries to muster its vital forces in a new and more effective cohesion. But at what point in the formative process did the city come into being? To understand the notion of the *polis*, the nature of this emerging type of community, and its precise relation to the appearance of sanctuaries, let us return to the other major role of the nonurban cults, for which we have already encountered omnipresent evidence: namely, social integration.

Social Integration and the Constitution of the Polis

We have noted the kourotrophic character of these extraurban deities who are also involved in frontier wars contaminated by practices of cultural inversion, but we have barely touched upon the subject of their role in the body of rites designed to effect the "vertical" integration of young people, that is to say, their accession to the status of adult members of the community. Now, not only do the nonurban cults all incorporate aspects of the rite of passage,[64] but furthermore, their integrating action also operates "horizontally," thereby shedding light upon the social constitution of the *polis*.

Let us first consider the transition from adolescence to maturity. This transition was expressed by a movement away from the inhabited area, followed by a return to it. Between the withdrawal and the return, the young people took part in rites that manifested a temporary inversion of values. In this fashion, they obliterated their old selves and allowed their new qualities to

---

64. These rituals have been the subject of numerous studies since the publication of Jeanmaire's *Couroi et courètes* (1939); among others, see Brelich, *Paides e Parthenoi* (1969); Calame, *Choeurs de jeunes filles*; Brulé, *Filles d'Athènes* (1987); Sourvinou-Inwood, *Studies in Girls' Transitions* (1988).

come into being. These rites took place outside civilized space, in the sanctuaries of Artemis situated out in the wild. As we have seen, the Spartan and Messenian stories of incidents that occurred in the sanctuary of Artemis Limnatis have the air of a historization of the myths upon which a rite of temporary segregation and initiatory death was founded. It took the form of symbolic disguises and murders (the Spartan boys dressed up as girls, the death of the Messenian girls) that wiped out their former status as boys or girls, allowing them to step into their new status as men and women. Similar myths and rituals characterized all the frontier sanctuaries of Artemis.[65] At Brauron, in Attica, too, Artemis protected human fecundity as well as natural fertility.[66] The ritual of the "Bears" involved little girls of between five and ten years of age and adolescent girls. The temporary segregation of the latter—a ritual death that expiated the death of Artemis' bear—and their participation in a veritable mystery that mimed the drama constituted the rite of passage through which they acceded to the world of adolescence, the first step toward marriage and reproduction. Parturition, another essential transition in a woman's life, was also presided over by the goddess, who would be presented with offerings in the shape of the clothes of a woman who had given birth to a healthy child.[67]

It may seem surprising, then, that the same functions were

65. For example: Artemis Hymnia between Mantinaea and Orchomenos, where the priest and priestess led a life completely foreign to the conventions and habits of normal human behavior (Pausanias 8.13.1); Artemis Hemerasia, at Lousoi, associated with the myth of madness, flight into the mountains, and the final healing of the Proïtidai (the daughters of Proitos were believed to have mocked Hera in her own sanctuary; afflicted by madness, they could not be cured and return to the domestic world of Hera except by sacrificing to Artemis [Bacchylides *Epinicians* 38.1.47 l Loeb]) (Pausanias 8.19.7); Artemis Alpheiaia, in Elis, where the goddess and the nymphs had covered their faces with mud, in order to escape from Alpheios (Pausanias 6.22.8); and the Artemis of the Elaphebolia of Hyampolis, in her warrior domain (Herodotus 8.27–28; Pausanias 10.1.3–11).

66. Kontis, "Artemis Brauronia" (1967).

67. Cf. Brelich, *Paides e Partenoi*, p. 240f.; Kontis, "Artemis Brauronia"; Kahil, "L'Artémis de Brauron" (1977); Vernant in *Annuaire du Collège de France*, 1981–82, p. 419; 1982–83, pp. 453–56; Sourvinou-Inwood, *Studies in Girls' Transitions*. In the classical period, a solemn procession left the Brauronion of Athens on the occasion of the goddess' great festival, which took place every four years.

also assigned to this goddess inside the civilized space. Thus, in Sparta, Artemis, already present in her frontier sanctuaries, was also Orthia, in her suburban sanctuary.[68] Here, for the boys, the trial in the rite of passage was flagellation or the rite of "initiatory death," which may have preceded it.[69] The feminine equivalent is to be found in myth: here, the phase of segregation and violence is represented by the rape of the young Helen, carried off by Theseus, who seized her while she was dancing with other adolescent girls in the sanctuary.[70]

The mention of dancing perhaps provides a clue as to the reasons for this eruption of initiatory rites and myths inside the civic space. The Artemis of the *eschatiai* is the goddess of temporary but absolute segregation, in which the adolescent loses his or her quality of *pais:* but how can the adult admitted by society, which is rooted in agrarian and cultivated space, be born in the isolation of the frontier regions? There was another high point in the integration of adolescents, which frequently took the form of their participation, for the very first time, in the solemn festivals held in the great sanctuaries on the relative edges (of the plain or the inhabited area). Here, too, their movement out of the town center represented a distancing or a change of status, but this time it took place without their altogether leaving the domain of civilization or separating themselves from the group of adults among whom they now had a place: this presentation of the younger generation to the goddess and the community was also—through the performance of dances and songs, designed to give pleasure to both—an integration into the cult and, thereby, equally into society. All the great nonurban deities thus act as protectors of this rite of passage. In Ephesus, where the deity once again was Artemis, the boys and girls, in two separate groups, each led by the most beautiful of its members, paraded in a majestic *pompē* along the short path leading to the Artemi-

---

68. "She Who Keeps Straight" whose statue had been found in a clump of *agnus castus* (on this plant, see Detienne, *Gardens of Adonis,* [1977], p. 94) and who helped young children to stand upright (Callimachus *Hymn to Artemis,* line 128).

69. In truth, flagellation is only attested by inscriptions and texts (Pausanias 3.26.7) in the Roman period: even if this was really a late ritual, it cannot have been introduced suddenly but must have followed on from some other procedure of "rupture."

70. Plutarch *Theseus* 31.

sion, accompanied by the whole citizen body.[71] Aphaia, another kourotrophic deity, received offerings characteristic of the rites of passage to adulthood in her sanctuary in Aegina, but in Argos it was of course Hera who presided over the transition from the world of childhood to that of adult life, through the institution of marriage: the virgin girls of Argos took part in a procession to the Heraia and there performed choral dances.[72]

Even Athena assumes these characteristics in her extraurban sanctuaries: at Elatea, the priest of the sanctuary of Athena Cranaia (twenty stades distant from the town) was a prepubescent boy whose mode of life separated him from the rest of the community.[73] At Troezen, girls who were about to marry went to make an offering of their belts to Athena Apatouria, on the island of Sphairia.[74] In Athens itself, the procession of the Oschophoria (a festival supposed to commemorate the return of Theseus and the other adolescents saved from the labyrinth of Minos) was led by two boys disguised as girls to the frontier sanctuary of Athena Skiras.[75]

But above all, Apollo was the other great deity in this domain. In Thebes, every eight years, the Daphnephoria (the bearing of the laurel) began with a procession that made its way from the town to the suburban sanctuary of Apollo Ismenios. The parade was led by a young boy, the laurel-bearer, accompanied by a chorus of girls carrying supplication branches and singing hymns.[76] Here, too, exceptional beauty seems to have been a decisive factor in the choice of the laurel-bearer.[77] The arrival at the sanctuary on the other side of the river Ismenios seems to have represented the moment of segregation, while the singing, on the

71. Xenophon of Ephesus *Ephesiaka* 1.2.2f.
72. Aphaia: Sinn, "Kult der Aphaia auf Aegina", 1988. Argos: Euripides *Electra*, line 172f.
73. Pausanias 10.34.7. His (ritual) bath was "in the old fashion."
74. Pausanias 2.33.1. On this cult, see Schmitt, "Athena Apatouria" 1977.
75. Jacoby *FGrH,*[2] (1957) 3b1 suppl., pp. 286–89; see the analysis by Vidal-Naquet in *Black Hunter,* pp. 114–16, and Calame, *Thésée* (1989), pp. 143–48 and 339–48. The terms *skiras, skiron* referred to the poor land of border regions, remote or frontier localities.
76. Pindar *Parthenaea* 2; Proclos ap. Photion *Bibl.* 321b30. Calame, *Chœurs de jeunes filles,* p. 190; Schachter, *Cults of Boiotia,* vol. 1 (1981), pp. 83–84.
77. Pausanias 10.10.4. In truth beauty is a gift of the kourotrophic goddess, a sign of her particular favor.

themes of local myths, constituted the criterion of admission into the adult world of the city. The rule that the parents of the child who led the procession should still be living emphasized the aspect of vertical integration, as it did in the Delphic festival of the Stepterion (or Septerion). In this ritual, the same condition applied to the boy who led the group of adolescents, whose task it was to set fire to the hut representing a palace, which had been set up in the sanctuary of Apollo, and who had to pass through a series of ritual trials that culminated in the ceremony of purification in the temple. The new young adults then carried the Apollonian laurel branch back to the sanctuary.[78]

The cult of Amyclaean Apollo, in Lacedaemonia, also seems to have retained the features of a rite of passage associated with the figure of the adolescent Hyacinthos. The ceremony commemorating him symbolized death followed by rebirth into a new life. Many features of the cult liken it to other rituals of adolescence: the solemn procession from Sparta to the sanctuary included a parade of girls carried along in specially decorated chariots; on the second day of the festival, before an audience composed of the entire city gathered in the sanctuary, the adolescents of both sexes took part in a performance of local dances and songs, which showed that they had been receptive to the education they had received and were now worthy to enter adult life.[79] The Hyacinthia as a whole constituted a festival of both natural and human renewal.

For boys, the transition through which they passed was also from the status of ephebe to that of adult warrior. The attributes of Amyclaean Apollo were, suitably, the bow and the spear. Now, for the Greeks, the bow was not a weapon of conventional warfare. Rather, it was used in the merciless hunts for either human or animal quarry that were associated with nature in the wild and terrifying avenging deities like Artemis, who would let fly her arrows at both beasts and men.[80] The spear, in contrast, was a weapon of civilized warfare and belonged to the ordered

78. Plutarch *Quaest. Graec.* 12. The celebration was supposed to commemorate and mime the struggle of Apollo against Python, his subsequent wanderings, his purification in the Vale of Tempe, and his return to Delphi.

79. Plutarch *Agesilas* 19.5; Athenaeus 4.138f. Cf. Brelich, *Paides e Partenoi,* p. 143f.; Calame, *Choeurs de jeunes filles,* p. 305f.

80. Callimachus *Hymn to Artemis,* lines 153–55.

and institutionalized human world.[81] From his extraurban sanctuary, Apollo took part in both those worlds and could thus preside over the passage of young people from the one to the other, that is to say, from "wild" adolescence to ordered adult life. In the Hyacinthia, this aspect was illustrated by the display of the breastplate of the Aegeid leader Timomachos, which served as a reminder that war meant hoplite combat—and perhaps also that the Spartans were the conquerors of Amyclae.

It is hard to tell whether it was really as a result of conquest (around the mid eighth century?) that Amyclae was integrated into Sparta, and even harder to determine whether the Amyclaeans were "Achaeans" who had resisted the Spartan pressure for a long time, unlike the other towns in Laconia (Pharis, Gerouthrai), as one late tradition held.[82] By the tenth century, already, there was nothing in its material culture to distinguish Amyclae from Sparta, but signs of persistent non-Dorian habitation have also been found near the sanctuary.[83] However that may be and whether this situation resulted from conquest, an agreement, or progressive assimilation, the important point to recognize is that Amyclae was not annexed but was integrated into the Spartan community and enjoyed the same standing as the four villages of Sparta. In the classical period, its inhabitants were full citizens, not *perioikoi* as were those of the Laconian towns.

That integration seems to have been what prompted the expansion of the cult, with the building of a sanctuary and the organization of the Hyacinthia, many features of which, in particular the solemn procession, cannot have predated the Spartans' growing interest in Amyclae. The cult, addressed to the hero Hyacinthos, is here associated with the cult of Apollo, although each deity retains his own particular individuality both in the myth, in which the two are similarly associated, and in the ritual: the sacrifice takes the chthonic form (*enagisma*) in the case

81. Bérard, "Le sceptre du prince" (1972), pp. 219–27 and n. 21 (Eretria); Brelich, *Paides e Partenoi*, p. 94 n. 129.

82. Pausanias 3.2.6; Huxley, *Early Sparta* (1962), p. 22, and *contra*, Cartledge, *Sparta and Laconia*, pp. 107–8.

83. For example, a bronze fish from the sixth century, bearing a dedication to Poseidon in the "Achaean" form "Pohoidan." Buschor, "Von Amyclaion" (1927), p. 37; Jeffery, *Local Scripts of Archaic Greece* (1961), p. 200, no. 34.

of Hyacinthos, the Olympian (*thysia*) in that of Apollo.[84] Perhaps
this duality reflects the twofold nature and at the same time the
unification of the social body, in which the Dorian component
predominated. If so, the acceptance of the adolescents into the
adult society could be seen as an obliteration of the old distinctions: all the young people, whether of Dorian origin or not, took
part in the same ritual.[85]

One episode in particular emphasizes that unificatory function of the cult by illustrating, *a contrario*, a case in which integration foundered. According to one tradition, it was at the sanctuary of Amyclae that the unsuccessful revolt of the Partheniai
took place. The Partheniai were the children to whom the Spartan women had given birth while their husbands were away
fighting in the First Messenian War. When the Spartan husbands
finally did return home, they refused to grant these young
people citizen status. The Partheniai had planned a revolt, timed
to take place during the Hyacinthia, but it was thwarted, and
being unable to gain recognition for their rights, the Partheniai
went off to found Tarentum.[86] This episode should be compared

84. Apollo kills Hyacinthos in the discus-throwing competition: Euripides
Electra, line 1471f. In the genealogies, the hero came under Lacedaemonian dependence: he was the son of Amyclas, son of Lacedaemon and Sparta (Apollodorus 3.10.3) or else his brother (Pausanias 3.1.3; Pausanias 3.19.3).

85. The role of the "Salaminians" in the festival of the Oschoporia and the
frontier sanctuary of Athena Skiras in Athens (cf. above, note 75) may have resulted from an identical process of religious integration at the time of the
Athenian conquest of the island. The name Skiras was supposed to refer to Salamis, and the "*genos* of the Salaminians" provided the bearers of branches in the
procession that linked Athens and the sanctuary. Might not this rite of integration for the younger generations also represent a means of fusing former conquerors and those they had conquered, through a religious agreement? A similar
episode involving feminine disguise was believed to have made it possible to
conquer the island through a trick (Plutarch *Solon* 8) and was a feature in the
ritual of the Skirophoria.

86. Strabo 6.3.2 (following Antiochos). The origin of the Partheniai has been a
subject of controversy since antiquity: were they the sons of Spartans who were
not fighting men (because of debility or by reason of their youth) or were they
the sons of slaves? The two essential studies on this subject are Pembroke, "Le
rôle des femmes: Locres et Tarente" (1970), and Vidal-Naquet, *Black Hunter,*
pp. 205–23. Whatever its veracity, or even its historicity, the episode certainly
makes the sanctuary and the cult instrumental in revealing problems affecting
the cohesion of the social body.

to another that occurred at about the same time: the founding of Syracuse by colonizers from Corinth who were similarly said to have set out from an extraurban sanctuary of Apollo, in this instance situated at Tenea, in the heart of the southern part of the territory of Corinth.[87] In each of these two cases, the sanctuary and the god's festival provided the venue and the timing for the staging of a challenge to the *polis,* in which what was at stake was either integration or exclusion (with the latter eventually leading to the creation of a new city).

The promotion of the cult at Amyclae into the greatest of all Laconian religious happenings and one endowed with all the territorial and agrarian as well as the warlike and initiatory characteristics we have noted, was thus the action that led to the founding of a new social organization. Although it is hard to make out exactly to what extent certain groups were, or were not, in a dependent position vis-à-vis the "Spartiates," the original distinctions became blurred once the various components merged into a single community through a common cult. The position, ritual, and promotion of that cult would have resulted from a decision taken in common if the Amyclaeans, far from being totally subjugated, were integrated on the basis of an agreement, an agreement primarily to do with the cult. Alternatively, the cult itself might have been the means of taking over and absorbing the conquered Amyclaeans. Whichever the case, the development of the sanctuary and the festival of Apollo and Hyacinthos, together with their role of both vertical and horizontal integration, was the act that established the Lacedaemonian *polis,* which took shape as a result of that early collective decision, the aim of which was to ensure the cohesion of the society.

Sparta thus provides an example of a division of tasks between Apollo and Artemis. For the goddess, too, was "political." One of the legends about the cult at the sanctuary of Orthia is extremely revealing. According to this, on the occasion of a sacrifice, the "Limnaians, Cynosurians, Mesoans, and Pitanaeans" came to blows and virtually wiped one another out on the very

87. Strabo 8.6.22. This story reduces the importance of another tradition (ibid., 6.3.3) that situated the Partheniai affair on the agora of Sparta: in particular, it confirms that the sanctuary was the place for large political gatherings, and the early agoras were no doubt the religious precincts of sanctuaries (see below, note 90).

altar. A fatal sickness then afflicted those who had survived. When consulted on the matter, the oracle declared that it would thenceforth be necessary to shed human blood upon the altar. A human sacrifice was accordingly organized, a sacrifice that the lawgiver Lycurgus later converted into the flagellation of the ephebes, which became an essential episode in the Orthia cult.[88] Now, Limnai, Cynosoura, Mesoa, and Pitane were the four townships that, throughout antiquity, together composed the town of Sparta. The introduction of a specifically Laconian aspect to the cult of Artemis thus marked the transition from a time of divisions and destruction to a time of unity, symbolized first and foremost by sacrifice. There had to be a "scapegoat" of unification, a victim necessary for the maintenance of social cohesion; and eventually that role was taken over by the body of ephebes, in whose hands the future of the entire social group lay.[89]

The two cults of Apollo and Artemis thus, through certain of their elements, reactivated a mythical or historical drama, the outcome of which was the birth of the city (the fighting between the inhabitants of the four villages, the fighting over Amyclae). But the Orthia cult provided the foundation for the unification of the hamlets of the center, while the cult of Apollo established the unity of all the inhabitants of the territory. (It is neither possible nor justifiable to deduce a priori which episode came first). The two sanctuaries also provided the framework for the first political assemblies.[90]

Similar elements are detectable in the rich festival of Artemis Triclaria and Dionysus Aisymnetes at Patras.[91] On the night of

88. Pausanias 3.16.7.

89. On the rites of Orthia and the role of the ephebes, see Vernant's very stimulating analyses in *L'individu, la mort, l'amour* (1989), pp. 173–209. The hypotheses of Carter, "Marks of Ortheia" (1987), and "Masks and Poetry" (1988), on the eastern origin of Ortheia/Orthia, who could not be assimilated to Artemis, do not seem well-founded to me, for reasons I have stated elsewhere ("Influence extérieure?" [1992], pp. 114–17).

90. The esplanade of the sanctuary of Orthia may have constituted the earliest agora of Sparta, before the shift to the site of the classical agora, further to the south and surrounded by cults founded at a later date. See Martin, *Recherches sur l'agora* (1951), pp. 207–11.

91. Pausanias 7.19–20.2. It has been studied by Massenzio, "Artemis Triklaria e Dionysos Aisymnetes" (1968), and also by Vernant, in *Annuaire de Collège de France*, 1982–83, pp. 445–49.

the ceremony, adolescents of both sexes, crowned with ears of wheat, would make their way to the sanctuary of Artemis, situated outside the town, close to the river Meilichios. There they laid their wreaths before the goddess, bathed in the river, and garlanded with ivy, returned to the town, to the sanctuary of Aisymnetes, where the priest would have set out the chest containing the statue of the god, while at the same time, three other statues—of Dionysus—Mesateus, Antheus and Aroeus—were brought there from another sanctuary.[92]

There was a great *hieros logos* to explain this celebration, and it was closely interwoven with the "history" of the city.[93] That history began with the autochthonous King Eumelos, who was rich in flocks but poor in subjects. Like many others, he was visited by Triptolemos, who in the name of the Eleusian Demeter, taught him the art of cultivating wheat and founding a town, which he called Aroe, after the word for ploughing the soil. Together, they then founded a second town, Antheia (The Flowery One), after the name of Eumelos' son. Finally, a third town grew up; it was called Mesatis (The Town in the Middle).

Then came the second phase. The Achaeans arrived, ejected the Ionians, and were settled by their king, Patreus, in the town of Aroe, which they surrounded by a wall and renamed Patras: an image of the founding synoecism of the *polis* of Patras. On to this is grafted the *aition* of the double cult of Artemis and Dionysus. According to myth, the cult of Artemis Triclaria (Of the Three Terrains) was founded by the Ionians of Aroe, Antheia, and Mesatis, but this ancient order was disrupted by a transgression. The goddess, angered by the guilty love affair between her priestess Comaitho and Melannippos, made the earth sterile and unleashed a series of death-dealing epidemics, which continued until, upon the advice of the oracle, an annual sacrifice was instituted, in which the victims were the most handsome boy and the most beautiful virgin girl. It was a savage rite that would not be abandoned until the arrival of a foreign king and a foreign god. This came to pass when Eurypylos, the son of Euaimon,

92. Pausanias 7.21.6, who also indicates that the sanctuary of Dionysus Aisymnetes was situated in the lower part of the town, nearer the sea, in what may originally have been a suburban position.
93. Ibid., 7.18.2–6.

was shipwrecked at Patras on his return journey from Troy and encountered the two victims for the year on their way to the sacrifice. He had brought with him as booty a box containing a statue of Dionysus, the sight of which had driven him mad. Eurypylos' reason was now restored, as the bloody ritual gave way to festivities in which Artemis, now mollified, became associated with Dionysus, the domesticated savior.

In their own ways, both the myth and the ritual make the establishment of this double cult the act that resulted in the founding of the city of Patras. First, they show a transition: the switch from a time of chaos to the time of civilization (when human sacrifices are discontinued) and also from a sacrifice in which life is destroyed to a rite of a kourotrophic and initiatory nature (the bathing in the river is not only a purification but also a symbol of the abandonment of the state of adolescence) with agrarian connotations (the crowns made of ears of wheat). But that transition is made possible and brought about by the union of a deity of the outlying territory, Artemis, with a deity of the town, Dionysus. The festival consists of a double procession between the two sanctuaries, and this connection maintains their balanced relationship, repeating the meeting that annulled or neutralized the harmful power of each deity (Artemisian savagery, Dionysiac madness).[94] Together these two become the protectors of the synoecism of Patras: the association of the Artemis of the Three Terrains and the Dionysus Mesateus, Antheus, and Aroeus recalls, maintains, and provides the foundation for the unification of the three *kōmai* into a single *polis*, while at the same time it brings about the indispensable symbiosis between the respective cults of the inhabited area and the outer territory. Dionysus' quality as Aisymnetes even imparts a specifically political character to his intervention, which finally brings the period of crisis to an end, for this was a title given to figures with exceptional

94. The change in the name of the river that is the scene of the festival evokes this mutual neutralization: at the time of the troubles, it was called Ameilichos, but became Meilichos when civic order was imposed. The ears of wheat in the wreaths were supposed to be what Artemis' victims wore; her anger brought into question the very foundations of the agricultural human society established by Triptolemos. The ivy garlands are Dionysiac, but here they are worn on the return to the town. All these "contradictions" serve to eliminate the frightening strangeness of the personalities of these deities.

powers who established a new order in cities torn apart by dissension.[95]

The ritual and myth of Artemis and Dionysus do not merge completely with the account of the "historical" synoecism attributed to the hero Patreus—an account that belongs to a different kind of discourse. However, in that they identify certain religious and political facts, they do constitute at the very least a religious formulation of the formation of the city. In Greek classical thought, the appearance of political order was without doubt always associated with the establishment of order that was characteristic of the human race. But by presenting the deities and the rites for the integration of the young as the creators of the first civic society, the stories and practices of Patras draw attention to cults that may well have constituted the principal means for uniting groups of different origins.[96]

At Sicyon we find an equally telling association: here, a local myth told of the coming of Apollo and Artemis, following the murder of Python. Having been ejected from a place called Phobos (Fear), they took refuge in Crete and a plague thereupon struck Aigialea (the ancient name for Sicyon). By way of a propitiatory rite, seven boys and seven girls were sent as suppliants to the nearby river Sythas, where they managed to persuade the deities to return to a sanctuary in their town: this was the sanctuary of Peitho (Persuasion). Ever since, in the festival of Apollo, children went to the river, then took the deities first to the urban temple of Persuasion and thence back to the temple of Apollo (no doubt situated just outside the town).[97] Peitho, an eminently political power, eliminates Phobos. The myth and the cult thus gave perfect expression to the ideal of relations within the city, where *philia* guarantees the cohesion of the community. The Sicyonian ritual established and perpetuated the virtues of the civic world, handed down from generation to generation.

Now, Fear and Persuasion were also the two antinomic poles

95. Aristotle *Politics* 3.14.8–10 (1285a). A Megarian magistracy also bore this name; cf. *RE*, s.v. Aisymnetes, 2 (Toepffer).

96. Perhaps from an ethnic point of view, the literary theme of the "expulsion of the Ionians" should not mask the probability of a more complex situation. Cf. Snodgrass, *Dark Age* (1971), p. 301.

97. Pausanias 2.7.7.

of the relationship between the two sexes, in which the quest for balance and its maintenance were conditions for the survival of the group and the perpetuation of its values. The integration of the female world implied by this balance was something else that was entrusted to cults that involved temporary exclusion and inversion.

In truth, the exclusion was twofold. In the first place, in normal circumstances, it kept women out of all public life: political life of course, but also sacrificial practices, for the two were linked where the major official cults were concerned.[98] However, even if this exclusion meant that women could not participate actively in citizen affairs, it could not go so far as to eliminate totally from the city those who alone could bring into the world its future generations. Through the intermediary of the husbands or brothers who represented them before the community and before the gods, women were indirectly admitted into the *polis*, in the position of "latent citizenesses."[99]

However, that passive integration, by which women were marginalized in the world of the community, was complemented by an active type of integration, in which women were positioned at the center of a sacred world that belonged to them alone: the world of the Thesmophoria of Demeter. The scene of these ceremonies in which, out of sight of the male city authorities, a veritable female city was set up, was a suburban sanctuary, the Thesmophorion. From the end of the eighth century onward, every city built one.[100] This sanctuary was never as monumentally imposing as the great sanctuaries in the city's outlying territory, nor did it take a similar form. Nevertheless, the Thesmophorion was clearly of great importance to the nascent city: that fact alone testifies to the truly civic impact of the cult of Demeter. The positioning of its sanctuary is illuminating. It would be situated at

98. See Detienne, "Violence of Wellborn Ladies" (1989).

99. To borrow Marcel Detienne's expression, *ibid.*, p. 196.

100. Apart from the many Thesmophoria known through literary and epigraphical sources (see *RE*, s.v. Thesmophoria, 4), excavations have also been carried out at those of Corinth, Cnossos, Thasos, and Cyrene (for the colonial West, see below), where the popularity of the cult culminated in the sixth century (see the references for each site in the Bibliography). On the exception constituted by the Thesmophoria of the acropolis of Megara and the Cadmaea of Thebes, see Polignac, "Déméter" (1990).

a point where the town adjoined the outlying territory, that is to say, between the place where the male assembly's power was exercised and the space that, when set in order, provided that power with its material bases and also its cultural models. Here, Demeter and the women stood guard over the indispensable unity of the two. Upon them depended on the one hand the generation of warriors and citizens of the future, on the other the reproduction of cereals and fruits of the cultivated territory. This association, central to the propitiatory cult addressed to Demeter, was more than simply a particular form of the traditional assimilation of the fecundity of the human race and the fertility of nature.[101] The relative isolation of the sanctuary, the secret nature of its rites, and the public nature of the procession in which the women betook themselves there all symbolized the crucial yet temporary responsibility of the women vis-à-vis the perpetuation of the community and the safeguarding of its identification with the city territory.[102] That responsibility conferred upon the women a latent citizenship of a religious nature, without which there could never have been any citizenship of the other, political, kind.

So there is nothing contradictory about the fact that women were excluded from public life while at the same time the political element was omnipresent in the cult of Demeter, as was manifest from the moment the city built this sanctuary for the goddess: for in it could be placed the altars of the *phratriai* upon which depended the renewal of the civic body, through the progressive integration of children and adolescents (as at Thasos); and here, too, the city could deposit sacred objects, which it protected as though its own destiny depended upon it (at Paros, for example).[103]

The integration thus effected was not a passive belonging, a posteriori, to a system already in place. Rather, it was necessary for that system's very constitution. The fact that the elaboration of a religious citizenship was a sine qua non condition for the

---

101. Detienne, "Violence of Wellborn Ladies," and *Gardens of Adonis*, pp. 78–90.

102. Callimachus *Hymn to Demeter*, lines 1–6, 118–33.

103. Thasos: Rolley, "Thesmophorion de Thasos" (1965); Paros: Herodotus 6.134.

formation of the city, or rather for the very process of the redefinition of social cohesion from which the *polis* resulted, can be
seen even more clearly in cases where non-Greek populations
were involved, that is to say, in Asia Minor—especially since
that "barbarian" presence would no doubt in many cases be female. Herodotus' account of the founders of Miletus marrying
the wives, sisters, and daughters of the Carians ejected from the
area is well known.[104] Another instructive account, in this respect, is the legend about the founding of the cult of Herakles at
Erythrae (opposite Chios).[105] It relates that the cult was set up
after a statue (described as "Egyptian") of the god was washed
up on a raft at Cape Mesate (The Middle Cape), between Chios
and Erythrae: the people of both places coveted it, but it eventually fell into the hands of the Erythraeans. A fisherman who had
had a prophetic dream had advised the women of Erythrae to
cut off their hair and with it fashion a rope to pull in the raft, but
the women of the *asty* (the *astai*) would not do this. Only the
Thracian women, the free and the slaves alike, were prepared to
sacrifice their hair. From that time on, only Thracian women
were admitted to the sanctuary of Herakles.[106]

In this tale, we once again find the theme of a clash over possession of a holy place "in the middle." It is analogous to all the
other conflicts involving a mimetic rivalry, which, as we have
noted, are so important in the formation of cities. This particular
religious *aition* may be read as an account of the foundation of a
colonial *polis* that depended upon the integration of "barbari-
ans," in this case Thracian women, excluded from public life on
two counts but eventually incorporated within the city (understood as a social entity), through their involvement in the cult.
These are women without whom, whatever their original circumstances, the city could not come into existence, for the simple
juxtaposition of even two whole communities, one Greek, the

104. Herodotus 1.146.
105. Pausanias 7.5.5–8. An *aition* of the cult of Herakles at Cos, designed to
explain why the priest wore feminine clothing when performing the sacrifice,
presents similar themes: the hero/god, having been shipwrecked, was supposed
to have been rescued by a Thracian woman (Plutarch *Quaest. Graec.* 58).
106. The complex question of the possible Phoenician origin of the "foreign"
Herakles, and also of Thasos, cannot be tackled here; see below, chap. 3, on the
Herakleion of Thasos.

other indigenous, did not constitute a city. A civic society could only be established on the basis of some form of integration of all the social components gathered in the territory, however remote they may have been from the decision-taking system. To that extent, organizing a cult was a way of founding a city.

This interaction between rites for the integration of young people, particular ways for women to take part in the cult, and the openings offered to non-Greeks, not only of the city itself but also from elsewhere, is strikingly illustrated by a sanctuary such as the Artemision of Ephesus. This suburban sanctuary, the scene of rituals of adolescence and also of ceremonies that gathered together the entire Ephesian community, was also the place where social cohesion was formed, according to the particular terms suited to this colonial city. Traditions had it that the cult was founded before the arrival of the Ionians—by the Amazons, according to some; by an autochthonous figure, Coresos, and Ephesos, the son of the river that flowed nearby, according to Pausanias.[107] When the Ionians, led by Androchos, the son of Codros, arrived upon the scene, they found Leleges, Lydians, and even Amazons dwelling in two separate areas. Androchos was said to have ejected those in the upper town but spared those who lived close to the sanctuary and under its protection.

Now, excavations have revealed that in its original state, right at the beginning of the seventh century, the Artemision consisted of several separate cult sites: the temple of Artemis proper, constructed as early as the eighth century, facing west; further to the west, a group of altars completed, toward the end of the seventh century, by a second temple, a *hekatompedos*, all facing south; and between the two, but more to the north, the foundations of a religious building or an altar constructed over eighth-century paving stones.[108] The presence of several cult sites here might well reflect the fact that a number of different peoples were incorporated in the archaic society. The coexistence of two major cult sites perhaps corresponded to the coexistence of

107. Callimachus *Hymn to Artemis,* lines 237–42; Pausanias, 7.2.7–8.

108. Bammer, Brein, and Wolff, "Das Tieropfer am Artemision" (1978), p. 107f.; Bammer, "Spüren der Phoniker" (1985), "Gold und Elfenbein von Kultbasis in Ephesos" (1988), and "Sanctuaires à l'Artémision d'Ephèse," (1991). The coexistence of several cult sites in the sanctuary seems to go back to the eighth century.

Greeks and Lydians in Ephesus, and here too, the two peoples may well have been united through the women, whose partici- pation in the cult seems to be attested by the discovery of instru- ments and objects of a specifically feminine nature among the sacrificial remains.[109] The northern foundations around which many offerings of foreign origin have been found (Phoenician figurines and ivories and ivory and gold animal representations characteristic of nomad art) indicate that the cult attracted for- eigners: Easterners and possibly Cimmerians. The discovery of the remains of Phoenician sacrifices of donkeys and dogs close to the western altar shows that these exotic offerings, or at least those from the Near East, were brought, not by Greeks—as would have been perfectly possible—but by foreigners who put in at the port alongside the sanctuary and practiced their own rites there, although without the benefit of any monumental buildings comparable to those of the other two religious cen- ters.[110] In contrast, the capture of the town by Croesos involved a total rearrangement of the sanctuary: the old temple was de- stroyed and the various cult sites were replaced by a single, large one: the great Artemision to one side and the former ancient altar to the other, separated by a wall that considerably limited the space available to those attending the sacrifices.

Women, young people, natives, and foreigners: the Artemi- sion of Ephesus is a perfect example of a sanctuary situated "on the edge," in a position where contact could be made with other peoples (either on the seashore or on the frontier). Here, deities oriented toward the outside ("wild" or "foreign") world pre- sided over ritual initiation and integration ceremonies, thereby affording a place inside the city's religious space to all the groups other than the adult *astoi*, who constituted an aristocracy of first- class citizens and tended to be more involved in the urban cults

109. Bammer, Brein, and Wolf, "Das Tieropfer am Artemision," p. 131; Aris- tophanes mentions the Lydian women's devotion to the Artemis of Ephesus (*Clouds* 1.589f.).

110. See note 108 above and Bammer, "Spüren der Phoniker," "Neue weib- liche Statuetten" (1985), and "Multikulturelle Aspekte" (1991/92). The Cimmer- ians' frequenting of the sanctuary may be at the origin of the legend of its foun- dation by the Amazons (Bammer, *Ephesos* [1988], pp. 212–20; "Sanctuaires à l'Artemision d'Ephèse" p. 67.

of the *polis*, where the rites and myths of sovereignty legitimated their own authority.[111] Clearly, there were gradations of integration, depending upon whether those affected were young, future citizens or citizens' wives honored by being included in the processions and choral dances or, in contrast, dependent natives or passing foreigners; and the forms that integration took would be more varied where the city engaged in trade with other peoples or was surrounded by non-Greek communities, as was the case in Asia Minor or in the colonies of the West. Thus, the Artemision of Ephesus demonstrates clearly how a city could define itself by the degree of participation in the cult that it allowed to noncitizens, integrating them into its society in some cases more, in others less. But before studying the role of nonurban sanctuaries in colonial foundations, we should try to understand the constitution of the early *polis* in the light of what is revealed by the importance ascribed to its cults.

The Greek city is frequently conceived in strictly institutional terms as a community of citizens with full rights, embodied by its sovereign assembly.[112] It is quite true that, in a *polis*, the political phenomenon always constitutes the axis of reference for social and economic life. However, to define it, as Aristotle does, solely in terms of a single form of expression, taking into account only the group that rules it (however varied its constitution) is a source of many difficulties, even in the city of the classical period, in which the various statuses of the population were more clearly distinguished than at any other time.[113] Such an approach clearly rules out understanding the *polis* during the process of its

111. Other examples have been analyzed by Simon, *Cults of Ionia,* (1986); see also Morgan, *Athletes and Oracles,* pp. 230–33, on the subject of Emporio of Chios. The abundance of foreign offerings at the Heraion of Samos (Kilian-Dirlmeyer, "Fremde Weihungen" [1985], pp. 236–43) should not be ascribed solely to the fact that the sanctuary was frequented by non-Greeks, for it may also reflect its central position in the world of Aegean trade. I have made a particular study of the role of these sanctuaries in contacts between Greece and the East in "Influence extérieure?" pp. 121–26.

112. Aristotle *Politics* 12521.6–7; 1276b.1–2.

113. These difficulties have been illuminated by the works of Claude Mossé: "La conception du citoyen" (1967); "Citoyens 'actifs' et citoyens 'passifs'" (1979). See also the reflections of Pečirka in "Crisis of the Athenian Polis" (1976), in particular p. 7.

formation. At that stage, it should be considered as a social entity founded upon a network of relations between the various members of a territorial community, all of whom are involved in the emergence of a new form of social coherence in which internal tensions, too, find a new framework of expression.[114] Accordingly, if our notion of citizenship is limited to its institutional, political aspects, we shall not be able to see beyond the concepts formed from a study of the Greek city in the classical period, concepts unsuited to a study of the initial form of the city. The truth is that the early city's components were extremely heterogeneous, sometimes even ethnically, and the positions (rather than statuses) of its inhabitants were more varied and less strictly defined than the distinctions that separated the citizens of the classical city from its women, children, foreigners, and slaves.[115] That imprecision surrounded even the elite from which the councils composed of *basileis* were drawn, and it also characterized the relations that existed between those *basileis* and the throng of warriors whom they led and who probably made up the very first *dēmos*.[116]

The remarkable development of the religious element in the Greek society of the late Geometric and early archaic period shows that the *polis* constituted the formal expression of a religious cohesion. It centered on cults that not only protected its integrity and growth, but were also capable of welding into a single community all the groups that had previously lived in geographical or social proximity without, however, being linked by any constricting cohesion. Now they were all included in a single stable structure. It was around these cults that, under the pressure of circumstances, a territorial solidarity eventually came to be established, and this brought in its train the dissolution of ancient cleavages and a redefinition of the relations between local elites, between conquerors and conquered, and in general, between dominators and dominated.

This is not to say that we should read into all this any deliber-

114. Cf. Pečirka, "Crisis of the Athenian Polis," and Nenci, "Spazio civico," p. 462.

115. The distinctions are even clearer in the "model city," Athens, than in the others (cf. Vidal-Naquet, *Black Hunter*, pp. 4–7 and 216–18).

116. See Mossé, "Ithaque," p. 11.

ate policy of integration or any subtle maneuvers prompted by a clear view of a definite goal or of some preexisting model of the city that sprang, like Athena, fully armed, from the minds of post-Homeric ideologues. The particular importance that every city ascribed to the cults that, as we have seen, were credited with powers of protection and integration, was neither artificial nor forced. On the contrary, that importance shows that these cults constituted the referential axis around which interacting conflicts and agreements created a new cohesion. Even more important, only those religious mediations could provide the terms for agreements, rejections, divisions, and exclusions, many of the details of which escape us but which fueled the dialectical process of the readjustment of, on the one hand, the external (spatial) frontiers and, on the other, the internal (social) ones from which cities emerged. The *polis* was thus based upon a "religious citizenship" shared in varying degrees and forms by the "kings" and their dependents, the *dēmos* of warriors and the women, the populations of the center and those of the conquered peripheries—in short, by all the inhabitants of the territory whose frontiers were established by the elite that assumed the function of leadership there. Clearly, that kind of citizenship did not itself imply anything approaching the exercise of power; nor did it rule out internal tensions and clashes. It did not, that is, succeed in masking conflicts. Indeed, it was at that level of citizenship that conflicts came out into the open and found expression, and it was, for that reason, the essential element in the reordering from which there emerged a social structure that was more coherent and also more efficient than any known in the dark ages of Greece.

The functional similarity of all the cults concerned relativizes some of the distinctions that we have noted in order to make this study more coherent. Although the great extraurban sanctuary generally symbolized territorial, religious, and cultural sovereignty and dispensed protection and social structuring, in some cities, where no such cult site existed, a monumental suburban sanctuary assumed the same characteristics. In Thebes, for example, it was the suburban (or perhaps "sub-Cadmean") sanctuary of Apollo Ismenios that received the offerings of the little cities of southern Boeotia that fell under Theban influence and

were eventually absorbed by synoecism, possibly as early as the
sixth century.[117] The difference in the location of such a sanctuary
was compensated for by the similarity of its functions. Equally,
where, in certain cities, two cults were present, they fitted into a
definite hierarchy and should not be regarded either as redun-
dant repetitions or as evidence of rivalry: in Lacedaemonia, the
integrating and founding roles of Artemis and Apollo complemented each other without overlapping or competing; and even
if, each in their own way, Hera and Pythaean Apollo both civilized and protected the territory, Hera alone ruled over the plain
of Argos, from her rural sanctuary, while Apollo, for his part,
wove a subtle network of connections and religious assimila-
tions that manifested the influence of the city in more or less remote areas.

Around that major pole, the great extraurban sanctuary, the
"minor" sanctuaries constituted two groups that, thanks to their
own particular attributes, served as an extension or a complement to it: on the one hand the suburban sanctuaries of Demeter,
on the other, Artemis' sanctuaries out in the *eschatiai*. However
distant they may seem from one another, they all, in their different ways, fulfilled the same function: that of ordering society
and setting up a political community. From this point of view,
the nonurban cult sites constitute a well-defined group whose
coherence becomes clear as soon as it is considered in relation to
the monumental sanctuary.

So the first thing that needs to be understood is the nature of
the monumental sanctuary, for it was there that the *polis* took
shape even as it gathered itself together around the cult and
forged its own consciousness of an identity that both itself and
others could recognize. There, in the sanctuary, the rites and the
architecture, together with the representations of local myths
and symbols, created a sacred space that was at once the heart
and the frontier of the city, the organ of its constantly renewed
constitution and the place of mediation in its relations—ami-
cable or hostile—with the external world, both human and divine. This essential combination of qualities explains why it is
that these sanctuaries were so famous: to know a city meant

117. Schachter, *Cults of Boiotia*, 1:82–83.

knowing the cult whose rites and image engendered the political society.

That is why we should revise our ideas about the role of urban cults and accept the image of a bipolar city in place of that of a monocentric one, the model for which, Athens, may have constituted its only example.

The Bipolar City and the Athenian Exception

The cities we have been considering so far generally had a sanctuary situated on the agora, usually consecrated to Apollo, or a sanctuary on an acropolis, usually dedicated to Athena. Because of the renown of the Athenian model of the monocentric city, that sanctuary is traditionally considered to have been the most important one for the city, and as a consequence of the urban Athena's usual title of Polias or Poliouchos, deities housed in such sanctuaries are known as "poliad," that is to say, city protectors.

Clearly, we should not minimize the role of these urban sanctuaries. The function of the first temples of Apollo, built in the late eighth century but soon to be replaced by some of the most remarkable monuments of archaic Greece, was to sacralize the center around which towns such as Eretria and Corinth gradually grew from an amalgamation of hamlets and various clusters of dwellings. Athena was assigned characteristics and attributes similar to those of other goddesses and played her part in safeguarding the city, if only by virtue of her warrior qualities. It was thus in Sparta, where she was Poliouchos, before becoming Chalkioikos when her temple was decorated with plaques of bronze at the end of the archaic period, and where she was honored by a procession of armed young men and offerings in the shape of shields—also in Tegea, in Gortyn, and in Argos, where an ancient shield, said to have belonged to Diomedes, was paraded in the procession that bore Athena Akria from the acropolis to the river Inachos.[118] This annual Argive ceremony of the

118. Sparta: Pausanias 3.17.2, 4.15.5; Polybius 4.22.35. Tegea: the chains worn by the Spartans conquered in a conflict at the beginning of the sixth century had been consecrated there to Athena Alea (Herodotus 1.66; Pausanias 8.47.1), who was, however, distinct from the Athena Poliatis close to the agora (Pausanias

Bath of Pallas, which resembled the Athenian Plyntheria, also draws attention to her interventions in the domain of fecundity.[119] In Gortyn and Axos, in Crete, her sanctuaries have been found to contain numerous archaic terra-cotta figurines of the goddess, who is sometimes represented naked, sometimes with her hands placed over her breasts or pubis, a gesture that later came to be reserved solely for Aphrodite.[120] In Lindos, another of Athena's famous sanctuaries, she is closer to the *potnia thēron* and rules over the wild, animal world.[121]

But there is nothing in any of this to suggest that the urban deity, even when situated on the acropolis, should be seen as the absolute immortal patron of the city, whose reign had metaphorically replaced that of the ancient kings. The effect of the monumental, liturgical, mythological, and historical importance of the great extraurban sanctuaries is to give the civic and religious space two poles, and it is not the case that the urban pole is the more important. It is, rather, a matter of a division of roles and a balance: Corinthia is consecrated not to Apollo but to Poseidon; the Athena Polias of the acropolis of Larissa in Thessaly faced competition from two Athenas "beyond the walls," the Athena Lageitara (People's Guide) and the Athena Patria, who protected the altars of the phratries, just as Demeter did in Thasos.[122] That division of roles and that balance are well illustrated by the frequent practice of displaying the city's decrees and treaties in the principal sanctuaries, the one in town and the one out

---

8.47.6). Gortyn: where some of the statuettes in the sanctuary of the acropolis represented her as an armed goddess (Rizza and Scrinari, *Gortina*, vol. 1 (1968), p. 249. Argos: Callimachus *Hymn to Athena* and *On the Bath of Pallas*.

119. In the Plyntheria, a procession of ephebes accompanied a *xoanon* of Athena to the Phaleros, where the deity was bathed by two young girls. Also, two adolescent girls consecrated to the goddess, the *arrēphoroi*, each year secretly descended from the acropolis to the gardens of the sanctuary of Aphrodite, carrying carefully hidden objects in their baskets (Pausanias 1.27.3; Plutarch *Alcibiades* 34.1).

120. Rizza and Scrinari, *Gortina*, 1:246f.; Rizza, "Terrecotte di Axos" (1967–68), p. 291f. One of these figures even represents Athena making the *anasurma* gesture, lifting her chiton up to her belt, another "privilege" that was later reserved for Aphrodite (in particular in the Hellenistic period).

121. Blinkenberg, "La déesse de Lindos" (1930–31), pp. 154–56.

122. Pausanias, 2.1.6; Helly, "A Larissa" (1970), p. 291.

in the territory, and of displaying agreements and treaties relating to external city affairs in the outlying sanctuary.[123]

The examples of bipolar cities are legion. In contrast, there is only one city that fully exemplifies the traditional monocentric concept of the city, and that is Athens itself, which provided that model. A comparison between two episodes will help us to appreciate the difference between the two models. After crushing the Argives in the battle of Sepeia, King Cleomenes of Sparta was arraigned by the ephors for not having attacked the town. He based his defense upon a miracle that he had witnessed in the temple of Hera.[124] Whatever the "truth" of the matter, this plea sufficed to clear the king, thereby showing that his march on the Heraion and the sacrifice that he offered there could be regarded as a strategy of symbolic conquest, for the fact that the sanctuary and its cult had fallen into the hands of the Spartans (the Argive priests having been ejected) signaled the end of Argive sovereignty in Argolis.

The opposite case is exemplified less than a century later during the Peloponnesian War. The armies of Sparta were repeatedly invading the Athenian territory, which they ravaged without managing to bring down the city, which had deliberately cut itself off from the land surrounding it but remained open to the sea. The Spartan army seemed to be wandering aimlessly through a space in which no point of orientation was provided by any cult site comparable to a Heraion (even Eleusis), the capture of which would have constituted a significant gain and a symbolic victory. For not only was Athens "an island within its terrain" as a result of the strategic, social, and economic policies made possible by Cleisthenes, sketched out by Themistocles, and implemented by Pericles; it was also a faithful continuation of a monocentric archaic city, the only city in Greece without a great nonurban sanctuary, which, had it existed, would no doubt have

123. See above, note 34. On a different note, it is equally significant that the Argives, having seized two statues of deities at Tiryns (probably during the wars of 460/458), placed one (the *xoanon* of Hera) in the Heraion and the other in the sanctuary of Apollo the Lycian, on the agora (Pausanias 2.17.5 and 7.46.3).

124. Where he had gone in the company of an elite group after the battle. The flame that he apparently saw emanating from the goddess made him understand that it would be vain to attempt an assault. Herodotus 6.81–82.

had the effect of a counterbalance. The imperial Athens of the fifth century would probably never have developed into what it became if the religious Athens of the eighth century had not been exceptional, focused as it was upon its acropolis consecrated to an Athena who truly did seem to represent an avatar of the Mycenaean palace goddess, the protector of royalty in the second millennium. It was around Athena that the Athenian *polis* took shape, and Cleisthenes' organization of the city space, which adopted that pattern, simply reinforced the concentric conformation of Attica.[125] Athens was the only city where the major civic and religious procession set off from the periphery and led to the heart of the town—the procession in which the whole society solemnly paraded before itself in a ceremony that manifested its own particular concept of its constitution and its space. In contrast to that Panathenaea festival, there were countless similar, but inverted, processions all over Greece, all of which set out from the center of the inhabited area to make their way to the great territorial or periurban sanctuaries of Hera, Apollo, or Artemis.

It is thus reasonable enough to draw a contrast between the many Athenian myths and rituals that reflect a centripetal structure of civic space and their equivalents in other cities—for instance, those that have to do with the double organizational action, both spatial and cultural, that instituted, on the one hand, ploughing and, on the other, blood sacrifice. The sequence of events in the Athenian Dipolia represented the progression from a primordial absence of differentiation for places and living beings to their disposition around a pole, namely, the acropolis, upon which the city's myths and its rites all converged.[126] In contrast, in Argos, the model par excellence of a bipolar city, the ceremony that enacted comparable religious concepts and ritual sequences was that of the Heraia, in which the *pompē* imposed form upon the Argive territory and society by orienting them toward the extraurban sanctuary. It is equally significant that the Ephesians, to defend themselves against Croesos, sought the protection of their suburban Artemis by linking their town to

125. See Lévêque and Vidal-Naquet, *Clisthène l'Athénien* (1964).
126. Durand, *Labour et sacrifice* (1986), pp. 43–66.

the sanctuary by means of a cable; and that, in Paros, the mysterious sacred objects whose possession ensured control of the city were secured in the Thesmophorion, whereas in Athens the city's precious objects and likewise its fate were entrusted to the *prostatai* heroes of the Erechtheion and the deities of its acropolis.[127]

However, it is not the case that Athens had no territorial sanctuaries at all.[128] By the end of the eighth century, the sanctuaries of Cape Sunion (Athena and Poseidon) were manifesting Athenian sovereignty at one extremity of its territory and at the same time constituted a point of access to the outside world, where seafarers could stop off and through which many Cycladic influences passed. The ceremonies associated with border sanctuaries such as those of Athena Skiras at Skiron, on the road leading to Eleusis and at Phaleron (Skirophoria, Oschophoria), the festivals of the Plyntheria in Phaleron and of Artemis Mounychia at Piraeus, where many of the myths and rites of segregation and integration for adolescents were associated with episodes in the Theseus legend, were all occasions marked by processions leading to the borders of the "close territory," the *pedion*.[129] Meanwhile, the popular cult of Artemis at Brauron had linked the city with its *eschatiai* at least since the sixth century, and possibly much earlier. Finally, the sanctuary of Eleusis, whatever the degree of autonomy enjoyed by the people of Eleusis in the management of the cult during the archaic period, symbolized the city's sovereignty over western Attica in a manner impossible for Megara and Boeotia to ignore. Nevertheless, neither the cults at the furthermost tip of Attica nor the mysteries of Eleusis, which were reserved solely for initiates or prospective initiates and so were quite different from purely civic cults, really played the same role for Athens as the great territorial sanctuaries of Hera or Apollo did for so many other cities. Right from the time of the formation of the city of Athens, its center was the acropolis.

This aspect of Athens' uniqueness may be set alongside another unique feature of which the Athenians were always boasting in their official speeches of the classical period: namely, their

127. Herodotus 5.72.
128. I provide a more detailed analysis in Polignac, "Sanctuaires et société en Attique" (forthcoming).
129. Calame, *Thésée*, pp. 291–396.

autochthony.[130] Although mythological in origin and exploited largely for ideological purposes, the theme of autochthony constituted a reminder that Attica was one of the rare regions of the Greek world in which some kind of historical continuity was suggested at the level of the institutions and cults, linking the archaic period to Mycenaean times. The switch from palace goddess to poliad deity and the transition, systematized by Aristotle's schema of how one kind of power gave way to another, passing from a monarchical authority progressively limited and fragmented to the distribution of the *archē* among several temporary magistracies, seem to be two aspects (all too often associated with all the Greek cities) of the historical peculiarity of Athens, which the violent upheavals of the end of the Helladic period did not affect with such intensity as other regions of Greece.[131] In Athens, the palace monarchy, although possibly weakened by those upheavals, was not swept away but probably found itself caught in a general movement of recession that undermined its authority little by little. That increasingly tenuous continuity would account for the exceptional importance, in the city of Athens, of the only acropolis where a truly poliad deity really did take over from the last vestiges of a disintegrating royal house.

So can Athens really be regarded as the model city? Far more likely, it was quite exceptional—as the Athenians themselves indeed proclaimed, for they alone were "autochthonous," they alone were designated by the name of their goddess. To accept that fact, even without going into the interplay of imaginary and ideological representations that expressed it, is to do justice to the other cities, in that it is a step toward establishing recognition of their particular identities. But it also poses the question of the role of the great urban sanctuary (whether on an agora or on an acropolis) and the validity of the notion "poliad."

What is the true significance of the protection afforded by the Polias, Poliatis, or Poliouchos deity, as opposed to the relation-

130. On this subject, see the works by Loraux, *Children of Athena* (1983), and *Invention of Athens* (1986).

131. Aristotle *Constitution of the Athenians* 3.2. On post-Mycenaean Attica: Desborough, *Late Mycenaeans* (1964), pp. 112–19, and Immerwahr, *Athenian Agora* (1971).

ship cities maintained with their nonurban deities? It could be understood as protection extended to the town, not to the city as a whole, for the *polis* element in those epithets could be taken to refer only to the urban center. The inhabited area was organized around sanctuaries that, situated at the heart of the hamlets clustered in the protourban space, testified to their symbolic union, which transcended whatever else might separate their inhabitants.[132] (Their material fusion into a veritable urban fabric was a very gradual process, not completed until later.) When a sanctuary was built, it sometimes took the place of the *megaron* of the *basileus* of the Geometric period, and it remained the center of the cults addressed to the deities who were the protectors of the aristocracy, the *astoi*, in their capacity as both a warrior elite (the armed Athena of the acropolises) and the political body that rules the city (Apollo, the protector of institutions). And the building of the sanctuary marked the birth of the town as the decision-taking center, recognized and frequented as such by the inhabitants of the territory. When the center of habitation acquired that new status, the agora would be marked out at the same time as the sanctuary was set up.[133] Whatever the meaning ascribed to *polis*, the urban sanctuary was thus to the political constitution of the city what the periurban and territorial sanctuary was to the city's social constitution brought about through the establishment of relations between different groups and the definition of social and spatial frontiers. The movement that gathered together the various components of the society around a cult whose external position made it acceptable to all was thus complemented and, as it were, reflected by the opposite movement, which created a political space by settling all those who wielded authority within the shelter afforded by the central urban cult.

So might there exist between the principal urban cult and the outer territory a symbolic link analogous to but the reverse of that which made the nonurban monumental sanctuary the emblem of the entire city? Such a link was, as we have seen, often created by periurban sanctuaries like the sanctuary of Pythaean

132. See discussion above of the rivalries supposed by myth to have taken place between the various small towns of Sparta.

133. See Martin, *Recherches sur l'agora,* chaps. 2, 3, and 4.

Apollo at Argos or that of Apollo Ismenios at Thebes.[134] Double cults, which introduced into the town a cult from the outer territory, as in the well-known case of Artemis Brauronia in Athens, were also established as early as the archaic period.[135] But the hypothesis that the central sanctuary might itself represent the territory in the heart of the town has been put forward in the case of the cult of Apollo in Eretria, where, in his capacity as the _daphnēphoros_ (laurel-bearer), the founding god of this Euboean city was associated with the Lelantine plain, where the Homeric hymn to him locates one of its episodes.[136] The Daphnephorion might thus be supposed to constitute a religious representation of the territory, in the center of the town. However, if we accept that Eretria originally stood on the site of Lefkandi / Xeropolis, it may in truth represent a lost territory from which, in about the mid eighth century, the population moved away, following defeats suffered in the wars with Chalcis, and then set up the new, historical city. If that is so, the establishment of the cult of Apollo and its symbolic representations in the center of the city was a normal founding act: through the cult, it preserved the memory of the place of origin evoked by the Daphnephoria at the heart of the community that had been obliged to move away from it. The case of Eretria can thus be assimilated to all the other colonial foundations and, thanks to the particular perspective offered by the history of cities created from scratch in non-Greek surroundings, a study of those foundations may deepen our understanding of the role of cults in the birth of the city.

134. In Thebes, some of the rites and deities associated with Apollo Ismenios may have originated from the region of Lake Copais (Schachter, _Cults of Boiotia,_ 1:78–80).

135. These pairs have been studied systematically in Arcadia by Jost, "Sanctuaires ruraux."

136. _Homeric Hymn to Apollo,_ line 216f. See Bérard, "Architecture érétrienne" (1971). The original temple was supposed to have been an exact representation of the "sacred hut" constructed by the god in the myth. However, that is perhaps a risky assumption. New discoveries invite a measure of caution in the interpretation of architectural particularities that may be of a purely secular nature.

CHAPTER THREE

Cults and Colonial Foundations

୶ ⁂ ৵

O
ne aspect of the Greek world's expansion in the eighth
and seventh centuries was the departure of expeditions
in search of new resources and the settlements that were established far away in the Aegean (Thasos, Thera), toward the Hellespont and the Black Sea and, above all, along the coasts of
southern Italy and Sicily. These settlements followed a phase of
preliminary contacts and possibly the establishment of scattered
individual outposts in the midst of indigenous societies, mainly
in the Etrusco-Latial area, from the beginning of the eighth century on.[1] The movement westward was both the earliest (the
very first settlements were installed there before the middle of
the century: Pithecussae in about 760, Naxos in 757, according to
the traditional chronology) and also the largest. New foundations proliferated in the second half of the eighth century and
the early seventh (Cumae, Sybaris, Rhegium, Tarentum, Metapontum, Locri, and Siris in Magna Graecia, Megara Hyblaea,
Syracuse, Leontini, Catania, Zancle, and Gela in Sicily). A second
wave of colonization (internal this time, since it was initiated by
cities that were themselves colonial: Sybaris, Croton, Syracuse,
Zancle, Megara, Gela, and Thera) resulted, in the seventh and
the early sixth centuries, in the creation of yet more cities (Posidonia, Caulonia, Himera, Agrigentum, Selinus, and Cyrene).

1. A Greek graffito recently discovered at Osteria del'Osa, near Rome, on a
fragment of a pot made locally, could well date from the end of the ninth century
or the first third of the eighth (Bietti-Sestieri, *Osteria del'Osa* [1992], p. 185). The
presence of Euboean artisans is also assumed at Veii, in about 760 (most recently
by Ridgway, "Demaratus" [1992], pp. 89–90).

The earliest colonies all resulted from the initiative of the Euboeans, in particular those from Chalcis (Pithecussae, Naxos, Rhegium, Zancle, Leontini, Catania), but hard on their heels came the Corinthians, who founded Syracuse in about 733, and the Megarians, who founded Megara Hyblaea in 728. The origins of the colonizers only really began to diversify at the end of the eighth century, with the arrival of Spartans (Tarentum), Messenians (Rhegium), Achaeans (Croton and Sybaris), Cretans and Rhodians (Gela), and Locrians (Epizephyrian Locri) and with colonization in the Aegean (Parians in Thasos).

The first of these settlements were prompted by the return of Greeks to long-distance trading routes, a return that, like the contemporary Phoenician expansion, was principally motivated by the quest for mineral ore (copper, iron) that originated in the Tyrrhenian world (Etruria in particular). Pithecussae was an emporium where Greeks and Phoenicians cohabited, and it was soon facilitating and stabilizing commercial contacts with the whole Etruscan and Etrusco-Campanian seaboard. The foundations of Zancle and Rhegium (like those of the Megarian colonies of the Hellespont, Astacus, Chalkedon, Byzantium, in the first quarter of the seventh century) testify to the Chalcidians' desire to secure a position on the straits that was as advantageous as the one they already enjoyed on the Euripus.[2] The other Euboean colonies and most subsequent colonies were established on sites backed by cultivable land. However, that does not mean that the colonies should be classified, in arbitrary fashion, in two different categories, the one commercial, the other agricultural. The colonization movement was a process of overall acquisition, and the choice of most sites was determined by a desire to ensure that the new cities benefited from the double advantage of a fertile territory and a coastal situation suitable for trading.[3] While colo-

---

2. On these questions, see Ridgway, *Magna Grecia* (1984), and the studies collected in Kopcke and Tokumaru, *Greece between East and West* (1992), together with an extensive bibliography.

3. See the remarks of Ducat in "Thèmes de la fondation de Rhégion" (1974), p. 112, and Lepore, in "Osservazioni" (1969), p. 184, on this "dynamic" interpretation of colonization in the overall framework of the expansion of Greek society. Phoenician colonization in the seventh century does not fall into the framework of this study; see Gras, *Trafics tyrrhéniens* (1988).

nization for the most part took the form of the conquest of new lands, the surplus of goods that resulted engendered new activities, new currents of exchange, thanks to which the entire Greek world, not solely the colonial cities, was in a position to sustain its growth.

In all probability colonization itself contributed to the reinforcement of the identity of the *polis* since, right from the start, it postulated the existence of a community framework within which it was possible to address the problem of dividing up society in a way accepted by all its members, and as we have seen, that framework and those terms were mediated by religion. Besides, what was ultimately required was a strong and lasting cohesion between all members of the colonizing expedition. Even if the point has been made elsewhere, it is important in the first place to stress that the social cohesion and political elaboration of the societies from which these colonizing expeditions started out were still in the process of evolving.[4] Expeditions with commercial ambitions and even the establishment of emporia could in many cases be ventures launched by private initiative. However, even if the decision to set forth was prompted by a particular individual or group of entrepreneurs, the actual departure of the founders of an *apoikia* involved the city as a whole, if only to the extent of its entrusting some of its religious objects and symbols to the would-be founder. The foundation of a colony may in many cases have constituted one of the city's earliest truly political decisions.

The group of colonizers thus had no ready-made references to hand, no preestablished frameworks to help them define and organize the type of society in which they were going to live. Now, these foundations certainly did give birth to cities, and in them the constitution of a *polis* resulted not from the gradual kind of evolution that took place in the Greco-Aegean world, but from a much shorter process that, in the confrontation of new problems, bypassed many of the stages that were characteristic of regions long populated by Greeks. Both the similarities and the differences make a comparative study worthwhile, as an inquiry into the sanctuaries immediately shows.

4. Bilinski, in *Atti Taranto 7 1967* (1968), p. 183.

Cults: Classifications and Interpretations

The importance of the nonurban sanctuaries of the colonial world, particularly Italy, has long fascinated archaeologists and historians. As one lists the cults of these colonial cities, one notices once again that the most famous sanctuaries (famous throughout the Greek world) are nonurban and also that, in most cities, the number and importance of those cults equal the number and importance of the urban cults. Their proliferation and diversity are such that it is difficult to classify them if one limits oneself to the categories of suburban or periurban and extraurban. It is no doubt convenient to make use of the idea of periurban sanctuaries as a category for all the cult locations in the immediate or less immediate neighborhood of the inhabited area, but a topographical description of this kind is not sufficient.

To establish meaningful categories, we need only return to the classification proposed at the end of chapter 2. In the colonies, as in the Greco-Aegean world, the following kinds of sanctuaries may be distinguished: (1) the monumental sanctuary of the urban pole of the colony; (2) the monumental sanctuary of the nonurban pole of the colony; (3) the nonmonumental periurban sanctuary; and (4) the nonmonumental sanctuary situated in the outer territory.[5] The first of those categories naturally includes sanctuaries situated on acropolises or at the center of the urban space. These were generally dedicated to Athena (Syracuse, Locri, Gela, Agrigentum, Thasos) or to Apollo (Metapontum, Selinus?, Cyrene, Thasos) or occasionally to Zeus (Locri). However, the principal sanctuary was sometimes situated in a corner or on the edge of the town, as at Naxos (Hera or Aphrodite?) and Posidonia (Hera), rather in the manner of an acropolis without any height.

Hera remained the principal deity for nonurban monumental sanctuaries, whether these were truly extraurban, as their Ae-

---

5. To clarify terminology, I should point out that, as earlier, the monumentality of a sanctuary is, obviously, gauged not in absolute terms (the kind of monumentality attested by the remains of the great temples of the classical age), but in relative ones, with respect to the style that distinguishes the *naos* from other archaic cult sites (*oikēma, megaron, sacellum,* etc.).

gean homologues were, as in Magna Graecia (Croton, Metapontum, Posidonia) or periurban, as in Sicily (Agrigentum, Selinus: Temple B at Marinella). But her place was taken by Zeus in Syracuse and Locri. Athena was also to be found within the outlying territory (on the hill of Francavilla Marittima in the Sybaris region) and Apollo on the outskirts of the territory (at Ciro Marina, to the north of Croton). Demeter (or occasionally Persephone) reigned over nonmonumental suburban sanctuaries (Siris, Locri, Posidonia?, Syracuse, Gela, Agrigentum, Selinus, Camarina, Helorus, Thasos, Cyrene), while frontier sanctuaries were devoted to Artemis or other feminine deities whose names are unknown to us but all of whom were associated with springs (San Biagio at Metapontum, Santa Anna at Croton, Palma di Montechiaro at Gela) or with ancient indigenous sites (the sanctuaries of the region around Sybaris). But Hera, in Croton and perhaps in Cumae, where she was the patron deity of the foundation, and possibly also Artemis in Metapontum, each had sanctuaries on the borders of town; and Zeus Meilichios, Hecate, and other goddesses were associated with Demeter in the sanctuaries to the west of Selinus. Finally, the cult of Herakles was well known in Thasos, where his sanctuary was in the southern part of the town, and it is also attested at Poggioreale, in the countryside behind Selinus.

The colonial cities thus present a wide variety of faces.[6] In some cities (Syracuse, Croton, Metapontum, Posidonia), the major sanctuary of the territory was sharply distinguished from the rest by its monumental nature and its wealth. In others (Megara Hyblaea, Agrigentum, Gela), the outstanding feature was the large number of small periurban sanctuaries surrounding the town. Selinus was distinguished by the perfect symmetry between its monumental temples dedicated to the Olympians (one of whom was Hera) to the east, and its chthonic sanctuaries that lay to the west, on the other side of the axis constituted by the town. However, the importance of nonurban sanctuaries and in particular of cults devoted to feminine deities in all these cities is a dominant feature that has given rise to a number of different explanations.

6. For an overall view, see Guzzo, Città scomparse, 1982.

Historiography, mainly Italian, has long taken an interest in this problem.[7] Three major interpretations have been advanced to account for the phenomenon, but they are all marred by their dependence upon an a priori assumption that can no longer be defended, namely, that the frequent nonurban positioning of major city deities was an exceptional phenomena peculiar to the western colonies and that the reason for it must accordingly lie in some feature peculiar to that region and its historical evolution.[8]

For instance, one often comes across the idea that the nonurban cults were of ancient indigenous origin, Hellenized when the Greeks arrived, and that the respective cities took them over and preserved them as important rites on account of their antiquity and the possibility of their making it easier to assimilate the indigenous people. It is suggested that, despite their Greek names, the deities, their attributes, and the rituals were really all indigenous and were only later given a Hellenized air: their continuing importance reflected the fusion of the two societies.[9]

Critical of the inadequacies of this theory, which is oversensitive to the "barbarian" features of some cults and is not applicable to all the sanctuaries,[10] another approach has taken note of the many associations between nonurban cults and legendary stories about sea voyages in the second millennium, or even vestiges of Mycenaean influences, which are interpreted as traces of a "precolonization" in the late Helladic period. It is true that the foundation myths of many sanctuaries and cities do feature heroes of Mino-Mycenaean origin—Argonauts, Homeric heroes, and so on—and many sites have been found to contain Mycenaean pottery, which testifies to the existence of relations

7. Since the works of Giannelli, *Culti e miti della Magna Grecia* (1906; 2d ed., 1963) and Ciaceri, *Culti e miti nella Storia di Sicilia* (1912; 2d ed., 1940).

8. A narrow view already criticized by Vallet in "La Cité et son territoire" (1968), p. 99. Edlund, *The Gods and the Places* (1987), has made a comparison between the rural sanctuaries of Magna Graecia and Etruria that likewise takes no account of the Hellenic background.

9. A thesis first presented by Giannelli and Ciaceri in their respective works, and one that would explain, for example, the reign of Demeter in Sicily and that of Persephone in Locri.

10. See the remarks of Bérard, *Colonisation grecque* (1957), p. 236, and Dunbabin, *Western Greeks* (1948), p. 181f.

between the Aegean and the Italic worlds in the Bronze Age.[11] Seen from this perspective, the Italic cults would appear to represent a renaissance of Aegean cults that were passed down either by the descendants of Mycenaeans who had settled in Italy or through the intermediary of autochthonous societies. The "indigenist" theory is thus opposed by a theory of affiliation and Greek continuity.[12]

Both these arguments are dismissed by those who reject any idea of a legacy behind the cults of the colonial cities and insist on regarding them purely as Greek cults of the historic period, whose nonurban positioning may be accounted for by more or less fortuitous reasons, such as the natural character of certain sites: an atmosphere conducive to the presence of particular deities (river mouths, caves, springs, narrow valleys), to which the colonizers must have been very responsive since their recent arrival in this unknown world rendered them particularly sensitive to supernatural manifestations, or a crucially important position from the point of view of shipping (on a headland).[13] Even without setting the above theories alongside the factual realities of the ancient world, they can be seen to present serious weaknesses.[14]

It is hard to believe that, in the religious domain, the Greeks were necessarily influenced by the Italic natives to the point of adopting their deities and rites, with no more than a Greek veneer, for all the evidence shows how rapidly the indigenous culture became deeply and lastingly Hellenized.[15] In the domains of

11. *Myths:* Cretans of the time of Minos in Tarentum and Sicily (Strabo 6.3.2), Nestor and the Neleids in Metapontum (ibid., 6.1.15), Jason in Posidonia (ibid., 6.251), Epeios and Philoctetes in Metapontum and Thurii (Justin 20.2.1), and of course Herakles in Croton and Sicily (Diodorus 4.22.6–24.6). *Mycenaeans: Atti Taranto 22, 1982,* (1983); Kilian, "Mycenaeans Up to Date" (1988); Vagnetti, "Présence égéenne en Italie" (1991).

12. The most ardent defender of this thesis in Italian historiography is Pugliese-Carratelli.

13. See, for example, Hermann, "Santuari di Magna Grecia" (1965), p. 47f.

14. They have also been refuted, at greater length, by Malkin, *Religion and Colonization* (1987), pp. 141–48, 160–64. See also Edlund, *The Gods and the Places* (1987), p. 29.

15. Cf. Brelich, "Religione greca in Sicilia" (1964–65). On the particular case of the *emporion* (eg. Pithecussae), where the cultural relations between Greeks and indigenous peoples were less rigid, and on the various seashore and harbor sanctuaries patronizing, as in the Aegean, the relations between local popula-

life-style, funerary customs, and art, the contact between the Greeks and the indigenous peoples most certainly did not take the form of an egalitarian syncretism or an "indigenization" of the Greeks. Although that does not exclude the retention of some indigenous features, their survival should not systematically be interpreted as having influenced the Greeks.

An archaeological argument joins forces with the cultural argument to refute that explanatory hypothesis. It is fair to say that not a single sanctuary has produced material proof of any continuity with a previous cult.[16] Many sanctuaries were established in a center of habitation from which the indigenous population had been ejected. The site and the urban cults of Syracuse were established on top of the ruins of a small autochthonous settlement, as were those of Rhegium, Locri, Selinus, and probably Gela.[17] The same applies to the sanctuaries in the region around Sybaris, such as Francavilla Marittima. But these establishments left no vestiges of religious activity, which suggests that the relevant societies never attained a level of development in which religion constituted an autonomous and public domain clearly indicated by special arrangements made to accommodate it. The Greeks, in contrast, set up sanctuaries soon after their arrival. That provides some indication of the gulf separating these two kinds of society and to a large extent renders the question of continuity meaningless.

It accordingly seems pointless to seek at all costs to establish the existence of a pre-Greek phase for the nonurban cults, which would provide an explanation for their importance. All these cults, by virtue of both their positioning and their functions, turn out to be rich in meaning if one but remembers that they were

---

tions and foreign seafarers, see Torelli, "Greci e indigeni" (1977), pp. 45–61; Olmos Romero, in *Atti Taranto 29, 1989* (1990): 419–420.

16. Contrary to what was for a time believed, it is not the case either at Francavilla Marittima, San Biagio at Metaponto, or the Heraion at Sele; cf. La Genière, "Grecs et indigènes" (1970), p. 672 n. 4. There is no evidence for ascribing to the autochthonous peoples who visited these places any specifically religious purpose, until after the arrival of the Greeks.

17. Vallet, "La Cité et son territoire," p. 110; and *AR* 23 (1976–77): 64–66 (Syracuse); Dionysius of Halicarnassus, *Rom. Ant.* Excerpta, 29.2 (Rhegium); Polybius 12.6.5 (Locri); *AR* 23 (1976–77): 72 (Gela, the zone of the temple of Athena); Parisi-Presicce, "Funzione delle aree sacre" (1984), p. 27 (Selinus).

either established or enlarged by Greeks who founded cities with territories attached, societies that were altogether new, even if they were inevitably forced to resolve the problems posed by the presence of indigenous peoples living there. These cults should not be considered from the point of view of the local populations. It was to the culture of the Greek city that they belonged, not to that of a Sikel, Oenotrian, or Iapygian village. Even if some of them may have taken over preexisting rituals, the formation of the *polis* that followed upon the arrival of the Greeks totally transformed both their importance and their meaning.

The thesis of a Mycenaean connection also presents difficulties. The presence of Aegeans (Mycenaeans, Cypriots) in the western Mediterranean and their creation of stopovers and trading ports did leave a mark upon the indigenous cultures. Their influence is detectable in the techniques and styles of certain pots (in Italy and Sardinia) and metalwork (in Sardinia and Sicily). However, the depth and duration of that influence following the disappearance of the Mycenaeans varies greatly from one site to another and, even if relations between the eastern and the western Mediterranean were not completely broken off, as is sometimes believed, it would be very risky to deduce that Aegean ideas and cults became implanted and survived in indigenous societies right down to the arrival of the Iron Age Greeks and that it was these survivals that were responsible for the creation of all the nonurban sanctuaries. For one thing, a society as deeply influenced by Cypriot metallurgical techniques as that of the Nouraghes of Sardinia does not appear to have adopted any Aegean religious practices; for another, the societies of southern Italy and Sicily underwent profound transformations in the early Iron Age (including population displacements), and these considerably altered their cultural *facies,* thereby diminishing the chances of the perpetuation of an earlier heritage.[18] In these circumstances, any cultural legacy would have been so tenuous that it could not possibly explain the behavior of the Greeks who landed on these same shores several centuries later and in a totally different context. In truth, in general, the idea of a

18. Guzzo, "Myths and Archaeology" (1990), gives a good general view of the problem.

Mycenaean legacy in the western Mediterranean reflects not a real continuity but an interpretation with a pro-Greek and would-be heroic bias of anything at all that, rightly or wrongly, could be taken as evidence for the presence of legendary Greek ancestors.[19]

As for the last of those theories, it relies too heavily on conjectural or even subjective elements to account for a structural phenomenon such as the preponderance of nonurban sanctuaries, which, furthermore, all three hypotheses wrongly take to be peculiar to the colonial world. What we need to do, then, is examine the significance of these sanctuaries in the light of what we know of the old Greek world.

Sanctuaries and Taking Possession of the Territory

As in the Aegean world, the nonurban sanctuaries of the colonial cities were linked first and foremost with the definition of the territory and the political space, sometimes according to modalities that were characteristic of the newly settled areas. What was new about the colonial situation was reflected in the order in which cults were founded.

That order was determined by the Greeks' way of installing themselves and organizing their territory. It is often suggested that there may have been a provisional phase of settlement, or even that trading posts may have been set up before the actual conquest of the terrain that heralded a definitive settlement. But the question is, when did a colonial foundation become a *polis* and what was the effect of that transformation upon the evolution of relations between the Greeks and the natives?

Greek colonization certainly was carried through at the expense of autochthonous populations, about whom quite a lot is

19. The theme of Herakles' exploits in the West provides an example of the way in which the localization of myths changed as the known—and "Hellenized"—world gradually expanded: see Croon, *Herdsman of the Dead* (1952) on the subject of the oxen of Geryon. The same phenomenon also lies at the origin of the legends of the Nostoi, in which many Homeric heroes are represented to have landed on the shores of Italy and Sicily, as they returned from Troy. See also Pearson, "Myth and Archaeology" (1975), and Murray, "Omero e l'etnografia" (1988–89).

now known, that is to say, the Thracians of the northern Aegean, the Iapygians of Apulia, the Oenotrians of Basilicata, the Chonians of Siris, the Sikels of Calabria and eastern Sicily, and the Sikanians and Elymians of western and eastern Sicily.[20] As a result of the arrival of the Greeks, these peoples were either expelled or submitted to servitude, possibly immediately, possibly following an attempt at coexistence that soon turned to their disadvantage.[21] In the West, the natives' withdrawal to defensive positions in the hills of the interior left the Greeks masters of the coastal plains. But if the abrupt disappearance of an indigenous settlement around the site of a future colony is a sure indication of the invasion of Greeks, it tells us nothing about how the newcomers organized themselves or about their attitude to the space of which they had seized possession. The establishment of cults, in contrast, certainly consecrated that seizure and the Greeks' efforts to set the territory in order.

The time taken to set up the various cults of a city was in most cases extremely short once the first religious gesture was made. Sometimes this took the form of consecrating the landing point: in Naxos, the Chalcidians, the first Greeks to settle in Sicily, set up an altar on the beach to Apollo, the founding god of their future city; the same may have happened in Gela.[22] But in general, all the religious sites of a city, both urban and nonurban, were established simultaneously or within the space of a single generation. In Syracuse, the earliest traces of a cult at the extraurban Olympieion (very early seventh century, at the latest) are only slightly later than those of the cult of Athena at Ortygia (last third of the eighth century).[23] There was a similar minimal time-

20. D'Agostino, "Civiltà del ferro" (1974); La Genière, "Grecs et non-Grecs" (1983), and "Ancient settlements" (1983); Bottini and Guzzo, "Greci e indigeni" (1986).

21. In Locri (Polybius 12.6.2–5), Leontini (Polyenus 6.22), between the Megarians and the Sikels in Thapsos before the foundation of Megara Hyblaea (Thucydides 6.4.1) and possibly in the region of Metapontum (the Incoronata) and in Selinus.

22. Naxos: Thucydides 6.3. Gela: Diodorus of Sicily 13.108.4 (a statue of Apollo on the shore).

23. The traditional chronology dates the arrival of the Corinthians to 733. For all these examples, see the references relating to archaeological sites in the Bibliography.

lag between the foundation of Croton (last third of the eighth century) and that of the cult of Hera Lacinia (around 700?), the foundation of Gela together with the cults of its acropolis (around 680), and that of the sanctuaries of Demeter (around 650). In Thasos, the acropolis cults (second quarter of the seventh century?) may have been set up slightly earlier than the cults of the Artemision, the Herakleion, and Aliki.[24] But in the case of the Sybarites, who set up cults as soon as they arrived (end of the eighth century) on the ruins of the indigenous settlements surrounding the plain of Crathis (Francavilla Marittima, Torre Mordillo), the simultaneity is quite remarkable.[25] The same applies to the foundations of the second generation of colonizers: at Metapontum, after 650, at Posidonia, around 620, and at Selinus, around 600, central and peripheral cults made their appearance simultaneously.

The appearance of border sanctuaries—for instance, at Metapontum, the sanctuary of San Biagio, seven kilometers distant from the town—could well mark the frontier of the territory initially claimed by the colony when it was first founded.[26] Their appearance might, on the other hand, mark a city's expansion. In some cases this was gradual, as at Croton, where the sanctuaries at Santa Anna, ten kilometers to the south of the town, and of Apollo Aleos, thirty kilometers to the north, both date from the second half of the seventh century. In contrast, the sanctuaries of Feudo Nobile and Palma di Montechiaro in the Gela territory, all dating from the seventh century, and the sanctuary of Poggioreale, on the frontier between Selinus and Segesta, dating from the

24. Attested in about 650; see Martin, "Thasos" (1978), p. 182f.

25. La Genière, "C'è un modello Amendolara" (1978), p. 345; "Grecs et non-Grecs."

26. San Biagio lies opposite the Incoronata hill, on the other bank of the Basento. It was an eighth-century indigenous site that may later have been occupied by Greeks living within the orbit of Siris, or have been reorganized by "hellenized" inhabitants who welcomed Greeks there. The Incoronata site was destroyed in the third quarter of the seventh century, possibly when the people of Metapontum founded their city and expanded their territory, and a sanctuary was established there in the early sixth century. The later conquests were also accompanied by the creation of sanctuaries, further inland, such as the sanctuary of Cozzo Presepe in the upper Bradano valley. See now Carter, "Sanctuaries in the Chora of Metaponto" (1994), 161–83.

late seventh or early sixth century, all testify to the rapidity with which the Greeks took possession of their environment. The term "environment" is used advisedly here, for the fact that in almost every case the little territorial sites were close to natural springs shows that dominion over water sources complemented dominion over the land when it came to determining the space within which the norms of Greek religion and civilization were to be established.

All these sanctuaries were thus associated with the symbolism of sovereignty, but that symbolism was oriented in two directions. The first, which is the better known, was in particular that of the urban sanctuaries, which represented the links connecting the new foundation with its metropolis, whose cults and even sacred objects it had transplanted.[27] Their presence at the heart of the settlement connected the colony with the familiar universe of Greek civilization in general and with its own motherland in particular. Apollo the founder and Athena the protector of towns were the guarantors of the Greekness of the expedition and the place where it settled. And more specifically, the Apollo of the Chalcidians of Naxos seems to be the god of Delphi;[28] the Apollo of Gela was the god of the Cretans who constituted one of its founding ethnic groups; Metapontum revered the Lycian Apollo of Achaia; while Thasos paid homage to the Pythaean Apollo of Paros. Gela was also indebted to the Rhodians, its other ethnic component, for the cult of Athena Lindia.[29]

In the representations that the colonizers constructed of the space in which they were implanting their own customs, urban sanctuaries were associated with institutions and myths such

27. Malkin, *Religion and Colonization*, pp. 114–33, and for the *aphidryma* carried with them by the Phocaeans who founded Marseille, "What Is an *Aphidryma?*" (1991).

28. This hypothesis seems preferable to that of Guarducci, "Nuova dea a Naxos" (1985), who suggests that the Apollo of Naxos should be recognized here: there was no reason why this deity should become the god of a pan-Siciliot cult, a role that would have been far better suited to the Archegetes god of Delphi, who guided many of the colonizing operations (Malkin, "Apollo Archegetes" [1986]).

29. Their influence remains detectable in Agrigentum, a colony of Gela: the Zeus (Atabyrios) and Athena of the acropolis were both Rhodian. The link with the symbolic metropolis was thus stronger than that with the actual metropolis (cf. Gabba and Vallet, *Sicilia antica* [1980], p. 276).

as the one at the fountain of Arethusa that, like an umbilical cord, connected the land and the gods of Greece with the new frontiers of the Greek world.[30] The gesture constituted by the foundation of the urban sanctuary, however impressive, was therefore oriented toward the world of the colony's origins: the cult that had provided protection for the colonizers during their voyage, their landing, and their first battles would also ensure the cohesion and protection of the small group of expedition members. As in Greece proper, an urban deity belonged first and foremost to the *astoi*, in this case the founding colonizers. However, to the extent that a colonial foundation involved an ordering of space, the organization of a new society whose components were often heterogeneous, the stabilization of relations with the surrounding neighborhood (both autochthonous peoples and other Greek cities), other deities were inevitably also involved.

The first problem for a new settlement, as can be seen even more clearly here than in the Greco-Aegean world, was the organization of space, and the modalities adopted show how cultural norms and social realities interacted. Let us for the time being leave aside the small sanctuaries of feminine deities that testify to the Greeks' systematic transformation of the space they divided among themselves into an agricultural terrain, for it was above all the nonurban monumental sanctuary that symbolized the fact that the land had acquired the status of a territory.[31]

Numerous colonial cities boasted cult sites founded outside the town in the earliest days of its existence and subsequently developed into monumental sanctuaries, some of them positively spectacular, all of them in the purest Greek style. The deity

30. This fountain was believed to be a resurfacing, from beyond the sea, of the river Alpheus, father of the nymph Arethusa (Pindar *Pythian* 2.5 and 12; Pausanias 5.14.6).

31. There is no need to go into details regarding the question of the division of land, a subject of many studies, including that of Asheri, *Distribuzioni di terre* (1966)—which, however, is more useful on the fourth century than on the archaic period (cf. Vallet, Villard, and Auberson, *Mégara Hyblaea* (1976), p. 405)— and the articles in Finley, *Problèmes de la terre* (1973) (in particular the chapters by Lepore, pp. 15–47; Adamesteanu, pp. 49–61; Martin, pp. 97–112). The general impression conveyed is that of an approximate equality between the earliest colonizers, as in the habitat of Megara Hyblaea (Vallet, Villard, and Auberson, *Mégara Hyblaea*, p. 410).

sheltered by the sanctuary was also entirely Greek, displaying no features at all to suggest the influence of any indigenous substrata or later contamination. The Hera of Magna Graecia was the same goddess as the Hera of Argos or Samos. On the Lacinian headland, near Croton, she was similarly associated with cattle: herds were consecrated to her in the sanctuary itself, and according to the myth of origins associated with the cult's foundation, it was Herakles who had founded it when he returned with Geryon's oxen.[32] In Posidonia, as in Croton, the goddess was the true poliad deity of the city while also presiding over cosmic harmony and civilizing order in the face of all that was barbarian, whether supernatural or human.[33]

Whether consecrated to Hera, as at Metapontum and at Selinus, on the Marinella plateau, or to Zeus, as at Syracuse, the Greek temple built in the heart or in the neighborhood of the *chōra* was clearly a deliberate statement of possession. Plenty of observations formulated about the sanctuaries of the "old" Greek world thus apply equally well to the colonial world. It is interesting to note, for instance, that this type of sanctuary tended to be founded in particular by cities whose neighbors— autochtonous peoples or other cities—by virtue of their higher than usual degree of sophistication and military and cultural dynamism, represented a greater than usual "challenge." The Heraion of the Tavole Palatine, five kilometers to the northeast of Metapontum and on the edge of the river Bradano, was thus "aimed at" Tarentum, whose territory began on the opposite bank and whose intentions were feared.[34] Locri built the sanctuary of Zeus on the river Halex to mark out and protect its frontier

32. Lacinios, the son of the indigenous hero Croton, who had offered Herakles hospitality, is supposed to have stolen some of Geryon's oxen. In the struggle that followed, Herakles killed the culprit but also his father, and to expiate the death of the innocent Croton, he set up the sanctuary of Hera (Diodorus 4.24.7, Servius ap. Aen. 3.552); the temple herds: Livy 24.3.3–7, 30.20.6. Obviously, Herakles' exploits were supposed to antedate the Greek conquest.

33. The heroes of order are represented as struggling against the forces of chaos, on the famous metopes known as the "Thesauros" metopes. Zancani-Montuoro and Zanotti-Bianco, *Heraion alla foce del Sele* (1951), p. 67f.

34. The Achaeans are supposed to have been invited by the Sybarites to settle there so as to block the territorial expansion of Tarentum (Strabo 6.1.15). However, it was Metapontum that eventually turned out to be more dangerous for Sybaris, which it destroyed at the end of the seventh century.

with powerful Rhegium.[35] The presence of thriving Etrusco-Campanian populations on the northern bank of the Sele around Pontecagnano helps to explain the importance of the Posidonians' Heraion, which stood on the southern bank, seven kilometers from the town.[36]

The outside world that was thus held in check was also, in every case, space upon which the agrarian order of civilization had never been imposed, space with no points of reference—in some cases, the sea. The Heraion of Sele stood close to the river mouth and presented a perfect image of the Greeks' orientation of space in the face of not only a barbarian expanse of land but equally the expanse of the sea. The Heraion of the Lacinian headland, fifteen kilometers to the south of Croton, constituted one of the most remarkable landmarks for shipping of the whole Ionian coast.[37]

Correlatively, the need for a monumental frontier sanctuary may not have been felt in cities that had rapidly taken possession of a large territory unthreatened by the close and pressing presence of dynamic neighbors. In their vision of space, the role of frontiers was less important. Their awareness of their territorial boundaries was less acute than it would have been in a more cramped city where the link between the town and the frontier sanctuary was given concrete expression by the processional path that appropriated the *chōra* through which it passed, attaching it to the city.[38]

Finally, in some cases, the absence of a monumental rural

35. This river was the scene of many confrontations (Thucydides 3.99.103.115). In the West, the rivers, which flowed parallel to one another, dividing the coastal plain into more or less regular bands, played an essential role in determining frontiers between the territories of the various cities and hence also in the positioning of sanctuaries. This may be a reason for the large numbers of cults of river deities in this region. Land relief, which in Greece constituted the frontier par excellence, played the same role in the colonial world, but with respect to the inland natives.

36. See Bibliography, Paestum.

37. Another example is the sanctuary of Demeter on the Leucopetra headland, in the Rhegium region (Vallet, *Rhégion et Zancle* [1958], p. 119f). At Posidonia, too, a Poseidonion similarly marked a double frontier, probably to the south, at Agropoli, hence in a symmetrical position to the Heraion.

38. Such as the road linking Posidonia with its Heraion.

sanctuary may reflect a form of colonization oriented not so much toward large-scale territorial conquest as toward establishing fruitful connections with the populations of the countryside around the colony. Thus, an opposition is often drawn between colonization of the Chalcidian type and colonization of the Dorian and Achaean type, for it is quite true that no large-scale sanctuaries are to be found in the Chalcidian cities. However, once again, it would be mistaken to be too categorical on the matter. In the first half of the seventh century, these same cities also embarked upon expansionist policies, as is attested by the destruction of indigenous sites and the establishment of small sanctuaries in the countryside around them (Morgantina, Montagna di Ramacca in the case of Leontini, Francavilla di Sicilia in the case of Naxos).[39] Conversely, cities notorious for the brutality of their conquests in the eighth century, such as Sybaris, subsequently extended their influence in a much more pacific fashion, and its increasing range was reflected in the appearance of small sanctuaries set up at intervals along the inland roads, signifying not appropriation but rather an effort at mediation with populations that had been drawn into the city's orbit.[40]

The role of the monumental temple, a symbol of Greekness in general and sovereignty in particular, was clearly to provide various forms of protection for the territory in which it was rooted by its *temenos:* protection against human aggression and protection for its fertility, which could be ensured by the feminine deities. Like its homologue in the Greco-Aegean world, the colonial nonurban monumental sanctuary was thus at once a symbol and a guardian of the civilized and city space whose values and institutions it both represented and protected.[41] The position that it occupied also made it the mediator between that space and the outside world and so, in the colonial context, a point of contact with the indigenous populations. Admittedly, in the case of these particular sanctuaries, the contact does appear

39. Procelli, "Ellenizzazione calcidese" (1988–89); Spigo, "Ricerche a Francavilla di Sicilia" (1984–85).

40. Guzzo, "Sibari" (1992), pp. 17–18.

41. Including political institutions: the sanctuary of Olympian Zeus housed the registers of the citizens of Syracuse (Plutarch *Nicias* 14); and its priests occupied the first rank in the religious hierarchy.

to take the imperious form of a proclamation of uncompromising and prestigious Hellenism, designed to cow the barbarian: the metopes discovered in the Heraion on the Sele all show scenes depicting the struggle against chaos and the achievements of the Greek heroes who set the world in order. However, that is but one aspect of a richer and more complex relationship in which the monumental sanctuary was complemented by other nonurban sanctuaries of a kind more suited to mediation between Greeks and natives.

Mediatory Cult Sites

In Asia Minor, another region where the nascent city was confronted with non-Greek populations living around it and within it, the great nonurban sanctuary fulfilled two functions: it stamped Greekness upon the place and it integrated "barbarian" people and, by so doing, was the principal vector of Hellenization to the outside world. In the colonial foundations, the same double-faceted problem of relations between Greeks and natives, both outside and within the city, elicited a response that was identical in spirit even if it took a variety of forms.

The destruction of Italic and Sikel villages that followed the arrival of the Greeks did not mean that all non-Greek peoples thereupon disappeared from the conquered territory. In some cases, some of the vanquished, those conquered on the very spot, constituted a servile labor force that farmed the land and performed other services for the Greeks, sometimes including the provision of women.[42] In other cases, the original inhabitants, having been ejected, subsequently returned to settle on the site of their former home, or not far off, on the edge of the plain, but henceforth in a position of dependence vis-à-vis the Greek city.[43]

In contrast, coexistence rather than rivalry characterized some

42. In Syracuse, the Kyllyrioi seem to have been the descendants of the Sikels who had been reduced to servitude and forced to farm the properties of the Corinthian colonizers (Herodotus 7.155). Mixed marriages are attested at Cyrene (ibid., 4.186) and in Sicily (Thucydides 6.17. 2, on the "mixed blood" of the population). Cf. La Genière, "C'è un modello Amendolara?" p. 348, and "Grecs et non-Grecs."

43. Amendolara and Francavilla Marittima, in the Sybaris region, are the best known cases (see La Genière, "Grecs et indigènes" pp. 633–35, and "C'è un modello Amendolara?" pp. 349–50). This population movement took place within

sanctuaries situated on the borders of the indigenous world, and these became places of contact and exchange rather than of exclusion. So let us now investigate the role that the extraurban sanctuary played in the Greeks' complex relationships with native populations. As we do so, however, it is important to draw a distinction between the effects of, on the one hand, *Hellenization*—the penetration of the Greek culture into the indigenous societies newly installed in the positions to which they had retreated or, further inland, pursuing their own lives quite undisturbed—and on the other, the *internal stabilization* of relations with non-Greek dependents living, at various levels, within the city's orbit.

It was in the process of Hellenization that the great territorial sanctuaries affected the relations between Greeks and natives. The material and cultural frontier that they marked out was neither closed nor defensive: the diffusion of Greek objects and customs, for which there is plenty of evidence in the early days of colonization, was rapid thanks to the prestige they soon acquired in the eyes of the local elites. These were quick to adopt many Greek customs, funerary ones, for example, and to benefit from the growing social distinction that they conferred, while at the same time the military pressure exerted by the colonizers strengthened the responsibilities and power of the indigenous warriors.[44] Access to the extraurban monumental sanctuaries of the Greek cities seems to have played an essential role in the pro-

---

the framework of a distribution of the settlement and organization of the territory that was common to all the archaic colonial cities. The Greek settlements remained clustered in the urban center; the surrounding cereal-producing plain, with open fields, remained virtually empty of dwellings (the first known form of a dispersed settlement, a disorderly scattering of farms in the *chōra* of Metapontum, dates from the mid-sixth century; see Carter, *Territory of Metaponto* [1983]); the surrounding hills were inhabited by dependent natives and sometimes by colonizers of the second wave (it is not known whether these were simply relegated to the poorest land or whether the poverty of the soil here was already being compensated for by the practice of arboriculture); finally, the *eschatiari*, with their frontier fortifications (*phrouria*) gave on to inland mountains, inhabited by natives. A city such as Posidonia provides a model of this arrangement, which, however, often underwent modification (see Greco, "Poséidonia" [1979], and "Chora poseidoniate" [1979].

44. D'Agostino, "Grecs et indigènes" (1977), and *Tombe principesche* (1977); Bottini, *Principi guerrieri* (1982); Ampolo, Bartoloni, Rathje, "Aspetti delle aristocrazie" (1984).

cess of confrontation-cum-seduction, a role of a kind to provide satisfaction both for the indigenous princes, whose authority and social and cultural superiority were thereby enhanced in the eyes of their "compatriots," and for the Greek cities themselves, which allowed independent societies to continue to exist on the peripheries of their own territories, keeping them at a distance but knowing that they were sympathetic to Greek solicitations and the Greek dynamism.

That, at any rate, is what is suggested, on the one hand by the diffusion of Greek beliefs and cult objects—from the Heraion on the Sele, for example [45]—and on the other, by the presence of indigenous offerings in sanctuaries such as the Athenaion of Francavilla Marittima and the Heraion of the Lacinian headland. These temples provide a perfect example of the double role sanctuaries sometimes played as symbols of conquest and points of contact, and they deserve our closer attention.

It is known that as soon as they arrived the Achaean founders of Sybaris seized control of the vast plain of Crathis, the basis of the future city's power, destroying the indigenous sites on the hills surrounding the plain: Torre Mordillo, Torano, Francavilla, and Amendolara. Having destroyed these sites immediately upon arrival, the colonizers proceeded to build sanctuaries on some of them, to consecrate the Greek conquest: probably at Torre Mordillo and certainly at Francavilla, whose Athenaion, situated ten or so kilometers to the northwest of the town, then became the recipient of a stream of not only Greek but also native offerings. [46]

Meanwhile, indigenous settlements reappeared not far away, on new sites, where they probably enjoyed a measure of autonomy, and participation in the cult of Athena now came to constitute the principal link between the Sybarites and these peoples in the outlying plain. However, a greater degree of integration

45. Cf. Zancani-Montuoro in *Atti e Memorie della Società Magna Grecia,* 1965–66, pp. 152–58. Other examples: La Genière, "Grecs et non-Grecs," pp. 268, 270.

46. See Bibliography, Sybaris, and La Genière, "C'è un modello Amendolara?" p. 345. Among these offerings were the inevitable "Dedalic" terra-cotta figurines and numerous bronzes, including one dedicated by the Olympic champion Cleombrotos, son of Dexilaos, from the sixth century (Foti, in *Atti e Memorie della Società Magna Grecia,* 1965, pp. 8 and 17).

into the culture and economy of the Greek city is indicated by the reconstitution of other, much more structured settlements, in the early sixth century, at Amendolara and Francavilla, at the foot of the Athenaion; here the tombs also testify to a far greater degree of Hellenization.[47] The Athenaion of Francavilla, at once a boundary mark and a pole of attraction, thus adopted various modes of religious mediation between the Greeks and native groups from both inside and outside the *polis*, for whom it constituted a meeting point, a place of mutual recognition.

This functional duality is even more evident as expressed in the veritable twofold attraction that the Greek religious world and its sanctuaries exerted, as at Croton, Metapontum, and Selinus. In Croton, a rich deposit of archaic votive offerings in the sanctuary of Hera contained precious Greek objects (a bronze horse in the Geometric tradition, a gold diadem, various bronzes) and also "princely" offerings of non-Greek origin: a little bronze boat from Sardinia, dating from the eighth or seventh century, and a Chonian or Oenotrian bronze ornament dating from the seventh century.[48] Whether diplomatic gifts or visitors' offerings, these objects confirm that Hera, as in Argos and Samos, protected and guaranteed the city's relations with the external world (and all three sanctuaries were among the principal places of *asylia* of the Greek world).[49] In the Greek sanctuaries, indigenous princes from a relative distance, rivaling one another for prestige, adopted the same pattern of behavior as that of the Greek *basileis* of the eighth century, a pattern that was no longer followed within the colonial cities, at least in the more or less egalitarian societies of the earliest generations of colonizers.[50] It is also remarkable that their offerings (the boat, the feminine ornaments) were of the very same type as those that the Greeks deposited in other sanctuaries dedicated to Hera. The much more modest sanctuary of Apollo Alleos, to the north of the town, was similarly oriented toward the non-Greek world, but in a quite different way. The region to the north of the Neto, with a much more mountainous landscape than the immediate countryside

47. La Genière, "C'è un modello Amendolara?" p. 349.
48. Lattanzi, "Recenti Scoperte" (1991) (Bibliography, Croton).
49. Plutarch *Pompey* 24. Maddoli, in *Atti Taranto 23, 1983* (1984), pp. 327–29.
50. Polignac, "Mediation, Competition, and Sovereignty" (1994), pp. 16–17.

beyond Croton, contained several important indigenous sites dating from the Iron Age that continued to develop quite independently after the foundation of Croton.[51] In the second half of the seventh century, the foundation of a small Greek settlement and a sanctuary at Ciro Marina, on the coast below these sites, constituted a marker indicating the extent of the range of influence of Croton, as it faced Sybaris, its powerful northern neighbor, and at the same time a means of stabilizing and regularizing relations with the autochthonous communities within its sphere of influence. The offerings and even the architecture of the temple, both modest and conservative, testify to the fact that this sanctuary was visited chiefly by the inhabitants of the inland areas.[52] Here it was a matter, not of sanctioning alliances with distant princes who thereby strengthened their own positions, but rather of integrating populations of the interior into the "religious territory" of the city; and the legends relating to Philoctetes that developed around the sanctuary, like those relating to Diomedes or Epeios that sprang up elsewhere (in Daunia and in the countryside behind Metapontum), seem to have acted as vectors for this process of acculturation.[53]

In Metapontum, the sanctuary of San Biagio clearly formed a pair with the Heraion of Tavole Palatine: each situated on the bank of one of the rivers that flowed round either side of the town (the Basento and the Bradano), they seemed to frame the city and its territory, marking its inner limits. But the great Heraion built in the Greek style on the frontier with Tarentum, to the northeast, was the official, sovereign conquerors' sanctuary. San Biagio, situated a little further inland, near a spring, was quite distinct from the Heraion by virtue of the modesty of its design, which in simple fashion reflected its orientation toward a far more popular, more agrarian, and more indigenous world. Many of the offerings brought to it were locally produced, whereas

51. At Ciro Superiore, Strongoli, and Murge di Strongoli: cf. Sabbione, "Murge di Strongoli" (1988), and La Genière, "Au pays de Philoctète" (1991) (Bibliography, Crotona).

52. Spadea, in *Atti Taranto 23, 1983* (1984), pp. 207–28.

53. Musti, "Mito di Filotette" (1991). All these heroes were supposed to have founded sanctuaries or small cities of the Italic populations, who were thus given a place in the Greek vision of "history."

those deposited in the Heraion were for the most part prestigious objects imported from Greece.[54]

At Selinus, an even more perfect symmetry obtained between the two sanctuaries on the edges of the town, the one to the east, the other to the west, the one on the Cottone River, the other on the Modione. The sanctuary of Demeter Malaphoros, close to the sources of the Gaggera, was one of a group of sanctuaries (Hecate, Zeus Meilichios, Temple M, for example) strung out in a line running from north to south at the foot of the plateau, as far as the mouth of the Modione (then further inland than today). It was an important center of popular piety but built in a quite modest architectural style typical of this kind of cult, the nature of which was at once agrarian and funerary (with a *megaron*). It was situated to the west of the town, that is to say, facing the great necropolis of Selinus, on the side of indigenous, already Punic Sicily, and close to the harbor.[55] The sanctuaries of the Marinella hill, in particular the most ancient of them, Temple E1 (Heraion?), were in contrast true Greek temples of orthodox design, and they housed purely Greek deities (whereas the Malaphoros deity was a Demeter suspected of "Sicilianism"). These temples were situated to the east of the town, the side giving on to the Sicily of Greek cities.

The sanctuary of Demeter Malaphoros, Temple E1, and the temple on the acropolis were all founded at the same time, toward the end of the seventh century. However, whereas Temple E1 (and those constructed later), on the Marinella hill, respected the east-west orientation of the orthogonal system of the streets of the acropolis and was thus positioned on the same axis as the urban temple, the sanctuaries in the western valley for the most part faced the Manuzza plateau (to the north), the axis of which was slightly inclined westward. This carefully designed

54. See, however, Carter, "Sanctuaries in the Chora of Metaponto" (1994), pp. 171, 174–75: the first counterpart to San Biagio may have been another sanctuary above the Bradano (at Salone), the Heraion being later.

55. See most recently Parisi-Presicce, "Funzione delle aree sacre" pp. 21–27, and Dewailly, *Statuettes* (1992), pp. 1–40 (Bibliography, Selinus). This study is especially helpful in clarifying the relations between different types of offerings, religious practices, and divine figures, which had seemed particularly confused in this sanctuary.

symmetry, which established a clear opposition between an Olympian, Greek, and conquering character and a chthonic, funerary, nocturnal character that also allowed access to non-Greeks constituted a perfect expression of the double face presented by all colonial cities.[56]

These examples clearly demonstrate the double orientation of the nonurban religious world of the city: on the one hand, there is a statement of sovereignty and the attraction exerted by the power of their monumentality and prestige; on the other, the religious access offered to the populations living on the cultural and political periphery of society. That accessibility was what was embodied by the many nonmonumental sanctuaries of the *chōra* and the urban periphery.

The sanctuary of San Biagio near Metapontum is thus the archetype of the cult sites scattered through the territory, most of them positioned more or less "on the edge," on the slopes of hills bordering the cultivated plain, and housing some feminine, chthonic, or agrarian deity or even one with healing powers (as at Croton's sanctuary of Santa Anna). Toward these sanctuaries many kinds of devotees would converge. Despite their modest architectural style, the cults were clearly extremely popular, for they attracted many offerings, the diverse styles and richness of which testify to the variety of their donors: Greeks, dependent natives whose settlements were dotted about in the same hilly zone, and peoples living further inland but still close enough to visit the sanctuary.[57]

56. The many lamps found in the sanctuary indicate that the cult of the Malaphoros deity involved nocturnal rituals. Dewailly, *Statuettes*, p. 153. Punic influences: Tusa, "Greci e non-Greci in Sicilia" (1983), pp. 302–5 (archaic metopes).

57. The sanctuary of the site known as Santa Anna, five kilometers from Agrigentum, appeared in the mid sixth century, apparently at the time the Sikels were being overcome and scattered throughout the territory (Fiorentini, "Santuario extra urbano di Santa Anna" [1969]). The sanctuaries of Feudo Nobile and Fonte, respectively in the territories of Gela and Posidonia, were situated close to archaic agricultural settlements, the ethnic origin of whose occupants is difficult to determine precisely (Adamesteanu, "Gela" (1960), p. 227f.; Greco, "Poséidonia" map on p. 227).

San Biagio provides an example "by default": indigenous offerings disappeared from the sanctuary around the middle of the sixth century, at the time when the expanding city was extending the boundaries of its territory further inland and Greeks were installing themselves in the many dispersed farms there. Cf. Torelli, "Greci e indigeni" (1977), p. 48.

The sanctuary of Malaphoros, for its part, is the archetype of a periurban cult site and more particularly of a sanctuary of Demeter or one of the other chthonic deities to which Sicily was supposed to be particularly devoted, but which were also to be found elsewhere. As in the Greco-Aegean world, the rituals of these sanctuaries allowed for the religious integration of women, who would celebrate the Thesmophoria here, outside the city of their menfolk; and they also possessed an agrarian importance by virtue of the way they associated the fertility of nature with that of human beings.[58] However, although the religious mechanisms were all fundamentally alike, both in the cities of Greece proper and in colonial foundations, the different context of the latter conferred a different orientation upon the ritual practices.

In the first place, the fact that the colonizers' wives, who might well be of indigenous origin, took part in religious ritual added an ethnic dimension to the function of integration that it fulfilled. It would no doubt be wrong to assume that the Greek colonial expeditions consisted solely of men, who were then obliged to take autochthonous wives, for the Greeks of the colonial cities were not all *mixobarbaroi*.[59] However, there must certainly have been unions between Greeks and natives, and these women, who had become a part of Greek life, as had the indigenous dependents who lived in the *chōra*, were, like the latter, indispensable to the viability of the society that was being developed. They thus enjoyed, albeit at a different level and with a different status, religious privileges that on the one hand balanced their responsibility in the perpetuation of the group and, on the other, assured their adhesion to the religious and cultural world of the Greek men. Thus, through their double identity as indigenous women who were also Greek wives, and the double protection they went to solicit from Demeter, they could, when necessary, act as an intermediary and link of solidarity between

58. The Thesmosphorion of Bitalemi, in Gela, was separated from the town by the river, which symbolized both interconnection and exclusion. The offerings deposited included, as well as statuettes of children and women, figurines of agricultural implements (cf. Orlandini, "Topografia dei santuari" [1968], p. 38f.).

59. Graham, "Religion, Women, and Greek Colonization" (1984), underlines the role of women in the transmission of certain cults of the metropolis in the new cities; the opposed arguments of Van Compernolle, "Femmes indigènes" (1983), make the point that the practice of mixed marriages may have been frequent, but they do not suffice to show that they were the rule in colonial circles.

the Greek urban world and the indigenous, rural one to which they were equally bound, sharing the preoccupations of both.

In a colony, the relationship of town and territory protected by the sanctuary of the chthonic deity, in its capacity as a cult site set up to mark the meeting of the two, was likely to be considerably more complex than in the old Greek world. There, dominion over the territory was not entirely in the hands of the urban society, for the city would be represented by clusters of local authorities that had formerly been autonomous. But in colonial foundations, the landed aristocracy, represented by the earliest colonists, constituted an urban kernel locked in conflict, initially at least, with a territory populated by the hostile non-Greeks whom they had conquered.[60] Although we should no doubt not overemphasize the possible effects of ethnic differences,[61] the relations between town and country really would appear to have been more delicate in the colonial situation: the mediation effected by the suburban sanctuary, particularly if consecrated to Demeter, was all the more necessary on that account, for the need to ensure the religious cohesion of the various social groups that combined to make society function was more imperative.

Because of this, despite the important part played by women in that mediation, the Thesmophorion was by no means the only periurban sanctuary, and its rituals were certainly not the only ones pertaining to the cult addressed to chthonic goddesses, particularly in the West. A single city might maintain several sanctuaries consecrated to Demeter: Gela boasted three, over and above its Thesmophorion, one of which, situated slightly to the north of the town, was composed of several *thēsauroi* grouped around a temple decorated by architectural terra-cotta ornaments, which made it the town's largest nonurban sanctuary.[62]

60. For example, in Sybaris, Syracuse, Gela, and Thasos.

61. To the extent that, in Greece itself, archaic society was familiar with widely varying forms of subjection and groups of dependents, and tribal cleavages, still detectable, posed problems similar to those encountered by the colonizers. It would be mistaken, furthermore, to exaggerate the cultural gap between the Greeks and the peoples of southern Italy and Sicily in the eighth and seventh centuries (cf. La Genière, "Grecs et non-Grecs," p. 272).

62. At the site known as Madonna dell'Alemanna. The other two, no more than *sacellae*, were at Predio Sola and Via Fiume, at the southern and northern limits of the settlement. See Orlandini, "Topografia dei Santuari," p. 33 n. 64.

Elsewhere, there were cities whose sanctuaries were arranged in a complex fashion in which a number of deities were associated: Zeus Meilichios, Demeter, and Hecate at Selinus; a number of chthonic deities at Agrigentum, where the many offerings and architectural improvements made in their sanctuary over the archaic period testify to its prime religious importance in the early days of the history of Agrigentum. Time and again the same architectural features are repeated: *megara* and *sacella*, separate from one another, and round altars, each with a central *bothros*. They are features that would no doubt be normal in Greek sanctuaries consecrated to such deities, and at the same time they were likely to be familiar to the indigenous religious world.[63]

Clearly, chthonic cults, addressed for the most part to Demeter and Kore, or even Persephone, as at Locri, were one of the principal vectors through which non-Greeks other than the princely elite became familiar with Greek cults and customs and managed to integrate them into their own cultures.[64] So much is attested by their wide diffusion in indigenous areas in the sixth century, both in Sicily and in Magna Graecia. At this time, their appearance usually coincided with a reorganization of the settlement and a transformation of the material culture indicating a general adoption of Greek models throughout the society.[65] This particular role of the chthonic cults may have stemmed from the individual characteristics of the deities and their cults, whose agrarian or even funerary connotations and sanctuaries, open to various types of practices, may have likened them to indigenous beliefs and customs. However, given that we know virtually nothing about the latter until the point when the adoption of a Hellenized form rendered them usable and recognizable, that is clearly but one aspect of the matter. What is certain is that, for the Greeks themselves, too, Demeter was the deity most suited to taming elements external to their own civilization: to

63. On this type of sanctuary, see Le Dinahet, "Sanctuaires chtoniens de Sicile" (1984).

64. The particular place of Persephone in Locrian religion has been best illuminated by Sourvinou-Inwood.

65. For example, in the countryside behind Catania and Leontini in Sicily (Procelli, "Ellenizzazione calcidese," p. 122); to the north of Croton (La Genière, "Au pays de Philoctète," [1991]); at Garaguso in Lucania and at Oria in the Salento region (see below, p. 126).

the extent that her myths and cults involved a temporary return to a more primitive life and a period before the establishment of the city, this goddess could bestow a familiar face upon anything that seemed foreign to Greek cultural norms, and she thereby made it possible to conceive of "otherness" in Greek terms.[66]

This quality was what brought Demeter close to Herakles, with whom she was often associated in colonial cities, as for example in the territory of Syracuse, where the hero, herding the cattle of Geryon, founded the cult of deities of the underworld at the spring of Cyanae.[67] On the face of it, Herakles' deeds in Sicily, in the countryside behind Syracuse and around Eryx, where he also founded cults after having overcome the local chieftains and heroes, seem to prefigure Greek colonization, just as they do at Croton. But those cults, unlike that of Hera Lacinia, were not manifestations of the Greek conquests. The places, figures, and rites with which they were associated indicate that one of Herakles' functions was that of a "mediator" who introduced foreign ideas and customs into the Greek culture: for instance, the strange sacrifices by immersion of the Cyanae spring, and the defeated Sikanian heroes, whose cult Herakles founded, evoked the world of the indigenous cult of the Palici in the Caltagirone region, although the form adopted by the cult of the Sikanian heroes was no doubt itself determined by Greek influences.[68] A sanctuary such as that of Poggioreale, situated between Selinus and the Elymian region of Segesta, was thus both a symbol of the Greeks' appropriation of the territory and a place where non-Greek religious practices could find new expression.

The above analysis is not altogether in agreement with the theory according to which Herakles is in some cases seen as a Hellenized version of a foreign god, such as the Phoenician Melquart of Tyre, notably in Thasos, where Herakles, at once hero

66. Breglia Pulci Doria, "Tesmoforie eretriese" (1979); Detienne, "Violence of Wellborn Ladies" (1979); Polignac, "Déméter et l'altérité" (1990).

67. Diodorus 4.23.

68. Martin, "Culte d'Héraclès en Sicile" (1979); Giangiulio, "Greci e non-Greci in Sicilia" (1983); Jourdain-Annequin, "Etre un Grec en Sicile" (1988–89). These developments in the myth of Herakles probably date from the fifth century rather than from the archaic period.

and god, is supposed to present this double character.[69] In this case the basis of the cult is foreign and only its appearance is Hellenized, whereas in Magna Graecia Herakles is never himself assimilated to a non-Greek deity. But even if it is possible that the Herakles of Gades, in Spain, and perhaps some of his cults in the Aegean (Erythrai) did have associations with the Phoenician god, the situation is much less clear in Thasos, where neither the sanctuary nor the religious practices display any of the obvious Phoenician characteristics that have been claimed to be detected.[70] It would therefore be mistaken to be too hasty in identifying Demeter and Herakles as foreign deities with a Hellenized veneer.

In truth, as we have seen, it is possible to account for many features that on the face of it seem surprising in the cults and sanctuaries of Demeter and Herakles if we replace them in their logical and symbolic relationship with the other city cults. It is not always necessary to appeal to "contaminations" or "legacies" from other cultures; nor of course is it possible to rule them out systematically, explaining them away by positing no more than a few incidental borrowings. The large number of sanctuaries of Demeter in Sicily should be considered relatively, in light of the evidence of their presence also in Magna Graecia and, indeed, throughout the Greco-Aegean world: the importance of these deities should be interpreted in the context of more general factors than the religious customs of one or another culture.

The wide diffusion of the Thesmophorion alone is thus not at all surprising, if that sanctuary answered a religious need felt just as keenly by colonial foundations as by their metropolises. But just as the appearance of a monumental sanctuary, Greek in both spirit and form, on the borders of the territory of a city in the west seems closely linked with the presence of a neighboring people who were relatively "advanced" or another Greek city,

69. Launay, *Sanctuaire d'Héraclès à Thasos* (1944); Pouilloux, "Héraclès thasien" (1977).

70. Bergquist, *Heracles on Thasos* (1973); Bonnet, *Melqart* (1988). A review of the matter has recently been produced in the light of the latest discoveries: des Courtils and Pariente, "Heracléion de Thasos" (1991). Herakles-Melquart at Gades: Van Berchem, "Sanctuaires d'Hercule-Melquart" (1967).

the proliferation of sanctuaries of chthonic deities in the territory surrounding a town could equally well result from the presence of large numbers of natives in that territory. Not all colonial cities set up such a superabundance of sanctuaries, but the development of many mediatory sanctuaries devoted to chthonic deities around Gela and Agrigentum, for example, was probably a response to the large numbers of Sikels and Sikanians used to farm the *chōra* and the consequent fragility of the latter's links with the Greek urban center.

If we approach the matter from this angle, we raise the question of the very constitution of the colonial *polis,* for whatever aspects of local cults the Greeks, on the strength of certain analogies and a similarity in certain fundamental religious preoccupations (agrarian, chthonic, iatric), may have deliberately integrated into the cults of their own deities, it is in connection with the formation of the colonial society that the religious mediation effected by the nonurban sanctuaries takes on its full significance.[71]

The Formation of a Colonial Society

The history of the sanctuaries of Demeter at Gela turns out to provide the most revealing evidence relating to the constitution of a colonial city. These cults did not make their appearance until the mid seventh century, when they did so all at once. The presence of chthonic deities in the city resulted from a religious shift that took place about one generation (thirty to forty years) after the arrival of the Cretan and Rhodian colonizers who had first founded the cults of Apollo and Athena.

Now these cults, so closely linked with the ethnic and geographical origins of the colonizers, were certainly suitable for affirming Greek sovereignty, but they were not of a kind to ensure the cohesion that was indispensable both between Greeks and indigenous people and between Greeks of different origins: the fact that they could not achieve this is noted in a well-known text of Herodotus' about the Deinomenid family (7.153), which is

71. See Brelich, "Religione greca in Sicilia" (1964–65), p. 48f.; and Martorana, "Recenti studi storico-religiosi" (1976–77).

most revealing about the role that chthonic goddesses played in the formation of a colonial society.

Herodotus relates that part of the population of Gela had split away and established itself on a site known as Mactorion, following a civil war (*stasis*). This secession came to an end only after the mediation of Telines, an ancestor of the Deinomenids, who was in possession of the *hiera* of chthonic deities and who, thanks to these objects, which were displayed prominently during negotiations, was able to persuade the rebels to return. He was then made the *hierophantos* of Demeter, a post that became hereditary and was passed on to his descendants.

This episode clearly demonstrates the integrating power of the chthonic cults, for armed solely with their *hiera*, Telines was able to persuade the dissidents to return: his principal arguments must have been of a religious nature, and the agreement reached by the two opposed groups probably also took a religious form. But whatever the terms of that agreement, it made Demeter and Kore the true guarantors of social cohesion and political harmony and also of the Deinomenid family, who became the hereditary *hierophantoi* of the dieties, figures of the first rank positioned at the heart of the process of mediation and equilibration upon which the city was based. This text could, of course, be regarded not so much as an example of the tensions of the archaic city but rather as a piece of fifth-century Deinomenid propaganda reflecting the policies of the tyrants of Syracuse, policies that were, precisely, based upon the cult of the chthonic deities, which was deemed to strengthen the social cohesion of their Sicilian empire.[72] Nevertheless, the evidence for the rise of the cult of Demeter in both Greek and indigenous circles before the fifth century shows that the religious policies of the Deinomenids did indeed partly stem from a preexisting situation that they systematized. So this episode, even when seen in the light of dynastic propaganda, may well tell us something about the archaic city. The incident has thus been interpreted as a clash between two influential groups divided by a social cleavage masked by an ethnic one. The Cretans and the Rhodians are believed to have been reconciled through the intervention of a

72. Privitera, "Politica religiosa dei Dinomidi" (1980).

third party, Telines, a native of Telos (opposite the Triopion headland), who acted as arbiter in a conflict between two Greek "families."[73] The Rhodians do indeed appear to have dominated the colony initially, as is suggested by the fact that it was their Lindia who was installed on the acropolis and also by the preponderance of imported Rhodian and eastern Greek objects or imitations of them until about the mid seventh century. At this point, which is when the chthonic cults made their appearance, a shift in the balance of power favored the Cretans—at least to judge by the origin or style of the objects that have been discovered there and that date from the second half of the century.[74]

But the middle of the seventh century was also a period of crucial importance in the relations between the Greek colonizers and the native societies here. Herodotus' account explicitly states that the rebels withdrew to Mactorion. Along with Omphake, this site was one of the major indigenous settlements on the edge of the plain of Gela. Omphake was believed to have been conquered by the first generation of colonizers, who were led by the city founder, Antiphemos. Now, the traces of the Greek conquest of the peripheral sites, such as the one where the modern town of Butera now stands, date from not long before the middle of the seventh century.[75] Whether or not Mactorion was among the sites conquered by the Greeks at the time of the secession, the dissidents' retreat to this spot suggests that perhaps not all—or even any—of them were Greek colonizers. But whatever the truth of the matter, the solution to this conflict certainly illuminates the whole process of the formation of Gelan society.

The chthonic deities were called in to salvage the city's threatened cohesion, and their sacred symbols were introduced as a signal of reconciliation, on the grounds that they might have the power to unite around them all the various components of the

73. Kesterman, "Les ancêtres de Gélon" (1970).

74. Meola, "Terrecotte orientalizzante di Gela" (1971), p. 79. The foundation of the city may have been preceded by a "precolonization," an informal settlement of a few Rhodians, in contact with the local natives, on the site of the future acropolis (end of the eighth century): Orlandini, "Ceramica greca di Gela" (1963), pp. 50–56. This acropolis was, furthermore, called Lindies (Thucydides 6.4.3).

75. Orlandini has suggested identifying this site of Butera, to the northwest of the plain, with the ancient Omphake ("Omphakè et Maktorion" [1961], pp. 145–49). This identification, like that of Monte Bubbonia, another site conquered at the end of the century, with Mactorion remains extremely hypothetical.

social body. The installation of their cult in the mid seventh century, which coincided possibly with the stabilization of relations between different groups of colonizers and certainly with the Sikels' becoming dependents within the city territory, constituted the foundation for a new social arrangement. Thus, the constitution of the *polis* of Gela was not simply a matter of the installation of Greeks there in about 680. It was only completed when the cult of Demeter, set up in a mediatory, neutral position, became the point upon which a number of different social groups converged and intermingled and found a modus vivendi. The urban deities' inability to assume that constitutive function is the reason why, later, they played no part in the crisis that made it necessary for the "political" society to be reestablished upon new foundations, once again by religious means.

That distinction drawn between the different stages in the formation of the Gelan society immediately calls to mind the case of Thasos, where the legendary and literary tradition depicts colonization in three phases, a portrait altogether too neat to be accepted without reservations.[76] The three phases recorded by tradition are as follows: first, a religious mission led by Tellis, who accompanied the Parian priestess of Demeter bearing the goddess' *hiera* to Thasos; next a wave of colonizers led by his son Telesicles in about 680; finally, a second wave of colonizers led by Glaucos in about 650 and made famous by the account of it given by Archilochus, Telesicles' son. The whole Parian operation of colonization seems too perfectly planned, over three generations of the family of the famous poet who recorded it, for it to be quite true. The legend of Tellis was no doubt invented after the colonization, and Telesicles was considered as a founder of Thasos only on the strength of a controversial document composed to redound to the credit of Archilochus.[77] This picture of

76. This tradition was derived from the evocation of the legend of Tellis in the frescoes of the Lesche of the Cnidians, at Delphi, a work by Polygnotus (Pausanias 10.28.3); the oracle inviting Telesicles to found Paros, mentioned in the *Monumentum Archilochi* of Paros (Kontoleon, "Neai epigrafai," [1952] and Sokolowski, *Lois sacrées des cités grecques*, 1:180); the fragments of Archilochus on the subject of Glaucos and his own battles (frags. 9, 13, 56, 60, 114, among others, CUF).

77. Tellis: Pouilloux, "Cultes de Thasos" (1954), p. 25. Telesicles: quite apart from the fact that the oracle mentioned in the *Monumentum* of the classical period may quite well be a pure invention, its interpretation is a very delicate matter:

colonization seems to systematize and spin out over a period of half a century an operation that was certainly complicated by bitter struggles against the Thracians and that was probably brought to a successful conclusion thanks only to the arrival of reinforcements, which, however, arrived within a much shorter period of time, no more than a generation later, if that.[78]

According to the legend about Tellis and Cleoboia taking sacred objects to the island prior to the foundation of the city and its urban sanctuaries, the cult of Demeter was the first to be established there; and the purpose of that legend was to ensure that Demeter would be regarded as the protector of the nascent Thasos. However, her propitiatory arrival there hardly corresponds to what we know of the history of cults generally. The cults of the acropolis (Athena Poliouchos, Pythaean Apollo) and those of the town (Artemis, Herakles) appeared when the Parians first settled there, while the only known sanctuary of Demeter, the Thesmophorion, to the north of the town, seems to date from no earlier than the sixth century.[79] The prestige of Demeter in Paros, where the Thesmophorion contained the sacred objects upon which the safety of the city depended, may have contributed to the creation of this story, but on the other hand there are a number of aspects to the *polis* of Thasos that could also explain the goddess's importance in the founding myth.[80] In the original structure of the town, the settlement was divided into two separate quarters, each centered upon a cult: the cult of Artemis in

---

the text may mean either that the god's order to found a colony was addressed to Telesicles himself or that it was addressed to all the Parians through his voice (Graham, "Foundation of Thasos" [1978], p. 61f.).

78. The Thasian ceramic material dating from the first half of the seventh century is Greek in the eyes of some, thus confirming the arrival of the first Parians in about 680–670 (Bernard, "Céramiques à Thasos" [1964], pp. 77–146; Martin, "Thasos," p. 182f.), and Thracian in the eyes of others, who push that arrival back to around 660–650 (Salviat, "Colonisation grecque dans la mer Egée" [1965], pp. 299–303; Graham, "Foundation of Thasos"). The demonstration by Grandjean, *Recherches sur l'habitat thasien* (1988), pp. 436–41, favoring the second of those interpretations, appears to be decisive.

79. The first ex-votos of the Artemision, which may have been brought from Paros, date from the first half of the seventh century: Weill, *Plastique archaïque de Thasos* (1985), pp. 205–12.

80. Herodotus 6.134. Archilochus is supposed to have composed a hymn to Demeter on Paros (frag. 296 CUF).

the north, the cult of Herakles in the south, and that split could be explained by two different origins or even statuses of the colonizers.[81] According to this hypothesis of a heterogeneous society, each of the urban sanctuaries was at first associated with a particular group. In contrast, in the classical period, it was in the Thesmophorion that the altars of all the *patrai* were placed, altars that constituted institutions essential for the cohesion and renewal of the civic body.[82] Ceremonies that were essential to the constitution of the society of Thasos thus took place in the sanctuary-beyond-the-walls; and that fact emphasizes the primordial mediation effected by Demeter in her capacity as founder and protector of the unity of the city, mediation that overrode both the initial cleavages and new divisions that were created by the installation of new inhabitants in the sixth century.[83] Thus, in its own way, the foundation myth would, after all, seem to illuminate the history of Thasos, even if it reversed the chronology.

We know of plenty of other, less explicit cases where a united society was similarly elaborated or failed to be elaborated, on a newly acquired territory, from a heterogeneous collection of groups. In Leontini, unsuccessful attempts were made to amalgamate first Chalcidians and Sikels, then Chalcidians and Megarians.[84] In Syracuse, Eleans seem to have accompanied the Corinthian colonizers.[85] Here the extraurban sanctuary, founded at the beginning of the seventh century, seems to have constituted both an affirmation of Greek sovereignty (it was consecrated to the Olympian Zeus, god of justice) and a place where the various social components of the city could intermingle and cohere. The choice of Zeus, whose influence was already spreading in the Peloponnese, may have been determined by the presence of Eleans, who included (or were led by?) an Iamid diviner.

Quite apart from the problem of relations with indigenous

81. Grandjean, *Recherches sur l'habitat thasien,* pp. 486–89.
82. Rolley, "Thesmophorion de Thasos" (1965).
83. It may have been at the time of the growth of the town in the sixth century that the Thracian element became a part of the population (Grandjean, *Recherches sur l'habitat thasien,* p. 473).
84. Thucydides 6.4.1.
85. Pindar (*Olympian* 6.1.4f.) mentions the Iamid diviner Agesias as being one of the founders of the city.

populations, the cohesion of a *polis* could be threatened by the arrival of new waves of colonizers: the earliest arrivals would set themselves up as a colonial aristocracy and relegate the latest arrivals to the outskirts of the town or would simply form a separate ethnic-religious entity. Mediation would then be arranged in exactly the same way: the suburban sanctuary of Herakles Mantiklos in Zancle/Messene and the extraurban sanctuary of Artemis in the territory of Rhegium were both erected at a point when Messenians settled in these two Chalcidian cities.[86] The fact that in Rhegium the Messenians, at first admitted to an inferior position, probably formed the lower class to which the tyrant Anaxilas turned in order to overthrow the Chalcidian oligarchy at the beginning of the fifth century shows how fragile the heterogeneous colonial societies were. This is why, despite the *aition* linking the arrival of the Messenians in Italy with the cult of Artemis Limnatis, the choice of Artemis and Herakles might be explained not so much by the Messenian religious traditions as by the part played by these two deities in the integration of newcomers and marginal populations.[87] In Syracuse, too, Artemis was supposed to have presided over a collective reconciliation of the countrymen (*agroikoi*) after a *stasis,* and the Herakleion in Messene was founded once the Zancleans and the Messenians sent there by Anaxilas to take the city had agreed to live together.[88]

All these examples show that the constitution of the *polis* is to be conceived not only in terms of access to the *archai* and partici-

86. Herakles Mantiklos: Pausanias 4.23.10; Artemis: Thucydides 43.3; Asheri, "A propos des sanctuaires extra-urbains" (1988), pp. 7–9; Vallet, *Rhégion et Zancle,* p. 69f., devotes an important passage to this question of the settlement of the Messenians and its religious aspects; Montepaone, "Artemis Phakelitis" (1984).

87. Strabo 6.1.6: the Messenians were supposed to have violently condemned the profanation of the sanctuary of Artemis Limnatis, which gave rise to the First Messenian War (see above) and ejected by their compatriots, owed their escape from their country's submission to the goddess's intervention. But the arrival of Messenians in Rhegium in fact probably dates from the sixth century (Asheri, "A propos des sanctuaires extra-urbains"); and the legend underlines the importance of the exclusion/integration motifs in the cult of Artemis.

88. Syracuse: *Schol. in Theocritus, Prolegomena,* p. 2. See Frontisi Ducroux, "Artémis bucolique"; Montepaone, "Artemis Phakelitis," pp. 94–96.

pation in political citizenship, but also as the gathering of different groups into a single effective body by allowing them all access to the same cults, assembling them around a number of common sanctuaries, and granting all of them the privilege of taking part in certain rituals: in short, the *polis* has to be considered also in terms of a religious citizenship.

Although the process of the formation of a colonial city, generally within one generation, seems to have been rapid compared with that of a city of the old Greco-Aegean world, the birth of a *polis* thus involved more than the foundation of a colony. That may seem contradictory in view of the nature of the colonial foundations, apparently carefully planned and organized even as early as the eighth century. Nevertheless, even in the case of a "model" foundation, Megara Hyblaea, a similar analysis could well be applicable. The orientation of the streets there certainly marked out five different quarters disposed around the agora in a manner reminiscent of the five villages of Megaris, the synoecism of which is supposed to have produced Megara Nisaia.[89] The unified space of the city would thus have respected the preexisting divisions in the society, the more so since the synoecism that resulted in the founding of the metropolis may have taken place at the same date as the founding of the colony, in which case the founders of Megara Hyblaea had perhaps never experienced communal urban life when they set out for Sicily. But in Sicily, right from the start, a space was reserved around the central square for the sanctuaries that were to symbolize the unity and identity of the city (a *hērōon* at one of the entrances to the agora, flanked by temples). However, the construction of the temples did not begin until about the middle of the seventh century, and no sacred spot in the agora has disclosed any votive deposit as rich as those found on the outskirts of the city. It is on the periphery of the urban space that the essential part of religious life seems to have taken place in the eighth and seventh centuries, in the sacred zones and the remains of sanctuaries discovered in the southeastern corner (on the cliff), on the northwestern edge, and in the northeastern corner, where the

89. This was pointed out by Svenbro, "Megara Hyblaea" 1982; see also Vallet, Villard, and Auberson, *Guide de Mégara* (1983), pp. 145–46.

offerings once again suggest that female deities were their recipients.[90] Could it be that this periurban distribution reflected the divisions of Megarian society, with each outlying sanctuary corresponding to one of the town quarters, or even to one of the founding villages? If so, Megara Hyblaea would provide an illustration of another kind of division of roles between the sanctuaries of the center and those of the periphery, a division suited to a society as yet barely unified. However, the data at our disposal do not make it possible to verify such a hypothesis.

In contrast, at the opposite geographical and chronological extremity of the archaic colonial western Mediterranean, the Messapian city of Oria does seem to present a reflection of the Greek cities' own history. In this region, until then not at all open to Greek influence, profound changes took place in the second third of the sixth century. The settlement of Oria, halfway between Tarentum and Brindisi, was reorganized, condensed, and surrounded by a town wall. Concurrently, a sanctuary of Demeter and Kore was founded outside the town, on the slopes of a hill facing it. This sanctuary then received a stream of offerings, some local but some Greek, from various places: Tarentum, Metapontum, Sybaris.[91] The suburban cult of the Demeter of Oria facilitated meetings and exchanges between Greeks and Messapians. This was a place where the natives set about appropriating the Greek cultural models (and the material objects that accompanied them), and it was a process in which every sector of the society took part. The foundation of this cult marked the reorganization of a Messapian "city" just as similar foundations betokened a reorganization in Greek cities, and it thereby provides extra confirmation of the central role that mediatory cults played in the consolidation of colonial societies.

The similarities and peculiarities of the situations in the new Greek world and the old thus resulted from the interaction of, on the one hand, unforseen experiences in new contexts and, on the other, the common attitude informing a process that was

90. Agora: Vallet, Villard, and Auberson, *Mégara Hyblaea* (1976); periurban sanctuaries: Vallet, Villard, and Auberson, *Guide de Mégara*, pp. 100, 133, 137; Gras, "Pianoro meridionale" (1984–85), p. 803.

91. D'Andria, "Greci e indigeni in Iapigia" (1983), pp. 292–95; Yntema, "Ricerca topografica" (1986).

identical wherever it took place within the sphere of the Greek civilization. Everywhere, the religious bases upon which the emergence of the city was founded underlined the importance of the interaction between urban cults and cults established in the outlying territory. It is a point that is confirmed by a study of another major religious transformation of the eighth century, namely, the diffusion of the cult of heroes.

CHAPTER FOUR

The Hero and the Political Elaboration
of the City

～ ✳ ⌐

*The Trojans had all foregathered, young and old alike, for a conference at
Priam's doors. Iris of the Nimble Feet came up to them and spoke in a voice
like that of Priam's son Polites [Citizen], who was posted as a lookout for the
Trojans on top of old Aesyetes' tomb.*

Iliad 2.786–93

As with the nonurban cults, the historians of the colonial
world were the first, besides Erwin Rohde, to connect the
appearance of cults of heroes with the birth of the city, on account of the customary heroization of city founders, who were
honored by being buried on the agora and by the establishment
of public cults devoted to them, as founders.[1] This practice began
at the same time as two other phenomena characteristic of the
period between 750 and 700. One was the increase in funerary
practices connected with heroization, practices that conferred an
exceptional status upon the deceased; the other was the appearance of offerings in Mycenaean tombs, some of which then became the center of a cult during the archaic period. To this extent, the cult of heroes seems to have been a fundamental aspect
in the transformation of Greek society that took place at the end
of the Geometric period. It is not so much the separate innovations on their own as the way they interacted that throws light
upon this transformation and the emergence of the archaic city.

Epigraph translation by E. V. Rien, Penguin Classics (Harmondsworth, 1950).
1. Rodhe, *Psyche* (1894), pp. 137–86, esp. pp. 140–49. Cults of founders: see
Malkin, *Religion and Colonization* (1987), pp. 189–266.

Each must nevertheless be reset in its historical context if we are to seize upon its effects and significance.

The Last of the Princes, the First of the Heroes

As early as the end of the middle Geometric period, the evolution of funerary customs was introducing new distinctions within the aristocracies of a number of regions in the Greek world. Attica was one of the first regions to be affected. Here tombs began to be distinguished by objects (craters, amphoras) that became increasingly monumental, and the mid eighth century saw the appearance of the first representations of funerary rituals and scenes of land or sea battles, which presented a partly idealized image of the lives and deaths of "princes," upon whom an epic dimension was thereby conferred.[2] Also in about 750, the first "royal tombs" made their appearance in Salamis, in Cyprus. They are distinguished by the unprecedented opulence of the funerary offerings and the traces of grandiose funerary rites (including the sacrifice of horses), which, it must be said, are reminiscent of the funerals of the heroes of the *Iliad*, in particular the famous ceremonies for Patroclus (book 23). The most sumptuous of these tombs (no. 79) dates from the end of the century.[3] Also in the mid eighth century, certain cist tombs of the Argive aristocracy began to be characterized by the inclusion of pieces of armor (in the first instance, helmets) and *obeloi* among the funerary offerings. This practice culminated in the late eighth century with the famous "panoply tomb" (Tomb 45, about 720–710).[4] The rise of these new customs testifies to a desire on the part of certain *basileis* to be assimilated to the epic heroes through their adoption of the epic model, transmitted principally by the *Iliad*. The historical context suggests that these pretensions to an exceptional status, which made these kings the equals of the kings

2. Coldstream, *Greek Geometric Pottery* (1968), pp. 29–90; Ahlberg, *Prothesis and Ekphora* (1971), and *Fighting in Greek Geometric Art* (1971); Whitley, *Style and Society* (1991), pp. 132–63.

3. Karageorghis, *Necropolis of Salamis*, vol. 1 (1967), vol. 3 (1973–74), vol. 5 (1978). Tomb 79: ibid. 3:4–122. Beer, "Contacts de Chypre" (1984), provides a useful synthesis on the whole collection of royal tombs in Cyprus.

4. Courbin, *Tombes géométriques d'Argos* (1974); Hägg, "Burial Customs" (1983). Tomb 45: Courbin, "Tombes géométriques d'Argos" (1957).

of former times, was one indication of the growing competitiveness that accompanied the formation of major political centers in regions where several different aristocracies were rivals for power and prestige. This is particularly evident in Cyprus, where the royal tombs were designed to proclaim the superiority of the Salamis dynasty over the island's other dynasties (which, for their part, also adopted these funerary practices in the late eighth / early seventh century). Similarly, in Argolis, the *basileis* of Argos sought by every means to consolidate their dominant position both within their city and vis-à-vis the aristocracies of other communities in the plain (Mycenae, Tiryns, Nauplia, not to mention Asine, which, having resisted Argos' influence, was destroyed in about 710).[5]

However, the case of Eretria provides the best illustration of the interaction between heroizing funerary practices and the establishment of a truly heroic cult. The rival Euboean aristocracies also resorted to imposing epic funerals as they competed for prestige. The funerary games of Amphidamas of Chalcis, in which Hesiod won the poetry competition, echoed the splendid ceremonies that marked the burial of a warrior of Eretria in about 720.[6] On that occasion, the deceased was displayed adorned with jewels and with his brow girt with a golden diadem. He was then cremated with his weapons on a pyre onto which ritually broken vases and sacrificed animals were cast.[7] This warrior was buried not far from the river that marked the city boundary to the west, close to the point where it was crossed by the road to Chalcis. His tomb contained a collection of funerary offerings that was particularly impressive by virtue of both the quantity and the quality of the objects: two great bronze bowls, six swords, and a dozen iron spears, one spear-tip of bronze (the "scepter"), a seal, jewels (a golden diadem). Be-

5. Cyprus: the interpretation of Snodgrass, *Cyprus* (1988), pp. 10–12, corrects that of Rupp, "Vive le roi" (1987), and "Royal Tombs" (1988), who regards this as a quest for legitimacy on the part of princes who had only recently acceded to a higher level of power. Argos: Hägg, "Burial Customs"; Polignac, "Cité et territoire" (forthcoming).

6. Hesiod *Works and Days* 650–60.

7. For this description and the accompanying analysis, see Bérard, *L'héroon à la porte de l'Ouest* (1970).

tween 720 and 680, there then developed around the "prince's" tomb what seemed to be a small, family necropolis. For those whose tombs gradually collected there, it was no doubt a way of manifesting the kinship that they claimed with this illustrious ancestor.

Around 680, at the very time the extension of the ramparts and the construction of the West Gate (leading to the Chalcis road) were incorporating this necropolis within the walls, right alongside the gate, burials here were discontinued. The funerary zone was covered over by a triangle of wide, massive paving slabs and was closed off on the southern side by a semicircular *peribolos*. The whole complex, which then remained untouched until the fifth century, was completed by an *oikos* dating from the end of the seventh century, later replaced by a second *oikos* and a series of five chambers toward the mid sixth century.

The addition of the triangle and the *peribolos* conferred a sacred character upon this place, which now became the *hērōon* of the princely occupant of Tomb 6, whose exceptional stature was confirmed in the eyes of the Eretrians by the richness of the objects deposited in the tomb, the grandiose funeral ceremonies that these conjured up, and the care with which the tomb had been constructed. The traces of a cult indicate that religious ceremonies continued to take place here right down to the early fifth century.[8] Throughout the entire archaic period, the warrior of the West Gate was considered one of the heroes of the Eretrian city, either by reason of his exploits in battle against the Chalcidians (through its very location, the tomb seemed designed to deter their attacks) or—if we accept that the city was heir to the legacy of the Lefkandi site, which was progressively abandoned in the course of the eighth century—owing to the part that he had played in the formation of Eretria. Even if the most ancient traces of occupation of the site go back to the ninth century, the

8. According to the offerings found in the *bothros* situated to the south of the triangular enclosure, the cult began at the beginning of the second half of the seventh century (Bérard, "Notes sur les fouilles" [1969], pp. 74–79). The objections raised by Martin, in "Erétrie" (1975), p. 48f., have been refuted by Bérard, "Topographie et urbanisme" (1978), pp. 89–94, who defends his own chronology against the later one (660–650) suggested by Martin for the installation of the triangle and the *peribolos*.

first urban constructions of Eretria (the sanctuary of Apollo, the port quarter, and the area around the West Gate) date from the middle and second half of the eighth century and could thus coincide with the *akmē* of the prince of the West Gate, making him, like the founders of the Euboean colonies in the western Mediterranean, and possibly following their model, the *archēge-tēs* of the city.[9] Indeed, Claude Bérard regards this prince as the last representative of the monarchy of the dark ages, interred with the symbols of his authority, in particular the bronze spear-head / scepter that had been handed down from one generation to the next and was eventually buried with the last figure to have exercised a personal form of power for which there was no longer a place in the *polis*. According to this theory, the prince's heroization thus placed on a metaphorical level the exercise of royalty that was eventually abolished when the *archai* were divided up among the aristocracy.[10] The last prince became the first hero.

This intriguing interpretation is both supported and modified if one compares the hero of Eretria with the contemporary her-oization of other city founders. A city founder did indeed pos-sess a monarchical kind of power. The authority conferred upon him by his leadership of the expedition, his choice of the site, his foundation of the colony, and his command in the battles fought was without equivalent in the society in which he now lived. His responsibility for the sacred objects reinforced the royal air of his power, which rested upon the cohesion of the group gathered around him, the kernel of the future city. But that unprecedented authority was in most cases shortlived,[11] for it ran contrary to the very bases of the *polis* over whose early days it had presided. The heroization of the city founder was thus not simply a gesture of

9. Bérard and Altherr-Charon, "Erétrie" (1981); Mazarakis Ainian, "Geomet-ric Eretria" (1987). On the heroization of city founders as a possible model for similar practices in Greece, see Malkin, *Religion and Colonization*, pp. 261–66. But the destruction of Lefkandi in about 720/710 may also be interpreted as the re-sult of an Eretrian conquest at the expense of Chalcis.

10. Claude Bérard speaks of an "allegory of royalty [making it possible] to recuperate certain prerogatives that had disappeared with the abolition of the exercise of monarchy" ("La mort du prince" [1982], p. 98). See also "Le sceptre du prince" (1972).

11. With a remarkable exception in the case of Battos, founder of Cyrene and of the Battiad dynasty.

gratitude; nor was it a transparent form of collective identification with him. It was a means of assimilating a situation of potential conflict in which the constitution of the framework for the existence of the community depended upon the temporary exercise of an individual authority that did not belong to that framework. Heroization symbolized both the need for a founder and the need for his personal *kratos* to disappear and be transferred to the whole body of leaders that took over from him. A founder was thus positioned at the crossroads of two worlds, that of the metropolis and that of the *apoikia*, where the time of "before the city" met with the time of the city.

Transitoriness was a feature common to all the candidates for heroization in the second half of the eighth century. The princes of the late Geometric period, rather than becoming the last in the Greek world (excluding Cyprus) to be buried along with their arms and other splendid funerary offerings, were in many cases the first to be buried along with their panoplies and the spits and andirons that betokened the importance of commensality and sacrifice in the constitution of the networks of power,[12] or with such large quantities of jewels and precious pots. Even where a continuity existed between themselves and their ancestors of the dark ages, they differed from them through their acquisition of unprecedented authority, prestige, and wealth. Their assimilation to the heroes of epic expressed the exceptional nature of their position. The presence of the spear-tip/scepter, a relic of the Bronze Age, in the tomb of the prince of Eretria did not, therefore, necessarily indicate that he was regarded as the last heir to a long monarchical tradition that went right back to the distant Mycenaean palace societies,[13] even if it is certainly possible that this insignia of power had been handed down in his family for several generations. It may equally possibly have indicated the prince's desire to show that he had been the first to exercise an authority that made him, in his capacity as war leader and, perhaps, leader of the new Eretria, the equal of the kings of epic.[14]

However, that exceptional prestige is not enough to explain

12. Murray, "Symposion" (1983), and *Sympotica* (1990).
13. Claude Bérard was too categorical on this point in his analyses.
14. The end of the Geometric period is characterized by a general tendency to assimilate the realities of the period, in every domain, to the imagined reality

the transition from a heroizing funeral to the establishment of an actual cult. The arrangement of the *hērōon* of Eretria indicates that there was a material and perhaps chronological break between the two worlds. Claude Bérard has explained the nature of that break and of the interaction between their respective practices in terms of the establishment of the egalitarian order of the aristocratic *polis*. However, that analysis posits too abrupt an opposition between two types of society, with one totally eradicating the other in the space of a single generation.[15] A comparison with what had happened not far away, still in Euboea, nearly three hundred years earlier, can sharpen our understanding of the phenomenon. The discovery at Lefkandi, at the top of the Toumba hill, of the remains of a "royal" burial dating from around 1000 B.C., that already presented many characteristics of the epic-style funerary practices of the late Geometric period (including the sacrifice of horses) forces us to reconsider the supposed relation between heroization and the city.[16] It is not that we should, as the discoverers of the site first suggested, regard as a *hērōon* the great edifice with its apse in which the royal couple had been buried, with their horses alongside. It is possible that this edifice was built, not immediately following the burial, to be destroyed soon after, but rather not long before the construction of the tomb and that it had constituted the royal *megaron*, at once a dwelling place and a hall for the banquets and ritual meals associated with the person of the *basileus*.[17] How-

---

of the heroic times made materially "present": cf. Snodgrass, *Archaic Greece* (1981), pp. 74–76; Schnapp-Gourbeillon, "Naissance de l'écriture" (1982); Hiller, "Rediscovery of the Mycenaean Past" (1983), speaks of the "constructive challenge" born of the confrontation of past and present for the Greeks of the eighth century. The spearhead may as well have been discovered in a Helladic tomb opened during the Geometric period.

15. Bérard, "La mort du prince." The same remark could be made on the analyses of Ian Morris, who likewise uses the expression "ideology of the *polis*" too systematically in what I consider to be an inadequate fashion for the earlier periods (*Burial and Ancient Society* [1987], p. 202; "Tomb Cult" [1988]; "Early polis as City and State" [1991]).

16. Popham, Touloupa, and Sackett, "Hero of Lefkandi" (1982); Popham, Calligas, and Sackett, *Lefkandi II* (1990).

17. Whitley, "Social Diversity in Dark Age Greece" (1991), p. 350; Calligas, "Hero Cult" (1988), p. 232.

ever, the destruction of this building and the construction of a tumulus on top of it also suggest a break that prefigures the *sēma* of Eretria; and the presence of funerary objects apparently from much more ancient times (a bronze vessel, a golden pendant) would seem to indicate that, as in the case of the scepter of Eretria, it was not possible to pass on to the heirs of the deceased certain symbols of cultural continuity with the past (whether or not that continuity was real or simulated is not relevant here). As in the case of the prince of Eretria, this sense of distance between one generation and the next may have been caused by the exceptional role played by the deceased at a crucial moment in the history of the community: not its physical foundation—its original establishment, at both Lefkandi and Eretria, happened earlier— but some decisive change. Just as the prince of Eretria was contemporary with the transformation of Eretria into a town and the colonial expeditions that enriched the city, so too the prince of Lefkandi had stood upon the threshold of the most brilliant period in his city's history, when fruitful contacts with Cyprus and the Near East were being resumed.[18]

There are thus grounds for thinking that the same scenario may have been played out twice, with an interval of three hundred years: once in each of the two cities, the second of which may have been a reformation of the first. Differences between the two cases remain, however. In both, a dynastic or family necropolis was created close to or around the founder's tomb over a certain period, forty years in Eretria, one hundred and fifty years in Lefkandi, where the Toumba "clan" was characterized both by the richness of its tombs and by a number of marked cultural peculiarities (pronounced links with Attica).[19] But in the first case, the necropolis existed before the closure of the site by means of the triangular area of paving, whereas in the second it developed after the creation of the tumulus. At Lefkandi, there is no sign of any organized cult such as the one at Eretria. The dead of Lefkandi were thus certainly "heroized," in the epic sense of the term, to the extent that their exceptional status was exalted by their funerals, the destruction of their dwelling place,

---

18. Popham, Sackett, and Themelis, *Lefkandi I* (1979), pp. 358–362.
19. Ibid.; Popham, Touloupa, Sackett, "Further Excavations" (1982).

and the erection of the monumental tumulus; and the reason for their heroization was no doubt the fact that they were the founders of a royal lineage that presided over the destiny of the community at a crucial moment in its expansion and that was determined to make its authority unchallengeable by placing the *archēgetēs* of the clan on the same level as the already legendary kings of the past. Nevertheless, all this was not enough to make them heroes in the religious sense.[20]

It is therefore important not to confuse the hero in the epic sense with the hero in the religious sense, yet neither should one draw too categorical an opposition between on the one hand "private" family strategies, which found expression in funerary practices, and on the other, "public" city strategies, which found concrete form in the establishment of a founder's cult. The cult at Eretria may have involved no more than a fraction of society, an aristocratic group, or even simply the families of the descendants, and not the whole city, as a state. But that would in no way diminish its importance, to the extent that the apparently private meetings constituted by the banquets of the various aristocratic groups were an essential feature of the public life of the city.[21] Even if it was managed by one particular aristocratic group, the Eretrian cult was political in that it was an essential element in the identity of the Eretrian aristocracy. By extending the protection of the prince not just to his direct descendants but also to all those who participated in the rites and the banquets, the cult clearly indicates a rearrangement in the aristocratic links of solidarity that appear to have constituted the basis of an archaic society.

There was, then, a fundamental difference between the situations of the tenth and the eighth centuries, a fact that is also shown by the evolution of funerary feasts in the Geometric necropolises of Naxos.[22] Here, in about 900, tombs were created in the ruins of Mycenaean buildings and walls were then constructed on top of them, designed to define particular enclosures

20. This fundamental distinction between ancestor and hero had already been drawn by Rodhe, *Psyche,* pp. 140–41, 148–49. Antonaccio, "Archaeology of Ancestors" (1933), pp. 51–52, gives a similar analysis.

21. Schmitt-Pantel, "Sacrificial Meal and *Symposion*" (1990); *La cité au banquet* (1992), pp. 17–113.

22. Lambrinoudakis, "Veneration of Ancestors" (1988).

where rites (about which we know little but that are attested by the accumulated remains of fires) followed by funerary feasts were subsequently practiced in continuous fashion right down to the late Geometric period. These forms of veneration appear to have been addressed to the founding ancestors of the local aristocracy, who, for their part, may have represented the generation of those who had returned to resettle in the neighborhood after it had been abandoned for an interval. The dead honored by these rites also had a particular link with the past: their installation amid the Mycenaean ruins was clearly a form of reappropriation aimed at effacing the historic break (for instance, a vase dated as Late Helladic III was placed on one of the tombs as an offering).[23] But toward the end of the eighth century, the family organization of this veneration was disappearing, a tumulus was raised over the funerary precincts situated close to the ancient town walls, and a cult may have continued to be practiced here until the seventh century. This pattern of developments thus seems to fall midway between the Lefkandi model and the Eretrian model. The rites and funerary feasts testify to an early form of heroization, of a family character. During a second phase, as at Eretria, the sēma established a break between the ancestors and those who honored them directly on top of their tomb, but made the location of the tomb, now visible and recognizable to all, a public place. The creation of a heroic cult of the dead thus always involved setting the ancestors at a distance and, at the same time, drawing their physical presence to the attention of the entire community. All this was effected by erecting a monumental point of reference that bestowed a public character upon a burial place whose history had until then been commemorated only by those who had a direct link with the dead.

Developments such as these influenced contemporary funerary customs in other places. In Athens, for example, the use of monumental vases as markers on certain tombs whose contents were relatively modest laid the emphasis on the collective memory, whereas only "family" memory could continue to honor deceased figures whose richly furnished tombs were not marked

23. Ibid., p. 235.

out visibly in any way. Even if the public display of the contents of the tomb and the presentation of offerings by close relations and kinsmen by marriage constituted an essential part of the funeral rites and provided a chance to demonstrate the authority and prestige of the deceased, he no longer enjoyed the same "presence."[24] But the greatest wealth of analogies with the phenomena described above is provided by the veneration devoted to Helladic tombs and the creation of the cult of ancient heroes.

The Masters of the Land: The Veneration and Appropriation of the Past

Depositing offerings in Mycenaean tombs—accidentally discovered or long known or deliberately excavated—was a practice that spread in the course of the last third of the eighth century; and for a long time this was considered to have been the most remarkable and widespread form taken by the cult of heroes in the archaic period. This view was particularly encouraged by Nicholas Coldstream's article that collected and systemized all the data.[25] As nobody any longer dreamed of regarding the phenomenon as a perpetuation of a Helladic funerary cult,[26] if only because of the hiatus of five or six centuries between the date of the tombs and the appearance of the offerings, discussion concentrated on the origin and significance of these cults. An initial explanation, which regarded the phenomenon as a consequence of the diffusion of epic poems, primarily the Homeric ones, definitely seems inadequate, even if the Homeric heroes had come from the very regions where these cults were concentrated (Attica, Argolis, Boeotia, Corinthia, Messenia—but not Laconia). Moreover, the only cults involving Homeric heroes were not centered on tombs and were practiced far from any burial grounds.

24. Whitley, *Style and Society*, pp. 161–62; and the very interesting suggestions of Houby-Nielsen, "Interactions between Chieftains and Citizens?" (1992).

25. Coldstream, "Hero Cults in the Age of Homer" (1976). Coldstream traced these cults to Attica (Aliki, Menidi, Thoricus, Eleusis), Boeotia (Thebes: Ismenion and Kastelli), Corinthia (Soligaea, at the beginning of the seventh century), Argolis (Argos: Deiras; Mycenae, Prosymna), Messenia (Nichoria, Volimedia, Vasiliko), Delos (Theke of the Hyperboraean Virgins).

26. Hypothesis of Nilsson, *Minoan-Mycenean Religion* (1950), p. 585.

In the "Menelaion" of Therapne, Menelaos and Helen, possibly associated with rites of adolescence, have the air of deities rather than heroes; and the Polis cult in Ithaca was a cave cult, possibly of nymphs (other such cases are known for the Geometric period), not a cult of Odysseus himself.[27] In this domain, as in that of myth, the correlation between practice and text is never that immediate. The coincidence of the diffusion of both epic poems and offerings in ancient tombs, far from pointing to a strictly causal relationship, testifies rather to a general interest in the memory of the "heroic ages" that took two close but separate forms. One can even find in Homer traces of this very kind of interest, an interest he is in fact believed to have encouraged.[28]

Besides, as a result of being represented on painted pots of the late Geometric and early archaic periods alongside great civilizing heroes such as Herakles, Perseus, Theseus, and Bellephoron,[29] the heroes of the Homeric poems also acquired a universal, Panhellenic dimension, which rendered them less amenable to the local interpretations and practices upon which heroic cults were based. Just as for other cults, the reappropriation of the past that led to the establishment of a cult tended to concentrate on secondary monuments and local heroes, which could be more freely "reinterpreted." So as Anthony Snodgrass has pointed out, it is altogether to be expected—indeed, I myself would say inevitable—that the Greeks who opened up a tomb in order to deposit offerings there should have had no idea of the true iden-

27. Menelaion: Herodotus 6.61. Catling, "Excavations at the Menelaion" (1976–77), pp. 36–37; the offerings in the sanctuary were very similar to those in the Artemision. Polis: cave cult comparable to those of Paros (Schilardi, "Paros II" [1975]); the presence of Odysseus (in a Hellenistic graffito: Benton, "Ithaca III" (1934–35), pp. 55–56, who also mentions archaic dedications to Hera and Athena) can be explained quite simply by *Odyssey* 13.345–71, where Athena reminds the hero that he has several times sacrificed to the Naiads in their cave, close to which he has just come ashore. Odysseus could thus be seen as the founder of the cult. On the "Agamemnoneion," see below.

28. See *Iliad* 3.326–32, where the Greeks ponder on the existence of an ancient tomb. See Snodgrass's remarks on the difference between the "epic" and "cultic" hero, in "Archaeology of the Hero" (1988). The difference between the "hero of epic" and the "hero of cult" has been stressed by Nagy, *The Best of the Achaeans* (1979), pp. 115–16.

29. Cf. Schefold, *Myth and Legend in Early Greek Art* (1971); Nagy, *The Best of the Achaeans*, pp. 115–16.

tity of the occupants, since the whole point was to confer upon them a heroic identity derived from the myths of their region or even of a particular canton of that region.[30] In this way, a cult established a link between the previous and the existing masters of the land and, through the sanction that the past thereby seemed to provide, legitimated the present state of things.

Anthony Snodgrass has also stressed the fact that these cults appeared predominantly in areas where a free peasantry developed in the archaic and classical periods (though this is not true of Messenia). So cults based on tombs, in many cases in a rural context, would have been set up as a way of legitimating claims to ownership of the land by communities or families of free peasants, at a time when property was becoming the basis for citizenship, a status that was gradually becoming more closely defined. On the other hand, these regions also constituted the Greece of cities, so such an appropriation may well have been instigated by a much larger community. Plenty of examples exist in which the discovery of the tomb of an ancestor or a legendary sovereign was used to justify a city's territorial claims: for instance, the bones of Orestes, opportunely discovered in Tegea by the Spartans, or the remains of Theseus that Cimon was so "divinely surprised" to unearth in Skyros, of which he had just taken possession.[31] Thus, the transformation of a tomb into a cult site might be a symbol of sovereignty just as was the construction of a frontier sanctuary.

However, none of the above interpretations sufficiently take into consideration the essential distinction between on the one hand the temporary veneration for a tomb expressed by the deposit of the occasional offering and, on the other, the establishment of a veritable, regular, and institutionalized cult.[32] The former involved individuals or families; the latter could only be the doing of an organized group, association, community, or

---

30. Snodgrass, *Archaeology* (1977), p. 30f.; *Archaic Greece*, p. 33f.

31. Herodotus 1.67; Plutarch *Cimon* 5, *Theseus* 36. The confusion between land (private) and territory (collective) in Snodgrass's analysis has been pointed out by Malkin, "Land Ownership" (1993).

32. On this subject see Antonaccio, *Archaeology of Ancestors* (1993). However, as Malkin, "Land Ownership," stresses, her use of the words "tomb cult" for the various forms of offerings at tombs also implies some kind of repeated activity, and can be misleading.

city. Upon closer examination, most "cults" turn out in truth to have amounted to no more than a temporary, even fleeting veneration, which led to no regular religious practices—and that is when they do not merely indicate the reuse of a tomb.[33] The true cults centered on tombs, which are attested by an abundance of pottery, figurines (horses, horsemen), terra-cotta "shields," and possibly small bronzes, are relatively few in number and are located essentially in either Attica (Menidi, Thoricus) or Messenia.[34] We should take a closer look at the relation between veneration for particular tombs and veritable heroic cults, in order to grasp their respective significances.

Argolis is one of the regions where that relation is most easily detectable.[35] Offerings appeared toward the end of the eighth century in Mycenaean tombs in Argos (Deiras), Mycenae (*tholos* tombs, Kalkani chamber tombs, Circles A and B), and between those two locations, in tombs of the necropolis to the northwest of the Heraion of Prosymna. This sporadic veneration lasted for no more than one generation and came to an end at the beginning of the seventh century. Now, the appearance of those offerings coincided, give or take a few years, with the last princely funerals of Argos (the tomb with the panoply),[36] and their disappearance coincided with the beginning of two cults that were particularly prominent in the seventh century: that of the small terrace at the northernmost point of the necropolis of Prosymna, close to the only tomb with a *tholos* and also to the road to Mycenae, and that of the "Agamemnoneion" situated one kilometer

33. At Eleusis, the enclosure dating from the late Geometric period that has been identified as the "*Hērōon* of the Seven against Thebes" could be simply a pseudo-ancestral enclosure built at the time of the reuse of a Helladic tomb; see Polignac, "Sanctuaires et société en Attique," n. 19 (forthcoming). For Prosymna, see below.

34. A comparative study of the offerings has been made by Abramson, "Hero Shrine for Phrontis at Sounion?" (1979), and Hägg, "Gifts to the Heroes" (1987).

35. What follows summarizes my analysis in "Cité et territoire" (forthcoming); see also the recent studies by Whitley, "Early States and Hero Cults" (1988), pp. 178–82, and Antonaccio, "Early Argive Heraion" (1992), pp. 98–104. See the references for archaeological sites in the Bibliography.

36. Their appearance also coincided with the funerary meals of the necropolis of Mount Barbouna at Asine, which were similar to those of Naxos (Hägg, "Funerary meals at Asine?" [1983]), which are not included in the analysis since the town was destroyed soon after.

to the south of Mycenae, close to the bridge by which the road to the Heraion crosses a ravine. The veneration of Helladic tombs and, in some cases, their reuse for new burials were clearly transitional practices, which may have begun as a kind of response to the heroizing funerals of the princes of Argos, a "counter-initiative" of other aristocratic groups. Those of Mycenae affirmed their individuality by the use of monuments of their own; others, at the Heraion, the regional sanctuary, manifested their claim to a local lineage of ancestors, which would increase their prestige (as well as their own rights in the sanctuary where the Argive princes were parading their supremacy by ritual means). The "clanic" logic behind the initiative of depositing offerings at tombs remained the same as that of heroizing funerals in a context of strong rivalry between the various groups of nobles. Conversely, the disappearance of the practice made room for institutionalized and therefore collective cults the nature of which is hard to determine but that certainly appear to have set the seal upon the formation of new aristocratic solidarities.[37] In the confrontation between the cult of the small terrace of Prosymna and the Agamemnoneion, the former seems to represent at least a symbolic appropriation of the Heraion and its heroes on the part of the Argive aristocracy, while the latter expresses the Mycenaean aristocracy's systematic recourse to its own mythical and religious traditions with the aim of defending its own collective identity.

This transition thus presents an exact parallel to the movement, in the same period, from heroizing funerals to the heroic cult of the historical dead. However, at least in Argolis, the cults to which it led were not necessarily cults centered on tombs. Attica presents a scene of even greater diversity. Here, cults with funerary or heroic connotations were flourishing at the end of

37. The small terrace of Prosymna might have been either a secondary sanctuary of Hera (Blegen, "Remains of Post-Mycenean Date" [1939]), "reserved" for an elite or the cult site of the hero of the *tholos* (Wright, "Old Temple Terrace" [1982], p. 194). The Mycenae cult is attributed to Agamemnon solely on the basis of Hellenistic descriptions that postdate the destruction of Mycenae in 468, and certain of the offerings could well denote the presence of a goddess in the sanctuary. Whatever the case may be, the richness of the offerings in both places and the traces of banquets in the Agamemnonaion leave room for no doubt as to the aristocratic nature of these cults.

the Geometric period, in the zone of the future agora with its wealth of ancient tombs, around tombs with a *tholos* out in the territory (Menidi, Thoricus) and in the temple of Athena at Sunium (Phrontis?). Even if the explanation for the appearance of these cults is not the same in all cases, most of them (except in Thoricus) present distinctive aristocratic features, including similarities with the funeral practices of the archaic Athenian elite.[38] In Messenia, too, the temporary veneration for certain tombs gave way to cults centered upon other tombs, and these continued down to the classical period. Here, the transition seems to have coincided with the period of the first Spartan conquest, but our limited knowledge of the context makes it impossible to decide whether recourse to the ancient masters of the sites involved was designed to legitimate the conquest or, on the contrary, to express opposition to Spartan domination.[39] Whatever the case may have been, though, the appearance of cults directly or indirectly associated with the memory and traces of the former masters of these sites did, in the territories where they were located, demonstrate the formation of the same kind of aristocratic association and solidarity as did the cult of the historic heroized dead within the urban space. Wherever they were associated with the emergence of a center of power, both kinds of cults contributed to the political elaboration of the city, for which the invention of a mythical founder provided the ultimate expression.

The Invention of the Mythical Founder

When the *Iliad* describes the meeting of the Trojan leaders, gathered around Hector at the foot of the tomb of Ilos, in the Trojan plain, the image of the council of the vast, legendary alliance,

---

38. Whitley, "Early States and Hero Cults" pp. 173–78, thus interprets the cults of Thoricus and Menidi as a defensive reaction on the part of ancient Attic communities faced with the appearance of new settlement centers. However, the two cults are not identical. See my remarks in "Sanctuaires et société." Also Houby-Nielsen, "Interactions between Chieftains and Citizens" (1992), pp. 354–57; and Whitley, "Monument before Marathon" (1994), pp. 220 76.

39. Snodgrass, "Archaeology of the Hero," p. 16; Morris, "Tomb Cult" (1988), p. 756. However, it is not certain that the first Spartan conquest extended to the region of these cults.

held under the auspices of a founding hero, seems to relate to a situation with which, at a local level, all the Greek cities must have been familiar in the early days of their existence.[40] The mythical founder of Troy was Ilos, one of the royal generations (Tros, Ilos, Laomedon) that had followed the time of Dardanos, when Troy was not yet a city but just a group of human beings living on the slopes of Mount Ida: "Holy Ilium had not yet risen in the plain as a city.[41]

Ilos' power stemmed from his legendary reputation as a local civilizer, the "colonizer" of the plain under threat from invaders, which he protected by means of his tomb, the location of which symbolized the Trojan sovereignty over the *chōra*. Ilos thus embodied the destiny of a whole series of regional civilizing heroes, each of whom was set up as a mythical founder of a *polis* thanks to a reinterpretation of his legendary personality and his deeply rooted presence, which in some cases gave rise to a cult, in a tomb whose location determined that of the very first organ of the *polis*, the aristocratic council. The figure of the founding hero is certainly one of those best defined by the series of typologies that have attempted to introduce some order into the vast world of heroic cults.[42]

Many of these heroes are known to us from the "national" traditions of the various cities, where foundation myths were of particular importance. In Megara, for instance, Alcathoos was not the first king; nor did he give his name to the city. Rather, he was the founder of the society of the *polis*, by reason of his actions both on the boundaries of the territory and in the heart of the community.[43] It was Alcathoos, the son of Pelops, who repelled the wild world by slaying the Citheron lion and, in consequence, founding the sanctuary of Artemis Agrotera and

40. *Iliad* 10.414f.; the tomb is mentioned again in book 11.166, 371 and book 24.350. And the place where the *dēmos* of Troy met, in front of Priam's palace, was where an "ancient," Aisyetes, was buried (2.786f.). Cf. Hadzisteliou-Price, "Hero-cult and Homer" (1973), p. 129f.

41. *Iliad* 20.216f.: the foundation myths of Troy. Referred to by Plato (*Laws* 3.68), and Strabo (13.1.25) in connection with the development of civilization, spreading from the mountains to the sea, by way of the plains.

42. Farnell, *Greek Hero Cults* (1921); Brelich, *Gli eroi greci* (1958).

43. Pausanias 1.39–44. See Bohringer, "Mégare" (1980); Polignac, "Déméter et l'altérité" (1990).

Apollo Agraios (both hunting deities) at Megara. Having established his sovereignty as a result of these exploits, he completed his founding act by moving the "center" from the acropolis of Caria to the western acropolis, where he set up a dwelling place for the Prodomeis gods, and by building new ramparts, with the aid of Apollo, who was then honored on the new acropolis as the city *archēgetēs*.[44]

By bringing to an end the chaos occasioned by the fierce lion, which nobody else had been able to overcome, Alcathoos established the symbolic equivalent of a frontier; and the introduction of order that he achieved involved not only creating the territory but also symbolizing its frontier, by founding the cult of the two hunting deities at the heart of this society. The association of the Apollo of the acropolis with the ramparts that enclosed and marked the outer limits of the city mirrored this equilibrium between the center and the periphery.

Whatever attributes and interpretations may have been added after the constitution of the city to form the later image of Alcathoos, to appeal to the hero by discovering his tomb or building him a *hērōon* close to the agora was thus to invent the figure of the mythical founder of the *polis*, a figure that the city then proceeded to honor by instituting local athletic games.[45]

Other heroes played a similar role. The agora of Megara displayed the tomb of the Argive Coroibos, the mythical founder of the sanctuary of Apollo of Tripodiscos, at the foot of the Geranian mountains, and that of Orsippos, presumed to be a champion of the Olympic Games in the late eighth century, who was supposed to have reconquered an outlying territory previously lost by his city.[46] Whether Orsippos was or was not a real person, his proximity to Coroibos and the fact that his exploits as an athlete and a warrior dated from the same period as the conflicts in the Isthmus out of which the cities of Megara and Corinth emerged, made him a protector of the city's southern frontier. Even more certainly, given that he was associated with a cult in the principal sanctuary of Megaris and with one of the founding villages of

44. On the acropolises of Megara, see Muller, "Megarika" (1980 and 1981).

45. Pindar *Isthmian* 7.67. The *hērōon* of Alcathoos lay not far from the agora (Pausanias 1.44.1).

46. Pausanias 1.43.7 and 44.1.

Megara, Coroibos personified the territory as a whole and also its cults at the center of the urban space.[47]

The figure of the founding hero is equally clearly defined in Argos, where the mythical sequence of events leading to the city's foundation bears close comparison to that of Megara. In Argos, too, we find first a prehuman phase (that of the rivers), then a "prepolitical" phase (a primitive human society assembled by Phoroneus, the father of Car) represented by the dynasty of the Phoronids, whose last prince, Gelanor, was defeated by a newcomer, Danaos of Egypt: the original society disappeared with Gelanor, for Danaos established not only a new royal lineage but also a new order.[48]

As a descendant of Io, the priestess of Hera seduced by Zeus, and also as father of the Danaids, whose rejection of marriage was to lead to their doom—with the exception of Hypermenestra, who then founded the lineage—Danaos first appears at the center of the vast Argive body of discourse on the institution of marriage and its importance in society as the basis of the human order: on that account, he qualifies as a civilizing hero par excellence and also as a local hero, since he plays a part in the corpus of legends that probably constituted the *hieros logos* of the Heraion. Finally, he was also the presumed founder of the cult of Lycian Apollo, whose title was supposed to refer directly to Danaos' victory over Gelanor and so to the establishment of his sovereignty.[49] His tomb lay close to the temple on the agora of Argos, where the god and the hero together protected the city institutions.

The image of the heroes who were founders of cults and organizers of the territory is clearly very close to the historical image of the city founder. But although the heroization of historical founders may have influenced similar practices in Greece itself, the archaeology of the urban centers of Greece provides no information on the dates and modalities of the establishment of tombs presumed to belong to founding heroes in the centers of

---

47. On Tripodiscus and the synoecism, see Rigsby, "Megara and Tripodiscus" (1987).

48. Pausanias 2.15.4f., 19.3.

49. The victory of a wolf (*lukos*), symbol of the foreigner, over a bull, symbol of the local king, would have announced Danaos' victory: Pansanias 2.19.3.

cities. The relevant texts even indicate that the latter process may sometimes have taken place at quite a late date: the bones of Theseus were not brought to Athens until the fifth century, which was when a number of similar operations also took place elsewhere.[50] The history of the Greek cities is frequently punctuated by "ideological foundations" that made use of a series of different heroes; and the establishment of the image and cult of the city founder was one phase of such foundations, the date of which varies from one city to another.[51]

A well-known example of such a process is provided by Athens, where the figure of the king Erechtheus and that of its political founder, Theseus, were both remodeled in conjunction with the image of the foundation of the city—rethought first at the time of Cleisthenes' reforms, then again at the time of Cimon's. Cleisthenes brought Erechtheus "down" from the acropolis into the new space shaped by *isonomia* by making him the eponymous founder of one of its ten tribes, and the simultaneous diffusion of representations of the cycle of myths about Theseus seems to have been inspired by the same antityrannical ideology. Cimon, by transferring Theseus' remains and burying them in a new *hērōon* in the heart of fifth-century Athens, completed the "democratic" interpretation of the ancient king's history handed down by Plutarch.[52]

But it was above all episodes of tyranny that favored all kinds of heroic manipulations. The most famous is that by which the tyrant Cleisthenes of Sicyon deprived the hero Adrastus of the cult that was addressed to him in the agora, and transferred the honors to the king of Argos' worst enemy, the Theban Melanippus whom he "had brought" there (*epagein* seems to indicate that the relics were transferred from Thebes to Sicyon).[53] This action of the tyrant fitted in with his anti-Argive policies as a whole. Now,

50. It is also possible that the tomb of Orsippos was not "established" on the agora of Megara until the fifth century (Piccirilli, *Megarika* [1976], pp. 127–30). The games of Alcathoos mentioned by Pindar show, on the contrary, that the hero already enjoyed a place of central importance in Megara at that time.

51. Bérard, "L'héroïsation et la formation de la cité" (1983), uses the expression "ideological foundations" in connection with the history of the cults in Athens.

52. Plutarch *Theseus*, in particular 36.2. On Theseus, see Calame, *Thésée* (1989).

53. Herodotus 5.67–68.

excavations in the agora of Argos have revealed the precinct of a "*hērōon* of the Seven against Thebes" bearing inscriptions that make it possible to date it to the same period as Cleisthenes.[54] This discovery dramatically illuminates the "mythological warfare" that set these two cities in opposition in the first half of the sixth century, when Argos installed in the center of its political space the heroes whom Sicyon was rejecting. But it also introduces new elements into the evolution of heroic cults in the archaic period. The fact is that the *hērōon* of the Seven did not contain any tombs of the legendary kings who had died beneath the walls of Thebes, whose remains Argos, unlike Athens, never claimed to have collected. The formulation of the inscriptions (*ton en Thēbais*) and the shape of the enclosure—similar to the (later) enclosure of the eponymous heroes of Athens, which did not contain any tombs either—indicate that by the early sixth century it was possible for veneration of ancient heroes to be unattached to any material relics in a tomb, which until then had frequently constituted an indispensable adjunct.[55] Instead of receiving offerings, the heroes could now be honored by athletic and musical competitions of the kind attested in Sicyon.

The urban space thus progressively acquired a wealth of monuments and a variety of heroic cults that gradually came to belong to the mythical space of the city.[56] Some of these protected the city by guarding the approach to its defenses: the tombs of the prince of Eretria, of Amphion and Zetos in Thebes, and possibly the first *hērōon* built for Theseus in Athens all stood sentinel at the town gates. Others marked out the main political space: the agora. Where the agora was established on the site of an ancient necropolis, the rediscovered tombs provided the basis for the heroic sanctuaries, so the presence of heroes in the public space did not always result from their remains being reburied there.

This was the kind of situation that gave rise to etiological stories such as the one that tells of the establishment of the principal

54. Pariente, "Monument argien" (1992).

55. But this separation already existed in some colonial foundations: in Megara Hyblaea, the *hērōon* housed no tomb; in Thasos, the monument to Glaucos at the entrance to the agora took the form of a cenotaph.

56. Piérart, "Argos 'assoiffée'" (1992).

buildings and political organs of Megara on top of the tombs of heroes. It is a text that, in its own way, gives a good account of how the authority of the heroes was always called upon to sanction the various phases in the political elaboration of Greek cities:

> They resolved no longer to be ruled by one king, but to have elected magistrates (*archontēs*) and to obey one another in turn. Then Aesymnus, who had a reputation second to none among the Megarians, came to the god in Delphi and asked in what way they could be prosperous. The oracle in its reply said that they would fare well if they took counsel with the majority (*en meta tōn pleionōn bouleusōntai*). This utterance they took to refer to the dead and built a council chamber in this place in order that the grave of their heroes might be within it.[57]

57. Pausanias 1.43.3 (trans. W. H. S. Jones, Loeb Classical Library [London and Cambridge, Mass., 1979]).

CONCLUSION

T he Greek renaissance: that expression, often applied to the eighth century, is a convenient way of referring to a collection of changes that imply a renewal, a certain break with the situation prevailing immediately before, and a deliberate, albeit partly illusory, reappropriation of a distant cultural heritage. But as in the case of the fifteenth and sixteenth centuries in Europe, there is a danger that it may distort our perception of the period in question by attempting to incorporate every aspect of it in one definition that ends up taking the place of historical analysis and becoming a convenient but deceptive label. For such reasons, some schools of thought and scholars insist, on the contrary, on manifest continuities throughout the Iron Age to such a degree that they underestimate the importance of the changes of the late Geometric period. To what extent, then, is it justifiable to speak of the emergence of the Greek city in the eighth century?

The answer to that question depends largely upon the meaning that one ascribes to the words "city" and *polis*. They are terms that are in general strongly marked by the image of the "classical city" that modern historiography has created. To use those concepts without qualification, or even to speak of a "city ideology" in the Geometric period, may lead to serious misapprehensions or to methodological impasses and sterile arguments in which disagreements over the words themselves stand in the way of new analyses. At the end of this work, it is thus worth asking what light the phenomena studied have cast upon Greek society and its evolution in the ninth and eighth centuries.

The characteristic arrangement in the "dark ages" seems to have been a horizontal juxtaposition in which, within the general

framework of a relatively low human density, traditional cleavages of various kinds (ethnic, tribal, geographic) kept the different social groups (small towns, villages clustering round a hand-
ful of noble households) in a state of relative autonomy, at the
same time limiting them to what was often a restricted circuit of
activities, exchanges, and influences (although there were a few
remarkable exceptions to this state of affairs). The structures
striving to emerge from this arrangement, such as a certain form
of somewhat vaguely defined royalty, could establish little hold
upon the local groups and "kings." This situation underwent a
profound transformation as a result of the many convergent
pressures created by demographic growth in Greece in the ninth
and eighth centuries. The new possibilities and difficulties that
resulted created new tensions, giving rise to or exacerbating
various kinds of rivalry and conflict but also facilitating new
forms of solidarity.

One aspect of increasing solidarity was a stronger cohesion
among those who bore arms and had to get along together if they
were to ensure the perpetuation or reinforcement of their authority. It was in this context that, gradually, an increasingly
clear hierarchy was established among the various centers of
power, the largest of which, the future great cities, acquired a
more or less complete regional preeminence. This ongoing consolidation of the structures of authority was accompanied by the
development of various forms of ritualized competition in the
funerary, religious, and agonistic domains and the eruption of
many armed conflicts that obliged the warring aristocracies to
reorganize their forces and power in a more systematic way than
in the clashes in the "epic" style of the past.

But despite its general implications, warfare, as well as the
exercise of power that went with it, was the business of only a
small fraction of society. The cohesion it encouraged could not,
on its own, extend beyond the limits of its original practical
framework, could not, *motu proprio*, reach beyond its own perpetuation and reinforcement in the course of increasingly bitter
conflicts. The creation of political organs that institutionalized
new modes of exercising public authority could in itself achieve
nothing unless it was backed up by a social body whose motives
and desire for unity were inspired by something other than war.
Warfare was a crystallizing agent, a factor of mutual reinforce-

ment in the societies that it set in opposition, and it did introduce
a collection of changes. But it could not itself make them produce
new social forms and attitudes. The elaboration of the first aristocratic phalanx certainly contributed to the emergence of a new
view of the needs of society, but it could not give them concrete
expression. And while conquest could overcome distances and
bring into contact groups that had previously lived apart, it did
so at the cost of creating new cleavages that undermined the unification it had imposed "from above."

In contrast, the "blossoming of religious life" we have noted
toward the end of the Geometric period shows that religion was
the only agent to effect the entire social body. It signaled the
emergence of a society that seemed to acquire self-awareness as
it retook possession of the past by endowing it with a sacred
character, organizing in an increasingly overt fashion collective
practices and sanctuaries in which rituals transformed a dispa-
rate collection of individuals or groups into a community active
and solid in its devotion to a particular cult. It was thus through
religious life that a new kind of social body was gradually to take
shape, one founded upon its members' common adhesion to the
same religious territory—religious territory not so much in the
sense of a symbolic representation of the actual territory as in the
way the social body envisaged its own cohesion (and its limits)
within a given space. Within that space, the relation between
social, demographic, and economic factors and religious ones
was not a link of dependence that bound a determining concrete
situation to its formal consequences, its "reflection" or "mask";
what was involved, rather, was the creation of a representation
of reality and of a pattern of behavior within it, formulated in
terms that were identical for all members of the society. The blossoming of cults in the ninth and eighth centuries introduced a
common language, a shared conception of reality, which then
modeled the forms of action that the society adopted.

That being so, when it came to redefining social and spatial
relations, the religious factor was at the heart of the debate.
Within the territorial framework marked out by war and the exercise of power, previously separate neighboring groups came to
be organized in a new way as some were integrated, others incorporated as dependents, others opposed and excluded; and attitudes toward those operations and their implementation were

determined by their respective implications vis-à-vis the religious cults. Participation in religious rituals guaranteed a mutual recognition of statuses and set the seal upon membership of the society, thereby defining an early form of citizenship. And it was in religious terms, through the gathering importance of rituals and the commitment to build sanctuaries for the deities who presided over this establishment of order, that the emerging society manifested its new cohesion and took its first collective—and hence political—long-term decisions. The religious space that was created in this way constituted the first civic space.

Given the historical circumstances of the formation of the city, there is nothing surprising or arbitrary about the fact that, in this process, that space was in many cases bipolar: within it the society took cognizance of itself and organized itself both at the center and on the geographical periphery. If only by reason of the fact that exclusive centrality tended to imply a dependent status for the periphery, the cults of the city center were unhelpful when it came to formulating and effecting the agreements and rejections that were essential to the constitution of a united and viable society throughout the territory as a whole. The great cult set up in the outlying territory was thus in many cases the one around which the social constitution of the city revolved, its importance being manifested by the centrifugal procession that brought the entire population to the very edge of the city space, to a point that was nevertheless the median point for the city society. However, that first movement was complemented by a second: namely, the movement that brought about the constitution of a collective power rooted at the center and that formalized the unification of the local aristocracies by bonding them into a concrete body of leaders that was "proto-isonomic" and, in its war-like behavior, also "proto-hoplitic." The central pole (which, in the Greek world, was to become the urban pole), through both its divine and its heroic cults, was the pole for the political constitution of the city, for it drew to it, from wherever they were scattered throughout the city territory, all the members of the *polis'* assemblies and councils.

In my view, we should not seek to determine which of those two simultaneous, indissociable, and mutually reinforcing movements came logically or chronologically first. The emergence of stable political institutions would have been inconceivable had not the bases of territorial solidarity been defined through the mediation of religion. The increasingly organized nature of the religious cults, which was reflected in the evolving pattern of offerings and ritual practices and the subsequent building of sanctuaries, was organically connected with the extension of the authority of the principal urban aristocracies over the greater part of society. It was by mutually fostering one another that those two movements linking the center and the city boundaries created the *polis.*

In the bipolar view of the city presented here, the idea of a *central point* is thus not abolished but complemented by that of a *median point.* The two were linked through the axis of relations by means of which the city was elaborated and around which the secondary cults, whether of gods or of heroes, in the settlement or on its fringes, within the territory or on its boundaries, delineated and defined the functions of appropriation, delimitation, interconnection, and integration and affirmed the city's identity and sovereignty as a *polis.* Some of those concepts were coordinated and synthesized in the great sanctuary out in the territory, others in the great sanctuary in the heart of the town. Clearly, this schema cannot be applied indiscriminately, without taking account of local variations, for, as we have seen, Athens presents the contrasting model of a city in which the two impulses leading to the formation of the *polis* merged into a single movement toward the center. Elsewhere, too, attention later became concentrated on a single central spot—the agora with its assembly, which now became the primordial means of self-identification and self-expression for the community. But even then, the separate and crucial development of quintessentially political thought and practice still did not dispense with the off-center religious pole where the city society continued to come periodically, to derive renewed strength from its origins, relive its foundation, and ensure its continuity. The political life of the city could not have existed without this median point where the religious agent that founded the civic society acquired concrete form. Right from the start, the Greek city depended upon mediation for its political life.

BIBLIOGRAPHY

❧ ✻ ☙

This bibliography comprises references consulted for this work, as well as others not mentioned explicitly in the notes. It is divided into two parts: a list of general references and a list of archaeological references organized by regions and sites.

The abbreviations of journals are from either the *American Journal of Archaeology* 90 (1986): 384–94 or the *Année Philologique*. The following conference publications are cited in abbreviated form:

Atti Taranto:
> Atti del . . . Convegno di studi sulla Magna Grecia, Taranto (the date is that of the conference):
>> 1. *Greci ed indigeni in Magna Grecia, 1961.*
>> 3. *Metropoli e colonie di Magna Grecia, 1963.*
>> 4. *Santuari di Magna Grecia, 1964.*
>> 7. *La città e il suo territorio, 1967.*
>> 10. *Taranto nella civiltà della Magna Grecia, 1970.*
>> 13. *Metaponto, 1973.*
>> 16. *Locri Epizefirii, 1976.*
>> 18. *Gli Eubei in Occidente, 1978.*
>> 20. *Siris e l'influenza ionica in Occidente, 1980.*
>> 22. *Magna Grecia e mondo miceneo, 1982.*
>> 23. *Crotone, 1983.*
>> 24. *Magna Grecia, Epiro e Macedonia, 1984.*
>> 27. *Poseidonia-Paestum, 1987.*
>> 29. *La Magna Grecia e il lontano Occidente, 1989.*

General References

Ahlberg, G. *Fighting on Land and Sea in Greek Geometric Art.* Stockholm, 1971.

———. *Prothesis and Ekphora in Greek Geometric Art.* Göteborg, 1971.

Alcock, S., and R. Osborne, eds. *Placing the Gods: Sanctuaries and Space in Ancient Greece.* Oxford, 1994.

Antonaccio, C. *An Archaeology of Ancestors: Hero and Tomb Cult in Early Greece.* London, 1993.

———. "The Archaeology of Ancestors." In *Cultural Poetics in Archaic Greece,* ed. C. Dougherty and L. Kurke, pp. 46–70. Cambridge, 1993.

Architecture et société de l'archaïsme grec à la fin de la république romaine. Actes du colloque international, Ecole française de Rome, 1980. Rome, 1983.

Asheri, D. *Distribuzioni di terre nell'antica Grecia.* Turin, 1966.

———. "A propos des sanctuaires extra-urbains de Sicile et Grande-Grèce: Théories et témoignages." In *Mélanges P. Lévêque,* ed. M.-M. Mactoux and E. Geny, 1:1–15. Paris, 1988.

Audring, G. "Proastion: Zur Funktion der Stadtnahen Landzone archaïscher Polis" *Klio* 63 (1981): 215–31.

Bérard, C. "Récupérer la mort du prince: Héroïsation et formation de la cité." In Gnoli and Vernant, *La mort, les morts* (1982): pp. 89–105.

———. "L'héroïsation et la formation de la cité: Un conflit idéologique." In *Architecture et société* (1983); pp. 43–62.

Bérard, J. *La colonisation grecque de l'Italie méridionale et de la Sicile.* 2d ed. Paris, 1957.

Bergquist, B. *The Archaic Greek Temenos: A Study of Structure and Function.* Lund, 1967.

———. "The Archaeology of Sacrifice: Minoan-Mycenean versus Greek." In Hägg, Marinatos, and Nordquist, *Early Greek Cult Practice* (1988), pp. 21–34.

———. "Sympotic Space: A Functional Aspect of Greek Dining-rooms." In Murray, *Sympotica* (1990), pp. 37–65.

———. "The Archaic Temenos in Western Greece." In Reverdin and Grange, *Le sanctuaire grec* (1992), 109–52.

Bietti-Sestieri, A.-M. *The Iron Age Community of Osteria del'Osa.* Cambridge, 1992.

Billot, M.-F. "Apollon Pythéen et l'Argolide archaïque: Histoire et mythes." *Archaiognosia* 6 (1989–90 [1992]): 35–100.

Bohringer, F. "Mégare: Traditions mythiques, espace sacré, et naissance de la cité." *Ant. Cl.* 49 (1980): 5:22.

Bölte, F. "Zu lakonischen Festen." *Rh. M.* 78 (1992): 124–32.

Bonnet, C. *Melqart: Cultes et mythes de l'Héraclès tyrien en Méditerranée.* Studia Phoenicia 8. Namur, 1988.

Bottini, A. *Principi guerrieri della Daunia.* Bari, 1982.

Bottini, A., and P. G. Guzzo. "Greci e indigeni in Magna Grecia dall'VIII al III sec. a.c." In *Popoli e Civiltà della Magna Grecia,* vol. 8, ed. C. Ampolo, A. Bottini, and P. G. Guzzo, pp. 11–390. Rome, 1986.

Bourriot, F. *Recherches sur le Génos: Etude d'histoire sociale athénienne.* Paris, 1974.

Bravo, B. "Sulân: Représailles et justice privée contre des étrangers dans les cités grecques." *Ann. Pisa,* ser. 3, 10 (1980): 675–987.

———. "Commerce et noblesse en Grèce archaïque." *DHA* 10 (1984): 99–160.

Breglia Pulci Doria, L. "Le Tesmoforie eretriese." In *Recherches sur les cultes,* vol. 1 (1979): pp. 53–63.

———. "Artemis Amarynthia." In *Société et colonisation eubéennes,* vol. 1 (1975): pp. 37–47.

———. "Demetra tra Eubea e Beozia e i suoi rapporti con Artemis." In *Recherches sur les cultes,* vol. 2 (1984), pp. 69–88.

Brelich, A. *Gli eroi greci.* Rome, 1958.

———. *Guerre, agoni, e culti nella grecia arcaica.* Bonn, 1961.

———. "La religione greca in Sicilia." *Kokalos* 10–11 (1964–65): 35–54.

———. *Paides e Partenoi.* Rome, 1969.

Brulé, P. *Les filles d'Athènes: La religion des filles à Athènes à l'époque classique.* Paris, 1987.

Calame, C. *Les chœurs de jeunes filles en Grèce ancienne.* Lausanne, 1977.

———. *Thésée et l'imaginaire athénien.* Lausanne, 1989.

Calligas, P. "Hero-Cult in Early Iron Age Greece." In Hägg, Marinatos, and Nordquist, *Early Greek Cult Practice* (1988), pp. 229–34.

Carter, J. "The Beginning of Narrative Art in the Geometric Period." *BSA* 67 (1972): 25–58.

Carter, J. B. "The Masks of Ortheia." *AJA* 91 (1987): 355–83.

———. "Masks and Poetry in Early Sparta." In Hägg, Marinatos, and Nordquist, *Early Greek Cult Practice* (1988), pp. 89–98.

———. "Sanctuaries in the Chora of Metaponto." In S. Alcock and R. Osborne, *Placing the Gods* (1994), pp. 161–98.

Cartledge, P. A. "Hoplites and Heroes: Sparta's Contributions to the Technique of Ancient Warfare." *JHS* 97 (1977): 11–27.

———. *Sparta and Laconia: A Regional History, 1300–366 B.C.* London, 1979.

Ciaceri, E. *Culti e miti nella storia di Sicilia.* Catane, 1911.

Ciccio, M. "Il santuario di Damia e Auxesia e il conflitto tra Atene ed Egina." In Sordi, *Santuari e politica* (1983), pp. 95–104.

Coldstream, J. N. "Hero Cults in the Age of Homer." *JHS* 96 (1976): 8–17.

———. *Geometric Greece.* Cambridge, 1977.

———. *Greek Geometric Pottery.* London, 1968.

Connor, W. R. "Tribes, Festivals, and Processions: Civic Ceremonial and Political Manipulation in Archaic Greece." *JHS* 107 (1987): 40–50.

Courbin, P. "La guerre en Grèce à haute époque." In Vernant, *Problèmes de la guerre* (1968), pp. 69–92.

Croon, H. *The Herdsman of the Dead: Studies on Some Cults, Myths, and Legends of the Ancient Greek Colonization Area.* Utrecht, 1952.

D'Agostino, B. "La civiltà del ferro nell'Italia meridionale e nella Sicilia." In *Popoli e Civiltà dell'Italia antica,* vol. 2 (1974), pp. 11–91.

———. "Grecs et indigènes sur la côte tyrrhénienne au VIIe siècle." *Ann. Econ. Soc. Civ.* 32 (1977): 3–20.

———. "Relations between Campania, Southern Etruria, and the Aegean in the Eighth Century B.C." In Descoeudres, *Greek Colonists* (1990), pp. 73–85.

Daverio-Rocchi, G. *Frontiera e confini nella Grecia antica.* Rome, 1988.

Démont, P. "Remarques sur les sens de *trepho.*" *REG* 91 (1978): 358–84.

Desborough, V. R. *The Late Myceneans and Their Successors.* Oxford, 1964.

———. *The Greek Dark Ages.* London, 1972.

Descoeudres, J.-P., ed. *Greek Colonists and Native Populations.* Proceedings of the First Australian Congress of Classical Archaeology. Canberra, 1990.

Detienne, M. "En Grèce archaïque, géométrie, politique, et société." *Ann. Econ. Soc. Civ.* 20 (1965): 425–41.

———. "La phalange: Problèmes et controverses." In Vernant, *Problèmes de la guerre* (1968), pp. 119–42.

———. *The Gardens of Adonis.* 1977.

———. "The Violence of Wellborn Ladies: Women in the Thesmophoria." In Detienne and Vernant, *The Cuisine of Sacrifice* (1989), pp. 129–47.

Detienne, M., and J.-P. Vernant. *Cunning Intelligence in Greek Culture and Society.* Hassocks, 1978.

———, eds. *The Cuisine of Sacrifice.* Chicago, 1989.

Dietrich, B. C. *Tradition in Greek Religion.* Berlin and New York, 1986.

Drerup, H. *Griechische Baukunst in Geometrischer Zeit.* Arch. Homerica 2, Kap. O, Göttingen, 1969.

Ducat, J. "La confédération béotienne à l'époque archaïque." *BCH* 97 (1973): 59–73.

———. "Kouros et Kolossos: Fonctions de la statue en Grèce archaïque." *BCH* 100 (1976): 239–51.

Dunbabin, T. J. *The Western Greeks.* Oxford, 1948.

Durand, J.-L. *Sacrifice et labour en Grèce ancienne.* Paris, 1986.

Edlund, I. E. M. *The Gods and the Places: Location and Function of Sanctuaries in the Countryside of Etruria and Magna Grecia.* Stockholm, 1987.

Ellinger, P. "Le gypse et la boue. 1, Sur les mythes de la guerre d'anéantissement." *Quaderni Urbinati* 29 (1978): 7–35.

———. "Les ruses de guerre d'Artémis." In *Recherches sur les cultes,* vol. 2 (1984), pp. 51–67.

———. *La légende nationale phocidienne: Artémis, les situations extrêmes et les récits de guerre d'anéantissement.* BCH Suppl. 27. Paris, 1993.

Etienne, R. "Autels et sacrifices." In Reverdin and Grange, *Le sanctuaire grec* (1992), pp. 291–319.

Etienne, R., and M.-T. Le Dinahet, eds. *L'espace sacrificiel dans les civilisations méditerranéennes de l'antiquité.* Paris, 1991.

Fågerström, K. *Greek Iron Age Architecture.* SIMA 81. Göteborg, 1988.

Farnell, L. R. *Greek Hero Cults and Ideas of Immortality.* Oxford, 1921.

Finley, M. I. *Early Greece: The Bronze and Archaic Ages.* London, 1970.

———. "The Ancient City from Fustel de Coulanges to Max Weber and Beyond." *Comparative Studies in Society and History* 19 (1977): 305–27.

———. *The World of Odysseus.* Rev. ed. London, 1977.

———, ed. *Problèmes de la terre en Grèce ancienne.* Paris, 1973.

Frontisi-Ducroux, F. *Dédale ou la mythologie de l'artisan.* Paris, 1975.

———. "Artémis bucolique." *RHR* 198 (1981): 29–56.

Gallet de Santerre, H. "Les statuettes de bronze mycéniennes au type dit du 'dieu Reshef' dans leur contexte égéen." *BCH* 111 (1987): 7–29.

Garlan, Y. "La défense du territoire à l'époque classique." In Finley, *Problèmes de la terre* (1973), pp. 149–60.

———. *Recherches de poliorcétique grecque.* Paris and Athens, 1974.

Gernet, L. *Anthropology of Ancient Greece.* Baltimore and London, 1981.

Giangiulio, M. "Greci e non-Greci in Sicilia alla luce dei culti e della leggenda di Eracle." In *Modes de contact* (1983), pp. 785–846.

Giannelli, G. *Culti e miti della Magna Grecia.* 2d ed. Florence, 1963.

Gnoli, G., and J.-P. Vernant, eds. *La mort, les morts dans les sociétés anciennes.* Cambridge, 1982.

Graham, A. J. "Religion, Women, and Greek Colonization." In *Religione e Città nel mondo antico: Atti 11, 1981,* pp. 293–314. Rome, 1984.

———. "Pre-colonial Contacts: Questions and Problems." In Descoeudres, *Greek Colonists* (1990), pp. 45–60.

Gras, M. *Trafics tyrrhéniens archaïques.* Rome, 1988.

Grecia, Italia, e Sicilia nell'VIII°–VII° sec. a.C. AS Atene 59 (1981): Boiotia, Eubea, Eubean colonies; 60 (1982); Megara, Peloponnesian cities, and their colonies; 61 (1983): Rhodes, Crete, Gela, Aegean, sanctuaries.

Greco, E., and M. Torelli. *Storia dell'urbanistica greca.* Rome, 1983.

Greenhalgh, P. *Early Greek Warfare.* Cambridge, 1973.

Guzzo, P. G. "Myths and Archaeology in South Italy." In Descoeudres, *Greek Colonists* (1990), pp. 131–41.

Hadzisteliou-Price, T. "Hero-Cult and Homer." *Historia* 22 (1973): 129–44.

———. *Kourotrophos: Cults and Representations of the Greek Nursing Deities.* Leiden, 1978.

Hägg, R. "Gifts to the heroes in Geometric and Archaic Greece." In *Gifts to the Gods,* ed. T. Linders and G. C. Nordquist. Boreas 15. Uppsala, 1987.

———, ed. *The Greek Renaissance of the Eighth Century B.C.: Tradition and Innovation.* Proceedings of the Second International Symposium at the Swedish Institute in Athens, 1981. Stockholm, 1983.

Hägg, R., and N. Marinatos, eds. *Sanctuaries and Cults in the Aegean Bronze Age.* Proceedings of the First International Symposium at the Swedish Institute in Athens, 1980. Stockholm, 1981.

———. *Greek Sanctuaries: New Approaches.* London, 1993.

Hägg, R., N. Marinatos, and G. C. Nordquist, eds. *Early Greek Cult Practice.* Proceedings of the Fifth International Symposium at the Swedish Institute in Athens, 1986. Stockholm, 1988.

Hermann, W. "Santuari di Magna Grecia." In *Atti Taranto 4, 1964* (1965), pp. 47–57.

Hiller, S. "Possible Historical Reasons for the Rediscovery of the Mycenean Past in the Age of Homer." In Hägg, *Greek Renaissance* (1983), pp. 9–14.

Houby-Nielsen, S. "Interactions between Chieftains and Citizens? Seventh Century B.C. Burial Customs in Athens." *Acta Hyperborea* 4 (1992): 343–74.

Huxley, G. L. *Early Sparta.* London, 1962.

Jeanmaire, H. *Couroi et courètes.* Paris, 1939.

Jeffery, L. H. *The Local Scripts of Archaic Greece.* Oxford, 1961.

Jost, M. *Sanctuaires et cultes d'Arcadie.* Paris, 1985.

———. "Sanctuaires ruraux et sanctuaires urbains en Arcadie." In Reverdin and Grange, *Le sanctuaire grec* (1992), pp. 205–45.

Jourdain-Annequin, C. "Etre un Grec en Sicile: Le mythe d'Héraclès." *Kokalos* 34–35 (1988–89): 143–66.

Kalpaxis, A. E. *Früarchaische Baukunst in Griechenland und Kleinasien.* Athens, 1976.

Khan, L. "Hermès, la frontière, et l'identité ambiguë. *Ktèma* 4 (1979): 201–11.

Kilian, K. "Myceneans Up to Date: Trends and Changes in Recent Research." In *Problems in Greek Prehistory,* ed. E. B. French and K. A. Wardle, pp. 115–52. Bristol, 1988.

Kilian-Dirlmeier, I. "Fremde Weihungen im griechischen Heiligtümern von 8. bis zum Begin des 7. Jahrhunderts." *JRGZM* 32 (1985): 215–54.

Kopcke, G., and I. Tokumaru, eds. *Greece between East and West. 10th–8th Centuries B.C.* Papers delivered at a meeting of the Institute of Fine Arts, New York University, 1990. Mainz, 1992.

Le Genière, J. de. "Contribution à l'étude des relations entre Grecs et indigènes sur la mer ionienne." *Mél. Rome* 82 (1970): 621–36.

———. "La colonisation grecque en Italie méridionale et en Sicile et l'acculturation des non-Grecs." *RA*, 1978, pp. 257–76.

———. "C'è un modello Amendolara?" *Ann. Pisa*, ser. 3, 8 (1978): 335–54.

———. "Entre Grecs et non-Grecs en Italie du Sud et en Sicile." In *Modes de contact* (1983), pp. 257–85.

———. "Contribution to a Typology of Ancient Settlements in Southern Italy." In *Crossroads of the Mediterranean*, ed. T. Hackens and R. R. Holloway, pp. 163–89. Louvain-la-Neuve and Providence, 1984.

———, ed. *Epeios et Philoctète en Italie.* Cahiers du Centre J. Bérard 16. Naples, 1991.

Le Dinahet, M. T. "Sanctuaires chtoniens de Sicile de l'époque archaïque à l'époque classique." In *Temples et sanctuaires*, ed. G. Roux, pp. 137–52. Lyons, 1985.

Legon, R. P. *Megara: The Political History of a Greek State to 366 B.C.*" Cornell, 1981.

Lepore, E. "Per una fenomenologia storica del rapporto città-territorio in Magna Grecia." In *Atti Taranto 7, 1967* (1968), pp. 9–66.

———. "Osservazioni sul rapporto tra fatti economici et fatti di colonizzazione in Occidente." *Dial. Arch.* 3 (1969): 175–88.

———. "Problemi dell'organizzazione dell *chora* coloniale." In Finley, *Problèmes de la terre* (1973), pp. 15–48.

Lepore, E., and A. Mele. "Pratiche rituali e culti eroici in Magna Grecia." In *Modes de contact* (1983), pp. 847–97.

Le Roy, C. "Mémoire et tradition." In *Aux origines de l'hellénisme: Mélanges H. Van Effenterre*, pp. 163–72. Paris, 1984.

Lévêque, P. "Continuité et innovations dans la religion grecque de la première moitié du premier millénaire." *PP* 28 (1973): 23–50.

Lévêque, P. and P. Vidal-Naquet. *Clisthène l'athénien: Essai sur la représentation de l'espace et du temps dans la pensée politique grecque.* Paris, 1964.

Lonis, R. *Guerre et religion en Grèce à l'époque classique.* Paris, 1979.

Loraux, N. "La belle mort spartiate." *Ktèma* 11 (1977): 105–21.

———. "L'autochtonie, une topique athénienne: Le mythe dans l'espace civique." *Ann. Econ. Soc. Civ.* 34 (1979): 1–25.

———. *The Invention of Athens: The Funeral Oration in the Classical City.* Cambridge, 1986.

————. *Children of Athena: Athenian Ideas about Citizenship and the Division between the Sexes.* Princeton, 1993.

Malkin, I. "Apollo Archegetes and Sicily" *Ann. Pisa* 16 (1986): 959–72.

————. *Religion and Colonization in Ancient Greece.* Leiden, 1987.

————. "What is an *Aphidryma?*" *Class. Ant.* 10 (1991): 77–96.

————. "Land Ownership, Territorial Possession, Hero Cults, and Scholarly Theory" In *Nomodeiktes: Greek Studies in Honor of Martin Ostwald,* ed. R. M. Rosen and J. Farrell, pp. 225–34. Ann Arbor, 1993.

Martin, R. *Recherches sur l'agora grecque.* Paris, 1951.

————. "Rapports entre les structures urbaines et les modes de division et d'exploitation du territoire." In Finley, *Problèmes de la terre* (1973), pp. 97–112.

————. *L'urbanisme en Grèce antique.* 2d ed. Paris, 1974.

————. "Introduction à l'étude du culte d'Héraclès en Sicile." In *Recherches sur les cultes,* vol. 1 (1979), pp. 11–18.

————. "L'espace civique, religieux et profane, dans les cités grecques de l'archaïsme à l'époque hellénistique." In *Architecture et société,* (1983), pp. 9–41.

Martorana, G. "Recenti studi storico-religiosi sulla Sicilia antica." *Kokalos* 22–23 (1976–77): 299–312.

Massenzio, M. "La festa di Artemis Triklaria e Dionysos Aisymnetes a Patrai." *Studi e Materiali di Storia delle Religioni* 39 (1968): 101–32.

Mazarakis-Ainian, A. "Contribution à l'étude de l'architecture religieuse grecque des Ages obscurs." *Ant. Cl.* 54 (1985): 5–48.

————. "Early Greek Temples: Their Origin and Function." In Hägg, Marinatos, and Nordquist, *Early Greek Cult Practice* (1988), pp. 105–19.

Mele, A. *Il commercio greco arcaico.* Cahiers du Centre J. Bérard 4. Naples, 1979.

Modes de contact et processus de transformation dans les sociétés anciennes. Actes du colloque de Cortone, 1981. Rome, 1983.

Moggi, M. "L'elemento indigeno nelle tradizioni letterarie sulle *ktiseis.*" In *Modes de contact* (1983), pp. 979–1004.

Montepaone, C. "Il mito di fondazione del rituale munichio in onore di Artemis." In *Recherches sur les cultes,* vol. 1 (1979), pp. 65–76.

————. "A proposito di Artemis Phakelitis." In *Recherches sur les cultes,* vol. 2 (1984), pp. 89–107.

Morgan, C. *Athletes and Oracles: The Transformation of Olympia and Delphi in the Eighth Century. B.C.* Cambridge, 1990.

————. "The Evolution of a 'Sacral Landscape': Isthmia, Perachora, and the Corinthian Gulf." In Alcock and Osborne, *Placing the Gods* (1994).

Morris, I. *Burial and Ancient Society: The Rise of the Greek City-State.* Cambridge, 1987.

————. "Tomb Cult and the 'Greek Renaissance': The Past in the Present in the Eighth Century B.C." *Antiquity* 62 (1988): 750–61.

————. "The Early Polis as City and State." In *City and Country in the Ancient World*, ed. J. Rich and A. Wallace-Hadrill. London, 1991.

Mossé, C. "La conception du citoyen dans la *Politique* d'Aristote." *Eirenè* 6 (1967): 17–22.

————. "Citoyens 'actifs' et citoyens 'passifs' dans la cité grecque." *REA* 81 (1979): 241–49.

————. "Ithaque ou la naissance de la cité." *Archeologia e Storia Antica* 2 (1980): 7–19.

Murray, O. "The Symposion as Social Organization." In Hägg, *Greek Renaissance* (1983), pp. 195–99.

————. "Omero e l'etnografia." *Kokalos* 34–35 (1988–89): 1–17.

————, ed. *Sympotica: A Symposium on the Symposion*. Oxford, 1990.

Murray, O., and S. Price, eds. *The Greek City from Homer to Alexander*. Oxford, 1990.

Mylonas, G. E. "The Cult of the Dead in Helladic Times." In *Studies Presented to D. M. Robinson*, ed. G. E. Mylonas and D. Raymond, 1: 64–105. St. Louis, 1951.

Nagy, G. *The Best of the Achaeans: Concepts of the Hero in Archaic Greek Poetry*. Baltimore, 1979.

Nenci, G. "Spazio civico, spazio religioso, e spazio catastale nella polis." *Ann. Pisa*, ser. 3, 9 (1979): 459–77.

Nenci, G., and S. Cataldi. "Strumenti e procedure nei rapporti tra Greci e indigeni." In *Modes de contact* (1983), pp. 581–606.

Neuen Forschungen in Griechischen Heiligtümern. Symposium in Olympia, 1974. DAI, Ath. Abt., 1976.

Nilsson, M. P. *Minoan-Mycenean Religion and Its Survivals*. Lund, 1950.

Orlandini, P. "Diffusione del culto di Demeter e Core in Sicilia." *Kokalos* 14–15 (1968–69): 334–38.

Osborne, R. *Classical Landscape with Figures: The Ancient Greek City and Its Countryside*. London, 1987.

Parisi-Presicce, C. "La funzione delle aree sacre nell'organizzazione primitiva delle colonie greche." *Arch. Cl.* 30 (1984): 19–132.

Pearson, L. "Myth and Archeology in Italy and Sicily." In *Studies in Greek Historians*, ed. R. Kagan, pp. 171–95. New Haven, 1975.

Pečirka, J. "The Crisis of the Athenian Polis in the Fourth Century B.C." *Eirenè* 14 (1976): 5–29.

Pembroke, S. "Le rôle des femmes dans la fondation des colonies grecques: Locres et Tarente." *Ann. Econ. Soc. Civ.* 25 (1970): 1240–70.

Petre, Z. "Premice ale formarii conceptuloi de *polis*." *St. Class.* 17 (1975): 7–15.

Pettersson, M. *Cults of Apollo at Sparta.* Stockholm, 1992.

Piccirilli, L. *Gli arbitrati interstatali greci.* Pisa, 1973.

————. *Megarika.* Pisa, 1975.

————. "Il santuario, la funzione guerriera della dea, la regalità: Il caso di Atena Chalkioikos." In Sordi, *Santuari e guerra* (1984), pp. 3–19.

Piérart, M. "Argos 'assoiffée' et Argos 'riche en cavales.'" In Piérart, *Polydipsion Argos* (1992), pp. 119–55.

————. "L'oracle d'Apollon à Argos." *Kernos* 3 (1990): 319–33.

————, ed. *Polydipsion Argos: Argos de la fin des palais mycéniens à la constitution de l'etat classique.* Acts du colloque de Fribourg, 1987. Athens, 1992.

Polignac, F. de. "Déméter et l'altérité dans la fondation." In *Tracés de fondation,* ed. M. Detienne, pp. 289–99. Louvain, 1990.

————. "Influence extérieure ou évolution interne? L'innovation culturelle en Grèce géométrique et archaïque." In Kopcke and Tokumaru, *Greece between East and West* (1992), pp. 114–27.

————. "Mediation, Competition, and Sovereignty." In Alcock and Osborne, *Placing the Gods* (1994), pp. 3–18.

————. "Cité et territoire: Un modèle argien?" In *Argos et l'Argolide: Topographie et urbanisme,* ed. A Pariente and G. Touchais. Ecole française d'Athènes, Recherches franco-hellénniques 3. Forthcoming.

————. "Sanctuaires et société en Attique géométrique et archaïque." In *Culture et société: L'avènement d'Athènes à l'époque archaïque,* ed. A. Verbanck-Piéard and D. Viviers. Brussels. Forthcoming.

Pourcet, J. "Le Latium protohistorique et archaïque." *Ant. Cl.* 47 (1978): 556–601.

Praudi, L. "L'Heraion di Platea e la festa dei Daidala." In Sordi, *Santuari e politica* (1983), pp. 82–94.

Pugliese-Caratelli, G. "Prime fasi della colonizzazione." In *Atti Taranto 1, 1961* (1962), pp. 136–49.

————. "Santuari extra murani in Magna Grecia." *PP* 17 (1962): 241–46.

————. "Culti e dottrine religiose in Magna Grecia." In *Atti Taranto 4, 1964* (1965), pp. 19–44.

Quiller, B. "The Dynamics of Homeric Society." *Symb. Oslo* 56 (1981): 109–55.

Recherches sur les cultes grecs et l'Occident. Vol. 1. Cahiers du Centre J. Bérard 5. Naples, 1979. Vol. 2. Cahiers du Centre J. Bérard 9. Naples, 1984.

Renfrew, C. *The Archaeology of Cult: The Sanctuary at Phylakopi.* BSA Suppl. 18. London, 1985.

Reverdin, O., and B. Grange, eds. *Le sanctuaire grec.* Entretiens sur l'Antiquité classique, Fondation Hardt, vol. 37. Geneva, 1992.

Ridgway, D. *L'alba della Magna Grecia*. Milan, 1984.

———. "The First Western Greeks and Their Neighbours, 1935–1985." In Descoeudres, *Greek Colonists* (1990), pp. 63–72.

———. "Demaratus and His Predecessors." In Kopcke and Tokumaru, *Greece between East and West* (1990), pp. 85–92.

Ringwood-Arnold, I. 'The Shield of Argos." *AJA* 21 (1937): 436–40.

Robert, F. "Dieux d'Homère et sanctuaires d'Asie Mineure." In *Mélanges L. S. Senghor: Langues, littérature, histoire anciennes*, pp. 417–27. Dakar, 1977.

Rohde, E. *Psyche: Seelencult und Unsterblichkeitsglaube der Griechen*. Vol. 1. Freiburg, 1894.

Rolley, C. "De la métallurgie aux sanctuaires: Rupture ou continuité?" In *Les trépieds à cuve clouée*, pp. 131–46. Ecole française d'Athènes, Fouilles de Delphes 5. Paris, 1979.

———. "Les grands sanctuaires panhelléniques." In Hägg, *Greek Renaissance* (1983), pp. 109–14.

———. "Argos, Corinthe, Athènes: Identité culturelle et modes de développement (IXᵉ–VIIIᵉ s.)." In Piérart, *Polydipsion Argos* (1992), pp. 37–54.

Roussel, D. *Tribu et cité*. Paris, 1976.

Rudhart, J., *Notions fondamentales de la pensée religieuse et actes constitutifs du culte dans la Grèce classique*. Geneva, 1958.

Rupp, D. W. "Reflections on the Development of Altars in the Eighth Century." In Hägg, *Greek Renaissance* (1983), pp. 101–7.

Rutkowsky, B. *Cult Places of the Aegean*. London, 1986.

Sarkady, J. "Outlines of the Development of the Greek Society (12th–8th Cent.)." *Acta Antiqua Academiae Scientiarum Hungaricae* 23 (1985): 107–25.

Sartre, M. "Aspects économiques et aspects religieux de la frontière dans les cités grecques." *Ktèma* 4 (1979): 213–24.

Schachter, A. *Cults of Boiotia*. 2 vols., London, 1981–86.

———. "Boiotia in the Sixth Century B.C." In *Boiotika*, ed. H. Beister and J. Buckler, pp. 73–86. Munich, 1989.

———. "Policy, Cult, and the Placing of Greek Sanctuaries." In Reverdin and Grange, *Le sanctuaire grec* (1992), pp. 37–51.

Schattner, T. G. *Griechische Hausmodelle*. AM-BH 15. Berlin, 1990.

Schefold, K. *Myth and Legend in Early Greek Art*. London, 1966.

———. "Poésie homérique et art archaïque." *RA*, 1972, pp. 9–22.

Schmitt Pantel, P. "Athéna Apatouria et la ceinture." *Ann. Econ. Soc. Civ.* 32 (1977): 1059–73.

———. "Sacrificial Meal and *Symposion*: Two Models of Civic Institutions in the Archaic City?" In *Sympotica* (1990), pp. 14–33.

————. *La cité au banquet: Histoire des repas publics dans les cités grecques.* Rome, 1992.

————, ed. *A History of Women.* Vol. 1, *From Ancient Goddesses to Christian Saints.* Harvard, 1992.

Schnapp-Gourbeillon, A. "Naissance de l'écriture et fonction poétique en Grèce archaïque." *Ann. Econ. Soc. Civ.* 37 (1982): 714–23.

Snodgrass, A. *Early Greek Armours and Weapons.* Edinburgh, 1964.

————. "Hoplite Reform and History." *JHS* 85 (1965): 110–22.

————. *The Dark Age of Greece.* Edinburgh, 1971.

————. "An Historical Homeric Society?" *JHS* 94 (1974): 114–25.

————. *Archaeology and the Rise of the Greek State.* Cambridge, 1977.

————. "Towards the Interpretation of the Geometric Figure Scenes." *AM* 95 (1980): 51–58.

————. *Archaic Greece: The Age of Experiment.* Cambridge, 1981.

————. "Les origines du culte des héros dans la Grèce antique." In Gnoli and Vernant, *La mort, les morts* (1982), pp. 107–19.

————. "The Greek Early Iron Age: A Reappraisal." *Dialogues d'Histoire Ancienne* 9 (1983): 73–86.

————. "The Archaeology of the Hero." *AION* 10 (1988): 19–26.

————. "The 'hoplite reform' revisited." *DHA* 19 (1993): 47–61.

Société et colonisation eubéennes. Vol. 1, *Contribution à l'étude de la société et de la colonisation eubéennes.* Cahiers du Centre J. Bérard 2. Naples, 1975. Vol. 2, *Nouvelle contribution à l'étude de la société et de la colonisation eubéennes.* Cahiers du Centre J. Bérard 6. Naples, 1981.

Sordi, M. "Il santuario di Olimpia e le guerre d'Elide." In Sordi, *Santuari e guerra* (1983), pp. 20–30.

Sordi, M., ed. *Santuari e politica nel mondo antico.* Contributi dell'Istituto di Storia Antica 9. Milan, 1983.

————. *Santuari e la guerra nel mondo classico.* Contributi dell'Istituto di Storia Antica 10. Milan, 1984.

Sourvinou-Inwood, C. "The Young Abductor of the Locrian Pinakes." *BICS* 20 (1973): 12–21.

————. "The Votum of 477/6 and the Foundation Legend of Locri Epizefirii." *CQ* 24 (1974): 186–98.

————. "The Boston Relief and the Religion of Locri Epizephyrii." *JHS* 94 (1974): 126–36.

————. Persephone and Aphrodite at Locri: A Model for Personality Definition in Greek Religion." *JHS* 98 (1978): 101–21.

————. *Studies in Girls' Transitions: Aspects of the Arkteia and Age Representation in Attic Iconography.* Athens, 1988.

Strøm, I. "Relations between Etruria and Campania around 700 B.C." In Descoeudres, *Greek Colonists* (1990), pp. 87–97.

————. "Evidence from the Sanctuaries." In Kopcke and Tokumaru, *Greece between East and West* (1992), pp. 46–60.

————. "Obeloi of Pre- or Proto-Monetary Value in the Greek Sanctuaries." In *Economics of Cult in the Ancient Greek World*, ed. T. Linders and B. Alroth, pp. 41–51. Boreas 21. Uppsala, 1992.

Torelli, M. "Greci e indigeni in Magna Grecia: Ideologia religiosa e rapporti de classe." *Studi Storici* 18 (1977): 45–61.

Tusa, V. "Greci e non-Greci in Sicilia." In *Modes de contact* (1983), pp. 299–314.

Vagnetti, L. "L'encadrement chronologique et les formes de la présence égéenne en Italie." In La Genière, *Epeios et Philoctète* (1991), pp. 9–18.

Vallet, G. "Métropoles et colonies." In *Atti Taranto 3, 1963* (1964), pp. 209–29.

————. "La cité et son territoire." In *Atti Taranto 7, 1967* (1968), pp. 67–142.

————. "Urbanisation et organisation de la chôra coloniale grecque en Grande-Grèce et en Sicile." In *Modes de contact* (1983), pp. 937–56.

Van Berchem, D. "Sanctuaires d'Hercule-Melquart." *Syria* 44 (1967): 76–108.

Van Compernolle, L. "Femmes indigènes et colonisateurs." In *Modes de contact* (1983), pp. 1033–49.

Vernant, J.-P. *Myth and Society in Ancient Greece.* New York, 1988.

————. *Myth and Thought among the Greeks.* London, 1983.

————. *Religion grecque, religions antiques.* Paris, 1976.

————. "Une divinité des marges: Artémis Orthia." In *Recherches sur les cultes*, vol. 2 (1984), pp. 13–27.

————. *L'individu, la mort, l'amour.* Paris, 1989.

————. *Mortals and Immortals: Collected Essays.* Princeton, 1991.

————, ed. *Problèmes de la guerre en Grèce ancienne.* 2d ed. Paris, 1985.

Vernant, J.-P., and P. Vidal-Naquet. *Myth and Tragedy in Ancient Greece.* New York, 1988.

Vian, F. *Les Origines de Thèbes: Cadmos et les Spartes.* Paris, 1963.

————. "La fonction guerrière dans la mythologie grecque." In Vernant, *Problèmes de la guerre* (1968), pp. 53–68.

Vidal-Naquet, P. "Valeurs religieuses et mythiques de la terre et du sacrifice dans l'Odyssée." In Finley, *Problèmes de la terre* (1973), pp. 269–92.

————. *The Black Hunter: Forms of Thought and Forms of Society in the Greek World.* Baltimore and London, 1986.

————. "The Black Hunter revisited." *PCPS* 212 (1986): 126–44.

Voyatsis, M. "Votive Riders Seated Side-Saddle at Early Greek Sanctuaries." *BSA* 87 (1992): 259–79.

Wasowicz, A. "Les lieux de culte des cités pontiques." In *Religione e Città nel mondo antico, Atti 11, 1981*, pp. 189–210. Rome, 1984.

Whitley, J. "Early States and Hero Cults: A Reappraisal." *JHS* 108 (1988): 173–82.

———. *Style and Society in Dark Age Greece*. Cambridge, 1991.

———. "Social diversity in Dark Age Greece." *BSA* 86 (1991): 341–65.

———. "The Monument that Stood before Marathon: Tomb Cult and Hero Cult in Archaic Attica." *AJA* 98 (1994): 213–30.

Zeithin, J. I. "The Argive Festival of Hera and Euripide's Electra." *TAPA* 101, (1970): 645–69.

References for Archaeological Sites

GREECE

Aegina

Sinn, U. "Der Kult des Aphaia auf Aegina." In Hägg, Marinatos, and Nordquist, *Early Greek Cult Practice* (1988), pp. 149–59.

Arcadia

TEGEA

Dugas, C. *Le Sanctuaire d'Alea Athéna à Tégée*. Paris, 1924.

Voyatzis, M. *The Early Sanctuary of Athena Alea at Tegea and Other Archaic Sanctuaries in Arcadia*. Göteborg, 1990.

Argolis

Courbin, P. *La céramique géométrique d'Argolide*. Paris, 1968.

Foley, A. *The Argolid, 800–600 B.C.: An Archaeological Survey*. Göteborg, 1988.

ARGOS

Archaeological Reports 14 (1978–79): Geometric tombs and cults.

Billot, M.-F. "Terres cuites architecturales d'Argos et d'Epidaure." *Hesperia* 59 (1990): 95–139.

Courbin, P. "Discoveries at Ancient Argos." *Archaeology* 9 (1956): 166–74.

———. "Tombe géométrique d'Argos." *BCH* 81 (1957): 322–86.

———. *Tombes géométriques d'Argos*. Vol. 1, Paris, 1974.

———. "Obéloi d'Argolide et d'ailleurs." In Hägg, *Greek Renaissance* (1983), pp. 149–56.

Croissant, F. "Note de topographie argienne." *BCH* 96 (1972): 137–54.

Des Courtils, J. "Note de topographie argienne." *BCH* 105 (1981): 607–10.

Deshayes, J. *Les fouilles de la Deiras*. Paris, 1966.

Hägg, R. *Die Gräber des Argolis in submykenischer, protogeometrischer, und geometrischer Zeit*. Uppsala, 1974.

———. "Burial Customs and Social Differentiation in Eighth-Century Argos." In Hägg, *Greek Renaissance* (1983), pp. 27–31.

Morgan, C., and T. Whitelaw. "Pots and Politics: Ceramic Evidence for the Rise of the Argive State." *AJA* 95 (1991): 79–108.

Pariente, A. "Le monument argien des 'Sept contre Thèbes.'" In Piérart, *Polydipsion Argos* (1992), pp. 195–229.

Vollgraff, W. *Le sanctuaire d'Apollon Pythéen à Argos*. Etudes peloponnésiennes 1. Paris, 1966.

ASINE

Hägg, R. "Funerary Meals in the Geometric Necropolis at Asine?" In Hägg, *Greek Renaissance* (1983), pp. 189–93.

Wells, B. "Apollo at Asine." In *Peloponnesiaka* 13 (1987–88): 349–52.

———. "The Asine Sima." *Hesperia* 59 (1990): 157–61.

HALIEIS

Bergquist, B. "Primary or Secondary Temple Function: The Case of Halieis." *Op. Ath.* 18, no 2. (1990): 23–27.

Jameson, M. H., "Excavations at Porto Cheli and Vicinity." *Hesperia* 38 (1969): 311–43; *Arch. Delt., Chronika* 26 (1971): 114–19; 27 (1972): 233–36.

HERAION / PROSYMNA

Amandry, P. "Sur les concours argiens." In *Études argiennes*, pp. 211–53. BCH Suppl. 6. Paris, 1980.

Antonaccio, C. "Terraces, Tombs, and the Early Argive Heraion." *Hesperia* 61 (1992): 85–105.

Blegen, C. W. *Prosymna: The Helladic Settlement Preceding the Argive Heraeum.* Cambridge, 1937.

———. "Remains of Post-Mycenean Deposits in Chamber Tombs." *Arch. Eph.*, 1937, pp. 377–90.

———. "Remains of Post-Mycenean Date." *AJA* 43 (1939): 410–44.

Caskey, J., and P. Amandry. "Investigations at the Heraion of Argos." *Hesperia* 21 (1952): 165–274.

Plommer, H. "The Old Platform of the Argive Heraeum." *JHS* 104 (1984): 183–84.

Strøm, I. "The Early Sanctuary of the Argive Heraion and Its External Relations." *Acta Arch.* 59 (1988): 173–203.

Waldstein, C. *The Argive Heraeum.* London, 1902–1905.

Wright, J. "The Old Temple Terrace at the Argive Heraion and the Early Cult of Hera in Argolid." *JHS* 102 (1982): 186–201.

MT KYNORTION / EPIDAUROS

Lambrinoudakis, V. "Remains of the Mycenean Period in the Sanctuary of Apollo Maleatas." In Hägg and Marinatos, *Sanctuaries and Cults* (1981), pp. 59–65.

———. "Staatskult und Geschichte von Epidauros." *Archaiognosia* 1 (1980): 39–63.

MYCENAE

Cook, J. M. "The Cult of Agamemnon at Mycenae." In *Géras A. Keramoupoullou*, pp. 112–18. Athens, 1953.

———. "Mycenae, 1939–1952: The Agamemnoneion." *BSA* 48 (1953): 30.

Wace, A. J. B. "The Epano Phono Tholos Thomb." *BSA* 48 (1953): 63.

NEMEA

Miller, S. G. "Excavations at Nemea." *Hesperia* 46 (1977): 1–26; 47 (1978): 58–88; 48 (1979): 73–103; 49 (1980): 178–201; 50 (1981): 45–67; 52 (1983): 70–95; 53 (1984): 171–92.

PHLIUS

Biers, W. "Excavations at Phlias: The Votive Deposit." *Hesperia* 40 (1971): 397–423 (hero cult).

Attica

ACHARNES

Lolling, H. G. *Das Kuppelgrab bei Menidi.* Athens, 1898.

Wolters, P. "Vasen aus Menidi." *Jd. I.* 13 (1898): 13–28; 14 (1899): 103–35.

ATHENS

Burr, D. "A Geometric House and Proto-Attic Deposit." *Hesperia* 2 (1933): 542–640.

Humphreys, S. C. "Family Tombs and Tomb Cult in Ancient Athens." *JHS* 100 (1980): 96–126.

Immerwahr, S. A. *Athenian Agora XIII: The Neolithic and Bronze Ages.* 1971.

Kübler, K. *Kerameikos V: Die Nekropole des 10. bis 8. Jahrhunderts.* Berlin, 1954.

———. *Kerameikos VI: Die Nekropole des späten 8, bis frühen 6. Jahrhunderts.* 2 vols. Berlin, 1959 and 1970.

Lalonde, G. V. "A Fifth-Century Hieron Southwest of the Athenian Agora." *Hesperia* 37 (1968): 123–33.

Oikonomides, A. N. *The Two Agoras in Ancient Athens.* Chicago, 1964.

Smithson, E. L. "The Grave of a Rich Athenian Lady ca. 850 B.C." *Hesperia* 37 (1968): 77–116.

Thompson, H. A. "Agora: A Favissa in the North Central Part." *Hesperia* 27 (1958): 148–53.

———. "Activity in the Athenian Agora, 1960–1965." *Hesperia* 35 (1966): 37–54.

———. "Activity in the Athenian Agora, 1966–1967." *Hesperia* 37 (1968): 58–60.

Thompson, H. A., and R. E. Wycherley. *Athenian Agora: A Guide to the Excavations.* Princeton, 1972.

Touloupa, E. "Bronzebleche von der Akropolis in Athens." *AM* 87 (1972): 57–72.

Young, R. S. *Late Geometric Graves and a Seventh-Century Well.* Hesperia Suppl. 2. Princeton, 1939.

———. "Sepulturae intra urbem." *Hesperia* 20 (1951): 187–252.

Academy

BCH, Chronique 83 (1959): 576–78; 86 (1962): 654; 88 (1964): 682.

BRAURON

Kahil, L. G. "Autour de l'Artémis attique." *Ant. K.* 8 (1965): 20–33.

———. "L'Artémis de Brauron: Rites et mystères." *Ant. K.* 20 (1977): 86–98.

Kontis, J. C. "Artemis Brauronia." *Arch. Delt.* 22 (1967): 156–206.

Travlos, J. "Tres naoi tou Artemidos." In *Neuen Forschungen* (1976), pp. 197–205.

ELEUSIS

Boardman, J. "Heracles, Peisistratos, and Eleusis." *JHS* 95 (1975): 1–12.

Darcque, P. "Les vestiges mycéniens découverts sous le télestérion d'Eleusis." *BCH* 105 (1981): 593–605.

Mylonas, G. "Anaskaphe nekrotapheiou Eleusinos." *Prakt.*, 1954, pp. 52–65.

———. *Eleusis and the Eleusinian Mysteries.* Princeton, 1961.

HYMETTOS

Langdon, K. M. *The Sanctuary of Zeus on Mount Hymettos.* Hesperia Suppl. 16. Princeton, 1976.

MOUNYCHIA

Palaiokrasia, L. "Neue Befunde aus dem Heiligtum des Artemis Munichia." *AM* 104 (1989): 1–40.

SOUNION

Abramson, H. "A Hero Shrine for Phrontis at Sounion?" *CSCA* 12 (1979): 1–19.

THORICUS

Mussche, H. F. "Recent Excavations at Thoricos." *Acta Classica* 13 (1970): 125–36.

Mussche, H. F., F. Bingen, and J. Servais. "Thoricos: Rapport préliminaire." *Ant. Cl.* 34 (1965): 5–46

Boeotia

Munn, M. H. "New Light on Panacton and the Attic-Boiotian Frontier." In *Boiotika*, ed. H. Beister and J. Buckler, pp. 231–44. Munich, 1989.

CABIRION

Schmaltz, B. *Metallfiguren aus dem Kabirionheiligtum bei Theben*. Berlin, 1985.

HALIARTES / ONCHESTOS

BCH, Chronique 98 (1974): 643–44.

Spyropoulos, T. G. "Some Boiotian Discoveries." *Teiresias* 3 (1973): 2–7.

Roesch, P. "Onchestos, capitale de l'état fédéral béotien." *Cahiers d'Histoire* 22 (1977): 82–83.

PTOION

Ducat, J. "Le Ptoion et l'histoire de la Béotie à l'époque archaique." *REG* 77 (1964): 283–90.

———. *Les kouroi du Ptoon: Le sanctuaire d'Apollon Ptoieus à l'époque archaique*. Paris, 1972.

Guillon, P. *Les trépieds du Ptoon*. Paris, 1943.

THEBES

Keramopoullos, A. "Thebaika." *Arch. Delt.* 3 (1917): 1–503.

Spyropoulos, T. G. "To archeion tou mykenaikou anactorou ton thebon." *AAA* 3 (1970): 322–27.

———. "Mykenaikos Basilikos thalamotos taphos en Thebais." *AAA* 4 (1971): 161–64.

Symeneoglu, S. *The Topography of Thebes*. Princeton, 1985.

Corinthia

CORINTH

Broneer, O. "Hero Cults in the Corinthian Agora." *Hesperia* 11 (1942): 125–61.

Butter, J. "The Last Myceneans at Corinth." *Hesperia* 48 (1979): 348–92.

Morgan, C. "Corinth, the Corinthian Gulf, and Western Greece during the Eighth Century B.C." *BSA* 83 (1988): 313–38.

Robinson, H. S. "Excavations: Temple Hill, 1968–1972." *Hesperia* 45 (1976): 203–39.

Roebuck, C. "Some Aspects of Urbanization in Corinth." *Hesperia* 41 (1972): 96–127.

Stroud, R., and N. Bookidis. *Demeter and Persephone in Ancient Corinth*. Princeton, 1987.

Williams, C. K., and J. E. Fisher. "Forum Area." *Hesperia* 41 (1972): 143–184; 42 (1973): 1–44; 43 (1974): 1–33; 47 (1978): 1–39.
———. "Corinth, Temple Hill." In *Neuen Forschungen* (1976), p. 239.

ISTHMIA

Broneer, O. "The Temple of Poseidon at Isthmia." In *Mélanges Charisterion eis A. K. Orlandos*, pp. 61–84. Athens, 1970.
———. "The Isthmian Sanctuary of Poseidon." In *Neuen Forschungen* (1976), pp. 39–62.
Gebhard, E. R., and F. P. Hemans. "Excavations at Isthmia, 1989." *Hesperia* 61 (1992): 1–23.

PERACHORA

Dunbabin, T. J. "The Oracle of Hera Akraia at Perachora." *BSA* 46 (1951): 61–71.
Payne, H. *The Sanctuary of Hera Akraia and Limenaia*. Oxford, 1940–62.
Sinn, U. "Das Heraion von Perachora: Eine sakrale Schutzzone in der korintische Peraia." *AM* 105 (1990): 53–116.
Tomlinson, R. "The Upper Terraces at Perachora." *BSA* 72 (1977): 197–202.
———. "Perachora." In Reverdin and Grange, *Le sanctuaire grec* (1992), pp. 321–51.

SOLYGAEA

Verdelis, N. M. "A Sanctuary at Solygeia." *Archaeology* 15 (1962): 184–92.

Elis

Sinn, U. "Das Heiligtum der Artemis Limnatis bei Kombothekra." *AM* 96 (1981): 25–71.

OLYMPIA

Heimeyer, W.-D. *Frühe Olympische Bronzefiguren: Die Tiervotive*. Deutsche Archäologische Institute, Olympische Forschungen 12. Athens, 1979.
Hermann, H. V. *Olympia: Heiligtum und Weltkampfstatte*. Munich, 1972.
Kyrieleis, H. "Neue Augsgrabungen in Olympia." In *Proceedings of an International Symposium on the Olympic Games*, ed. W. Coulson and H. Kyrieleis, pp. 19–24. Athens, 1992.
Maas, M. *Die geometrischen Dreifüsse von Olympia*. Deutsche Archäologische Institute, Olympische Forschungen 10. Athens, 1978.

————. "Die geometrischen Dreifüsse von Olympia." *Ant. K.* 24 (1981): 6–20.

Philipp, H. *Bronzeschmuck aus Olympia*. Deutsche Archäologische Institute, Olympische Forschungen 13. Athens, 1981.

Etolia

THERMOS

Bundgaard, J. A. "A propos de la date de la peristasis du Mégaron B à Thermos." *BCH* 70 (1946): 51–57.

Euboea

Auberson, P. "Chalcis, Lefkandi, Érétrie au VIIIe siècle." In *Société et colonisation eubéennes*, vol. 1 (1975), pp. 9–15.

AMARYNTHOS

Knoepfler, D. "Carystos et les Artemisia d'Amarynthos." *BCH* 96 (1972): 283–301.

ERETRIA

Auberson, P. *Le temple d'Apollon Daphnéphoros: Architecture*. Vol. 1 of *Erétria: Fouilles et recherches*, Berne, 1968.

————. "La reconstitution du Daphnéphorion d'Érétrie." *Ant. K.* 17 (1974): 60–68.

Bérard, C. "Notes sur les fouilles au sud de l'hérôon." *Ant. K.* 12 (1969): 74–79.

————. *L'hérôon à la porte de l'Ouest*. Vol. 3 of *Eretria: Fouilles et recherches*. Berne, 1970.

————. "Architecture érétrienne et mythologie delphique." *Ant. K.* 14 (1971): 59–73.

————. "Le sceptre du prince." *Mus. Helv.* 29 (1972): 219–27.

————. "Topographie et urbanisme de l'Erétrie archaïque: L'hérôon." In *Erétria: Fouilles et recherches*, 6:89–94. Berne, 1978.

Bérard, C., and A. Altherr-Charon. "Érétrie: L'organisation de l'espace et la formation d'une cité grecque." In *L'Archéologie aujourd'hui*, ed. A. Schnapp, pp. 229–49. Paris, 1981.

Martin, R. "Erétrie: Problèmes de topographie et d'évolution urbaine." In *Société et colonisation eubéennes*, vol. 1 (1975), pp. 48–52.

Mazarakis Ainian, A. "Geometric Eretria." *Ant. K.* 30 (1987): 3–24.

Metzger, J. R. *Das Thesmophorion von Eretria*. Vol. 7 of *Erétria: Fouilles et recherches*. Berne, 1985.

Schefold, K., and D. Knoepfler. "Forschungen in Eretria." *Ant. K.* 19 (1976): 51–58.

Themelis, P. G. "An Eighth-Century Goldsmith's Workshop at Eretria." In Hägg, *Greek Renaissance* (1983), pp. 157–65.

LEFKANDI

Popham, M. R., L. H. Sackett, and P. G. Themelis. *Lefkandi I: The Iron Age. The Settlement and Cemeteries.* London, 1979–80.

Popham, M. R., P. G. Calligas, and L. H. Sackett, eds. *Lefkandi II: The Protogeometric Building at Toumba.* Vol. 1, *The pottery,* by R. W. Catling and I. S. Lemos. London, 1990.

Popham, M. R., E. Touloupa, and L. H. Sackett. "Further Excavations of the Toumba Cemetery, 1981." *BSA* 77 (1982): 213–48.

———. "The Hero of Lefkandi." *Antiquity* 56 (1982): 169–74.

Ithaca

Benton, S. "Excavations at Ithaca III." *BSA* 35 (1934–35): 45–73.

Laconia

AMYCLAE

Buschor, E., and W. Von Massow. "Von Amyclaion." *AM* 52 (1927): 1–85.

KYNOURIA

Christien, J. "De Sparte à la côte est du Péloponnèse." In Piérart, *Polydipsion Argos* (1992): pp. 157–72.

Faklaris, P. B. *Archaia Kynouria.* Thessaloníki, 1985.

SPARTA

Boardman, J. "Artemis Orthia and Chronology." *BSA* 58 (1963): 1–7.

Coulson, W. D. E. "The Dark Age Pottery of Sparta." *BSA* 80 (1985): 29–84.

Dawkins, R. M. "Artemis Orthia: History of the Sanctuary." *BSA* 16 (1909–10): 18–53.

———. *The Sanctuary of Artemis Orthia at Sparta.* London, 1929.

Dickins, G. "The Hieron of Athena Chalkioikos." *BSA* 13 (1906–7): 137–54.

Lamb, W. "Notes on Bronzes from the Acropolis." *BSA* (1926–27): 82–95.

———. "Notes on Bronzes from the Orthia Site." *BSA* (1926–27): 96–106.

Wace, A. J. B. "The Herôon." *BSA* 12 (1905–6): 288–94.

Woodward, A. M. "The Acropolis." *BSA* (1926–27): 37–48.

THERAPNE

Catling, H. W. "Excavations at the Menelaion." *AR*, 1976–77, pp. 24–42; 1980–81, pp. 16–19.
Dawkins, R. M. "A Mycenean City near the Menelaion." *BSA* 16 (1909–10): 4–11.
Wace, A. J. B., et al. "The Menelaion." *BSA* 15 (1908–09): 108–57.

Megara

"Chronique d'une journée mégarienne." *MEFRA* 95 (1983–84): 617–50.
Muller, C. "Megarika." *BCH* 104 (1980): 83–92; 105 (1981): 203–25; 106 (1982): 379–407; 107 (1983): 157–79.
Rigsby, K. J. "Megara and Tripodiscus." *GRBS* 28 (1987): 93–102.

Messenia

Fagerström, K., "Finds, Function, and Plan: A Contribution to the Interpretation of Iron Age Nichoria in Messenia." *Op. Ath.* 17 (1988): 33–50.
Macdonald, W. A., ed. *Excavations at Nichoria*. Vol. 3, *Dark Ages and Byzantine Occupations*. Minneapolis, 1983.
Mazarakis Ainian, A. "Nichoria in the South-Western Peloponnese: Units IV-1 and IV-5 Reconsidered," *Op. Ath.* 19 (1992): 75–84.
Pantelides, M. "Taphoi tes Pylou." *AAA* 3, (1970): 115–36.

Phocis
DELPHI

Daux, G. "Fouilles de Delphes." *BCH* 87 (1963): 191f. (hērōon of Phylakos).
Pouilloux, J. *La région nord du sanctuaire*. Ecole française d'Athènes, Fouilles de Delphes 2: Topographie et architecture. Paris, 1960.
Rolley, C. *Les trépieds à cuve clouée*. Ecole française d'Athènes, Fouilles de Delphes 5, no. 3: Monuments figurés. Paris, 1979.

HYAMPOLIS / KALAPODI

Ellinger, P. "Hyampolis et le sanctuaire d'Artémis Elaphebolos dans l'histoire, la légende, et l'espace de la Phocide." *AA* 42 (1987): 88–99.
Felsch, R. C. S. "Mykenischer Kult im Heiligtum bei Kalapodi?" In Hägg and Marinatos, *Sanctuaries and Cults* (1981), pp. 81–89.
———. "Zur Chronologie und zum Stil geometrischer Bronzen aus Kalapodi." In Hägg, *Greek Renaissance* (1983), pp. 123–29.
———. "Tempel und Altäre im Heiligtum der Artemis Elaphebolos von Hyampolis." In Etienne and Le Dinahet, *L'espace sacrificiel* (1991), pp. 85–91.

Felsch, R. C. S., et al. "Apollon und Artemis oder Artemis und Apollon?" *AA* 35 (1980): 38–118.

——. "Kalapodi: Bericht über di Grabungen im heiligtum der Artemis Elaphebolos und des Apollon von Hyampolis." *AA* 42 (1987): 1–99.

Thessaly

Kilian, K. *Fibeln in Thessalien vonder mykenischen bis zu archaischen Zeit.* *PBF* 14, no. 2, (1975).

——. "Weihungen aus Eisen und Eisenverarbeitung im Heiligtum zu Philia." In Hägg, *Greek Renaissance* (1983), pp. 131–46.

LARISSA

Helly, B. "A Larissa, bouleversements et remise en ordre de sanctuaires." *Mnemosyne* 23 (1970): 250–96.

PHERAI

Bequignon, Y. *Recherches archéologiques à Phères de Thessalie.* Paris, 1937.

CRETE

Demagne, P. *La Crète dédalique.* Paris, 1947.

Faure, P. *Fonctions des cavernes crétoises.* Paris, 1953.

Levi, D. "Caratteri e continuità del culto cretese sulle vette montane." *Parola del Passato* 181 (1978): 294–313.

Van Effenterre, H. "Querelles crétoises." *REA* 44 (1942): 31–51.

AXOS

Rizza, G. "Le terrecotte di Axos." *AS Atene* 45–46, n.s. 29–30 (1967–68): 211–302.

CNOSSOS

Brock, J. K. *Fortetsa: Early Greek Tombs near Knossos.* Cambridge, 1957.

Coldstream, J. N. *Knossos: The Sanctuary of Demeter.* London, 1973.

Callaghan, P. J. "Excavations at a Shrine of Glaukos, Cnossos." *BSA* 73 (1978): 1–30.

DREROS

Marinatos, S. "Le temple géométrique de Dréros." *BCH* 70 (1936): 214–85.

GORTYN

Cassimatis, H. "Figurines dédaliques de Gortyne: Essai de typologie." *BCH* 106 (1982): 447–64.

Rizza, G., and V. Santa Maria Scrinari. *Il santuario sull' acropoli di Gortina.* Vol. 1. Rome, 1968.

AEGEAN

CHIOS

Boardman, J. *Excavations in Chios: Greek Emporio.* London, 1967.

DELOS

Courbin, P. "Le temple archaïque de Délos." *BCH* 111 (1987): 63–78.
Gallet de Santerre, H. *Délos primitive et archaïque.* Paris, 1956.
Poursat, J.-C. "Ivoires de l'Artémision: Chypre et Délos." *BCH* 93 (1973): 415–25.
Robert, F. "Le sanctuaire de l'archégète Anios à Délos." *RA*, 1953, pp. 8–40.
Rolley, C. "Bronzes géométriques et orientaux." In *Etudes déliennes,* pp. 491–524. *BCH* Suppl. 1. Paris, 1973.
Roux, G. "Le vrai temple d'Apollon à Délos." *REG* 90 (1977): xxii–xxiv.
Vatin, C. "Théke d'Opis et Argè." *BCH* 85 (1965): 225–30.

LESBOS

Robert, L. "Recherches épigraphiques." *REA* 62 (1960): 300–311.

NAXOS

Lambrinoudakis, V. K. "Veneration of Ancestors in Geometric Naxos." In Hägg, Marinatos, and Nordquist, *Early Greek Cult Practice* (1988), pp. 235–46.
Lambrinoudakis, V. K., and G. Gruben. "Das Neuendeckte Heiligtum von Iria aus Naxos." *AA* 42 (1987): 569–621.

PAROS

Kontoleon, N. "Neai epigrafai peri tou Archilochou ek Parou." *Arch. Ep.* (1952): 32–95.
Schilardi, D. H. "Paros II." *JFA* 2 (1975): 83–96.
———. "The Decline of the Geometric Settlement of Koukounaries at Paros." In Hägg, *Greek Renaissance* (1983), pp. 173–83.
———. "The temple of Athena at Koukounaries. Observations on the cult of Athena on Paros." In Hägg, Marinatos, and Nordquist, *Early Greek Cult Practice* (1988), pp. 41–48.

RHODES

Blinkenberg, C. "La déesse de Lindos." *Arch. RW* 28 (1930–31): 154–66.

SAMOS

Kron, U. "Kultmahle im Heraion von Samos archaischer Zeit." In Hägg, Marinatos, and Nordquist, *Early Greek Cult Practice* (1988) 135–48.

Walter, H. *Das Heraion von Samos*. Munich, 1976.

THASOS

Bergquist, B. *Heracles on Thasos*. Uppsala, 1973.

Bernard, P. "Céramiques de la première moitié du VIIᵉ siècle à Thasos." *BCH* 88 (1964): 77–146.

Des Courtils, J., and A. Pariente. "Problèmes topographiques et religieux à l'Héracléion de Thasos." In Etienne and Le Dinahet, *L'espace sacrificiel* (1991), pp. 67–73.

Graham, A. J. "The Foundation of Thasos." *BSA* 73 (1978): 61–98.

Grandjean. Y. *Recherches sur l'habitat thasien*. BCH Suppl. 12. Paris, 1988.

Launey, M. *Le sanctuaire et le culte d'Héraclès à Thasos*. Ecole française d'Athènes, Etudes thasiennes 1. Athens, 1944.

Martin, R. *L'agora*. Ecole française d'Athènes, Etudes thasiennes 6. Athens, 1959.

———. "Thasos: Quelques problèmes de structure urbaine." *CRAI* (1978): 82–197.

Picard, C. *Les portes sculptées à images divines*. Ecole française d'Athènes, Etudes thasiennes 7. Athens, 1962.

Pouilloux, J. *Recherches sur l'histoire et les cultes de Thasos*. Ecole française d'Athènes, Etudes thasiennes 3. Athens, 1954.

———. "Glaucos, fils de Leptine, Parien." *BCH* 79 (1955): 75–86.

———. "L'Héraclès thasien." *REA* 76 (1974): 305–16.

Rolley, C. "Le sanctuaire des dieux pâtrooi et le Thesmophorion de Thasos." *BCH* 89 (1965): 44–83.

Salviat, F. "La colonisation grecque dans la mer Égée: Céramique parienne orientalisante, céramiques précolonials à Thasos." In *Actes du 8ᵉ Congrès International d'Archéologie Classique*, pp. 299–303. Paris, 1965.

———. "Demeter Eleusinie Patroie." In *Thasiaca*, pp. 407–10. BCH Suppl. 5. Paris, 1979.

Salviat, F., and N. Weill. "The Sanctuary of Artemis in Thasos." *Archaeology* 13 (1960): 97–104.

EASTERN GREECE

Sakellariou, M. B. *La colonisation grecque en Asie Mineure*. Athens, 1958.

CLAZOMENAI

La Genière, J. de. "Recherches récentes à Clazomènes (mission franco-turque)." *Revue des archéologues et historiens d'art de Louvain* 15 (1982): 82–96.

EPHESOS / CLAROS

Bammer, A. "Spüren der Phöniker im Artemision von Ephesos." *Anat. St.* 35 (1985): 103–8.

———. "Neue weibliche Statuetten aus dem Artemision von Ephesos." *ÖJh.* 56 (1985): 39–58.

———. "Gold und Elfenbein von einer Kultbasis in Ephesos." *ÖJh.* 58 (1988): 1–23.

———. *Ephesos: Stadt an Fluss und Meer.* Vienna, 1988.

———. "Les sanctuaires des VIIIe et VIIe siècles à l'Artémision d'Ephèse." *RA,* 1991, pp. 63–83.

———. "Multikulturelle Aspekte der frühen Kunst im Artemision von Ephesos." *ÖJh.* 61 (1991–92): 18–54.

Bammer, A., F. Brein, and P. Wolff. "Das Tieropfer am Artemisionaltar von Ephesos." In *Festschrift F. K. Dörner: Studien zur Religion und Kultur Kleinasiens,* edited by S. Sahin, E. Schwertheim, and J. Wagner, 1:107–57. Leiden, 1978.

Hogarth, D. G. *The Archaic Artemision.* London, 1908.

La Genière, J. de, ed. *Cahiers de Claros.* Vol. 1. Paris, 1992.

Picard, C. *Ephese et Claros.* Paris, 1922.

MILETUS / DIDYMA

Tuchelt, K. "Tempel-Heiligtum-Siedlung: Probleme zur topographie von Didyma." In *Neuen Forschungen* (1976), pp. 207–18.

———. "Der Heiligtümer von Didyma unf ihre Grundzüge." *RA,* 1991, pp. 85–98.

CYPRUS

Beer, C. "Quelques aspects des contacts de Chypre aux VIIIe et VIIe siècles avant n.e." *Opus* 3 (1984): 253–71.

Karageorghis, V. *Excavations at the Necropolis of Salamis.* Nicosia, 1967 (Vol. 1); 1973–74 (vol. 3); 1978 (vol. 5).

———, ed. *Archaeology in Cyprus, 1960–1985.* Nicosia, 1985.

Rupp, D. W. "Vive le Roi: The emergence of the State in Iron Age Cyprus." In *Western Cyprus: Connections,* ed. D. W. Rupp. SIMA 77. Göteborg, 1987.

Snodgrass, A. *Cyprus and Early Greek History.* Nicosia, 1988.

AFRICA

CYRENE

Chamoux, F. *Cyrène sous la monarchie des Battiades.* Paris, 1953.

Stucchi, S. *L'agora di Cirene.* Vol. 1. Rome, 1965.

White, D. *The Extramural Sanctuary of Demeter and Persephone in Cyrene.* Philadelphia, 1984.

WESTERN GREECE

CROTON

Atti Taranto 23, 1983: Crotone. 1984.

La Genière, J. de. "Au pays de Philotecte: La montagne des Murge." In *La Genière Epeios et Philoctète* (1991), pp. 75–116.

Lattanzi, E. "Recenti scoperte nei santuari di Hera Lacinia a Crotone e di Apollo Aleo a Ciro Marina." In *La Genière, Epeios et Philoctète* (1991), pp. 67–73.

Musti, D. "Lo sviluppo del mito di Filotette da Crotona a Sibari." In *La Genière, Epeios et Philoctète* (1991), pp. 21–35.

Sabbione, C. "L'insediamento delle Murge di Strongoli." In *Per un identità culturale dei Brettii,* ed. P. Poccetti, pp. 195–200. Naples, 1988.

CUMAE-PITHECUSSAE

Albore-Livadie, C. "Remarques sur un groupe de tombes de Cumes." In *Société et colonisation eubéennes,* vol. 1 (1975), pp. 53–57.

Buchner, G. *Pithekoussai.* Accad. Lincei, Mon. Ant. Rome, 1993.

D'Agostino, B. "Ideologia e rituale funerario in Campania nei secoli VIII e VII." In *Société et colonisation eubéennes,* vol. 1 (1975), pp. 107–10.

Johannowsky, W. "Problemi relativi a Cuma arcaica." In *Société et colonisation eubéennes,* vol. 1 (1975), pp. 98–105.

Ridgway, D. "The Foundation of Pithekoussai." In *Société et colonisation eubéennes,* vol. 2 (1981), pp. 45–56.

LOCRI

Atti Taranto 16, 1976: Locri Epizefirii. 1977.

De Franciscis, A. *Stato e società in Locri Epizeffirii: L'archivio dell'Olympieion locrese.* Naples, 1972.

Gigante, M. "Le tavole di Locri." *PP* 31 (1976): 417–32.

Musti, D. "Città e santuario a Locri Epizefirii." *PP* 29 (1974): 1–21.

———. *Le tavole di Locri.* Rome, 1979.

Zancani-Montuoro, P. "Il tempio de Persefone a Locri." *Accad. Lincei, Rendiconti,* 1959, p. 226f.

METAPONTUM

Atti Taranto 13, 1973: Metaponto. 1974.

Adamesteanu, D. "Le suddivisioni di terra nel Metapontino." In Finley, *Problèmes de la terre* (1973), pp. 49–62.

———. "I santuari metapontini." In *Neuen Forschungen* (1976), pp. 151–66.

———. "Greeks and Natives in Basilicata." In Descoeudres, *Greek Colonists* (1990), pp. 143–50.

Adamesteanu, D., A. De Siena, and D. Mertens. "Metaponto: Santuario di Apollo, Tempio D." *Bolletino d'Arte* 60 (1975): 26–49.

Adamesteanu, D., and C. Vatin. "L'arrière-pays de Métaponte." *CRAI* (1976): 110–23.

Carter, J. C. *The Territory of Metaponto.* Austin, 1983.

———. "Metapontum—Land, Wealth, and Population." In Descoeudres, *Greek Colonists* (1990), pp. 405–41.

———. "Sanctuaries in the Chora of Metaponto." In S. Alcock and R. Osborne, *Placing the Gods* (1994), pp. 161–98.

I Greci sul Basento: Mostra degli scavi archeologici all'Incoronata di Metaponto. Como, 1986.

Mertens, D. "Metapont: Ein neuer Plan des Stadtzentrums." *AA* 40 (1985): 645–71.

Olbrich, G. "Ein Heiligtum der Artemis Metapontina? Zur Ikonographie der Terrakotta-figuren von San Biagio bei Metapont." *PP* 31 (1976): 376–408.

POSIDONIA / PAESTUM

Atti Taranto 27, 1987: Poseidonia-Paestum. 1988.

Greco, E. "Poséidonia entre le VIe et le IVe siècle av. J.-C.: Quelques problèmes de topographie historique." *RA,* 1979, pp. 219–34.

———. "Richerche sulla chora poseidoniate: Il 'paesagio agrario' dalla fondazione dell città alla fine del sec. IV a.C." *Dial. Arch.,* n.s. 1 (1979): 7–26.

———. "Qualche riflessione ancora sulle origini di Poseidonia." *Dial. Arch.,* n.s. 1 (1979): 51–56.

Greco, E., and D. Theodorescu. *Poséidonia-Paestum.* Vol. 1, *La curia.* Vol. 2, *L'agora.* Rome, 1980 and 1983.

———. "Continuité et discontinuité dans l'utilisation d'un espace public: L'exemple de Poséidonia-Paestum." In *Architecture et société,* (1983), pp. 93–104.

Pedley, J. G. "Excavations at Paestum." *AJA* 89 (1985): 53–59 (Sta Venera).

Van Effenterre, H. "La fondation de Paestum." *PP* 35 (1980): 161–75.

Zancani-Montuoro, P., and U. Zanotti-Bianco. *L'Heraion alla foce del Sele.* Rome, 1951.

Pontecagnano

D'Agostino, B. *Tombe principesche di Pontecagnano.* Accad. Lincei, Mon. Ant., Miscell. 2, no. 1. Rome, 1977.

D'Agostino, B., and P. Gastaldi. *Pontecagnano II: La necropoli del Picentino 1.* Naples, 1988.

De Natale, S. *Pontecagnano II: La necropoli di S. Antonio.* Naples, 1988.

RHEGIUM

Ducat, J. "Les thèmes des récits de la fondation de Rhegion." In *Mélanges helléniques offerts à G. Daux*, pp. 93–114. Paris, 1974.
Vallet, G. *Rhégion et Zancle*. Paris, 1958.

SIRIS

Atti Taranto 21, 1981: Siris. 1982.
Pianu, G. "Scavi nel santuario di Demetra a Policoro." In *Studi su Siris-Eraclea*, pp. 95–112. Archeologia Perusina 8. Rome, 1989.

SYBARIS

Guzzo, P. G. "Sibari e la Sibaritide." *RA*, 1992, pp. 3–35.
La Genière, J. de. "C'è un modello Amendolara?" *Ann. Pisa*. ser. 3, 8 (1978): 335–54.

Francavilla-Marittima

Foti, G., and P. Zancani Montuoro. "Scavi a Francavilla Marittima." *Atti M. Grecia* 6–7 (1965–66): 7–13; 11–12 (1970–71): 38–74.
Stoop, W. M. "Note sugli scavi nel santuario di Atena sul Timpone della Motta." *BA Besch*. 54 (1979): 76–79; 55 (1980): 163–89; 58 (1983): 16–52; 62 (1987): 21–31.

TARANTO

Atti Taranto 10, 1970: Taranto. 1971.
Lo Porto, F. G. "Satyrion." *Not. Sc*. 23 (1969): 177–219.

Iapygia

D'Andria, F. "Greci e indigeni in Iapigia." In *Modes de contact* (1983), pp. 287–97.
———. "Greek Influence in the Adriatic: Fifty Years after Beaumont." In Descoeudres, *Greek Colonists* (1990), pp. 281–90.
Yntema, D. "La ricerca topografica nel territorio oritano." *Archivio Storico Pugliese* 39 (1986): 3–26.

SICILY

Di Vita, A. "Town Planning in the Greek Colonies of Sicily." In Descoeudres, *Greek Colonists* (1990), pp. 343–63.
Gabba, E., and G. Vallet, eds., *La Sicilia antica*. Vol. 1, *Indigeni, Fenici-punici, e Greci*. Vol. 2, *Le città greche di Sicilia*. Vol. 3, *Città greche e indigene di Sicilia: Documenti e storia*. Naples, 1980.

AGRIGENTUM

De Miro, E. "La fondazione di Agrigento e l'ellenizzazione del territorio." *Kokalos* 8 (1962): 128–52.

———. "I recenti scavi sul pogetto di San Nicolo." *Cron. Catania* 2 (1963): 57–63.

De Waele, J. *Akragas Graeca: Die historische Topographie des griechischen Akragas I.* Gravenhague, 1971.

Fiorentini, G. "Il santuario extra urbano di S. Anna." *Cron. Catania* 8 (1969): 63–80.

Marconi, P. *Agrigento arcaica: Il santuario delle divinità chtonie e il tempio detto di Vulcano.* Rome, 1933.

Rizzo, F. "Akragas e la fondazione di Minoia." *Kokalos* 13 (1967): 117–42.

Siracusano, A. *Il santuario rupestre di Agrigento in località San Biagio.* Rome, 1983.

CAMARINA

Giudice, F. *La stipe di Persephone a Camarina.* Accad. Lincei, Mon. Ant. Miscell. Rome, 1979.

Pelagatti, P. "Sul parco archeologico di Camarina." *Bolletino d'Arte* 61 (1976): 122–32.

———. "Camarina." *Kokalos* 26–27 (1980–81): 712–32.

ELORO

Voza, G. *Kokalos* 18–19 (1972–73): 181–82; 26–27 (1980–81): 685–88.

GELA

Adamesteanu, D. "Gela." *Not. Sc.* 14 (1960): 67–246.

Caputo, G. "Tre xoana e il culto di una sorgente sulfurea in territorio geloo-agrigentino." *Accad. Lincei, Mon. Art.* 37 (1938): 631–84.

Griffo, P., and L. Von Matt. *Géla: Destin d'une cité.* Paris, 1964.

Guarducci, M. "L'heroon di Antiphemos." *AS Atene* 37–38, n.s. 21–22 (1959–60): 264f.

Kron, U. "Frauenfeste im Demeterheiligtümern: Das Thesmophorion von Bitalemi." *AA* 47 (1985): 609–50.

Meola, E. *Terrecotte orientalizante di Gela.* Accad. Lincei, Mon. Ant. 48, Miscell. Rome, 1971.

Orlandini, P. "Omphakè e Maktorion." *Kokalos* 7 (1961): 145–49.

———. "La piu antica ceramica greca di Gela e il problema dei Lindioi." *Cron. Catania* 2 (1963): 50–56.

———. "La stipe votive del Predio Sola." *Accad. Lincei, Mon. Ant.* 46 (1963): 1–78.

———. "Scavo del Thesmophorion di Bitalemi." *Kokalos* 12 (1966): 8–5; 13 (1967): 117–79.

———. "Topografia dei santuari e documentazione archeologica dei culti." *Riv. Ist. Arch.* 15 (1968): 20–66.

The Deinomenids and Demeter

Kestermann, J. P. "Les ancêtres de Gélon." *Ant. Cl.* 39 (1970): 359–413.

Privitera, G. A. "Politica religiosa dei Dinomidi e ideologia dell'optimus rex." In *Perennitas: Studi in onore di A. Brelich*, 393–431. Rome, 1980.

Van Compernolle, R. "Les Deinoménides et le culte de Déméter à Géla." In *Hommages W. Deonna*, 474–79. Brussels, 1957.

White, D. "Demeter Sicilian Cult as a Political Instrument." *GRBS* 5 (1964): 261–79.

HIMERA

Bonacasa, N. "Pinakes fittili di Himera." *AS Atene* 45–46 (1967–68): 303–25.

———. "Scavi di Himera." *Kokalos* 22–23 (1976–77): 701–12.

LEONTINI

Procelli, E. "Aspetti e problemi dell'ellenizzazione calcidese ai margini della piana di Catania." *Kokalos* 34–35 (1988–89): 121–24.

Rizza, G. "Siculi e Greci sui colli di Leontini." *Cron. Catania* 1 (1962): 3–27.

MEGARA HYBLAEA

Gras, M. "Nécropole et histoire." *Kokalos* 21 (1975): 37–53.

———. "Ricerche sul pianoro meridionale dell'abitato." *Kokalos* 30–31 (1984–85): 801–4.

Orsi, P. "Sur une très antique statue de Mégara Hyblaea." *BCH* 19 (1895): 307–17.

———. "Mégara Hyblaea, 1917–1921." *Accad. Lincei, Mon. Ant.* 27 (1921): 109–80.

Svenbro, J. "A Mégara Hyblaea, le corps géomètre." *Ann. Econ. Soc. Civ.* 37 (1982): 953–64.

Vallet, G. "Espace privé et espace public dans une cité coloniale d'Occident (Mégara Hyblaea)." In Finley, *Problèmes de la terre*, (1973), p. 83–94.

———. "Travaux et recherches à Mégara Hyblaea." *Kokalos* 26–27 (1980–81): 796–804.

Vallet, G. and F. Villard. "Fouilles de Mégara Hyblaea." *Mél. Rome* 65 (1953): 33–38; 66 (1954): 13–24.

Vallet, G., F. Villard, and P. Auberson. *Mégara Hyblaea*. Vol. 1, *Le quartier de l'agora archaïque*. Rome, 1976.

———. *Guide de Mégara.* Rome, 1983.

NAXOS

Guarducci, M. "Una nuova dea a Naxos in Sicilia e i legami della città siciliota con l'omonima isola delle Cicladi." *MEFRA* 97 (1985): 7–34.

Pelagatti, P. *Kokalos* 22–23 (1976–77): 537–45; 26–27 (1980–81): 635–706.

Spigo, U. "Richerche a Francavilla di Sicilia." *Kokalos* 26–27 (1980–81): 777–86; 30–31 (1984–85): 863–904.

SELINUS

Dewailly, M. *Les statuettes aux parures du sanctuaire de la Malophoros à Sélinonte.* Cahiers du Centre J. Bérard 17. Naples, 1992.

Gabrici, E. *Il santuario della Malophoros.* Accad. Lincei, Mon. Ant. Rome, 1956.

Kerenyi, K. "Le divinità e i templi di Selinunte." *Kokalos* 12 (1956): 3–72.

La Genière, J. de. "Réflexions sur Sélinonte et l'Ouest sicilien." *CRAI* (1977): 251–64.

———. "Sélinonte: Recherches sur la topographie urbaine (1975–1981)." *Ann. Pisa,* ser. 3, 12 (1982): 469–79.

Martin, R. "L'histoire de Sélinonte d'après les fouilles récentes." *CRAI* (1977): 46–63.

———. "Recherches sur l'acropole de Sélinonte." *Kokalos* 26–27 (1980–81): 1009–1016.

Tusa, V. "Le divinità e i templi di Selinunte." *Kokalos* 13 (1967): 186–93.

Tusa, V., and A. Rallo. "Scavi e ricerche nella città antica di Selinunte." *Kokalos* 22–23 (1976–77): 660f., 720f.

SYRACUSE

Olympieion

Orsi, P. *L'Olympieion di Siracusa.* Accad. Lincei, Mon. Ant. Rome, 1903.

Ortygia

Cultrera, G. "L'Apollonion-Artemision di Ortigia in Siracusa." *Accad. Lincei, Mon. Ant.* 41 (1951): 701–860.

Orsi, P. "Gli scavi intorno all'Athenaion di Siracusa." *Accad. Lincei, Mon. Ant.* 25 (1919): 354–762.

Pelagatti, P. In *Kokalos* 22–23 (1976–77), 548f; 26–27 (1980–81): 635–706.

Thesmophorion de Piazza Vittoria

Voza, G. *Kokalos* 22–23 (1976–77): 551f; 26–27 (1980–81): 680–85.